THE WORD OF KNOWLEDGE IN ACTION

THE WORD
OF KNOWLEDGE
IN ACTION

Terry Atkinson

New Living Publishers
Manchester

First Published 2008

British Library Cataloguing in Publication Data
A catalogue record for this book is available
From the British Library

Scripture quotations are from the King James Version of the Bible,
unless otherwise stated.

Cover design by Roger Judd

ISBN 978-1-899721-11-5

Produced and printed in England for
NEW LIVING PUBLISHERS
164 Radcliffe New Road, Whitefield
Manchester M45 7TU England

Printed in Denmark
by Norhaven Paperback A/S

Contents

	About the Author	9
	Introduction	11
1	GOD SPEAKING TO US	23
2	DISCERNING THE WILL OF GOD FOR YOUR LIFE	34
3	THE EXPANSION OF A GROWING CHURCH	42
4	THE HISTORY AND SPIRITUALITY OF A CHURCH	48
5	A DISTORTED VISION	55
6	THE CHURCH ON THE MOVE	63
7	TRYING TO ACCOMPLISH THE IMPOSSIBLE	69
8	THE SINGING TREE	76
9	DEALING WITH CULTURAL DIFFERENCES	84
10	SAND, SWEAT AND STONES	92
11	THE SOUND OF MANY WATERS	101
12	RESIST THE DEVIL AND HE WILL FLEE FROM YOU	109
13	CARDBOARD CHRISTIANITY	117
14	THE SINKING ARK	125
15	THE MINISTRY OF HELPS	133
16	THE BURDEN BEARER	141
17	THE RESCUE MISSION	149
18	THE POWER OF THE CROSS OF JESUS CHRIST	157
19	MRS NOAH	164
20	THE LIVING AMONG THE DEAD	171

21	VISION AND APPLICATION	179
22	SHOES THAT DO NOT FIT	186
23	THE ISOLATIONIST	195
24	THE DIRECTOR OF COMMUNICATIONS	204
25	AFRAID OF LEADERSHIP	212
26	FINDING THE MISSING PIECE AND COMPLETING THE PUZZLE	221
27	FILLING THE CUP TO THE BRIM	229
28	THE MULTI-COLOURED RAINBOW	236
29	THE ATHLETE	244
30	THE OINTMENT OF LOVE	253
31	ONE DROP OF BLOOD	261
32	THE BEST BOOK OF ALL	268
33	THE LAST CHAPTER	276

DEDICATION

This book is dedicated to all who seek to be 'being filled' (Greek tense of Ephesians 5:18) with the Holy Spirit. There are those in the Christian faith who long to operate in the fifth dimension. They know about the height, length, breadth and depth of Christian experience, but desire to 'launch out into the deep.' They feel a need through hunger and thirst to move from what can only be known by the human mind into the expansion and demonstration of the Holy Spirit.

Where appropriate, names have been changed to safeguard anyone mentioned in the book.

DEDICATION

ABOUT THE AUTHOR

Terry Atkinson, one of ten children, came to faith in Christ in Yorkshire, England as a teenager. His early years in the ministry were spent founding churches in Perth, Western Australia. From Australia, Terry returned to England to study theology in Kenley, Surrey. He has been a minister of the gospel since the age of twenty-one, first pioneering a church in Gainsborough, Lincolnshire, England. He has been involved in Christian ministry for nearly fifty years, holding pastorates as far apart as Shrewsbury, Shropshire and Maryport in Cumbria. Now based in Manchester, England, he is at present engaged in itinerant ministry in the north-west of England and in Canada.

Terry is married to Margaret, whom he met while a theological student. She accompanies him during his ministry engagements, being used of the Lord to help and direct the lives of others who are in need. They have one daughter, two sons, and four grandchildren.

The author's writings cover many topics and include: *Dying Is Living* (on life after death); *In Sickness and in Health*; *The Growing Pains of Peter*, *Peter —the Mature Man* and *Diamonds in David.*

INTRODUCTION

The *word of knowledge*[1] is a gift of the Holy Spirit, and for all who believe that the Lord can and will use them, this gift will be placed at their disposal. God is faithful to those who will trust Him. When we are filled with the Holy Spirit, and as the promise of the Father comes upon and into us, then we have the Source of all the gifts of the Holy Ghost (Guest). (Luke 24:49.) The gifts are not in us, but in the Giver of every good and perfect gift.[2] If we are baptised in the Holy Spirit we have the Source of the gifts. As we ask God to use us, we take the supply given and apply it as the Almighty intended.

Jesus prefaced one remark by saying 'Do you believe that I am able to do this?'[3] More than ever we need weapons in the gifts of the Holy Spirit to fight the 'good fight' of faith. We have no need to face any battle or challenge clad in silk, we face such in armour that has been provided for us. After the armour mentioned in Ephesians 6 comes 1 Corinthians 12 and 14, putting a sword, spear, shield, gun, tank, flame-thrower, heat-seeker and missiles into our hands to be used on the battlefield. The gifts of the Spirit are not carnal weapons but are spiritual, enabling us to draw back the thin curtain between this world and the spiritual world. These gifts are mighty through God to the pulling down of strongholds, (strong, hold) principalities and powers.[4] 'Strongholds' are arguments of Satan falsely called evolution and science. It is that held within a 'fort', and to conquer him in the stockade we have the 'com' 'fort' of the Holy Ghost. We need to take a 'stronghold' on him who holds people within his power. We must counteract the 'wiles' (skilful tricks) of the devil by being part of the acts of the Apostles. Truth is always greater than tricks. In the English television series 'All Creatures Great and Small', there is a dog named 'Tricky', and that says it all about the devil.

God has used me in the *word of knowledge*, and I have never seen this gift operated in the way that God operates in me. I have not read about it in any book apart from the Bible. No one has taught me; I have never sat at the feet of Gamaliel. There has been no influence from others, only the Holy Spirit. In a unique way I see pictures that God reveals to me of the life of a person or a church. Then, under the anointing of the Spirit I describe what I am seeing. It is like an artist painting a picture, stroke after stroke that comes from the mind and spirit, what is revealed to me comes from the Holy Spirit. The inspiration involved is above the inspiration of music, the artist or any creative ability. Sometimes it is a succession of pictures, almost like watching a film. When I have described one thing, the picture sometimes changes to another subject connected to that which has already revealed. When a person is considering refusing to carry out what God is saying, the Lord shows me their disobedience in another picture form, and I go on to describe that. God has a scrapbook on lives, and is able to reveal each stage one moment at a time. It seems as if a flower is opening its petals as the sun shines, and I see in my spirit the complete action. Sometimes in prayer I see what I am going to describe at a future meeting —even two or three weeks beforehand. The more time you spend waiting on the Lord the clearer the picture becomes. You have to frame that picture in your own words. God provides the picture, you are the canvas which it appears and is seen through. It is as if the Divine Artist is adding the final colours before it is presented. I have received such things when travelling in a motor car, on a bus, walking along a country lane, or travelling on an aeroplane. The gifts of the Spirit are a 'manifestation'[5] and an 'operation' which is an 'unveiling,' as if something that has had a dark cloth over it until it is revealed.

When the Lord reveals things of an eternal and practical nature, involving insight and foresight through the *word of knowledge*, He is revealing truths about a life or a situation, or circumstances. What is revealed is so different to that normally thought about in the human mind. It stands as a king among men. It is as different from the Queen's English as that spoken with an accent. When it is in operation you feel like taking a sharp intake of breath, because you are left aghast, and with Daniel and others who have been used by the Lord in this manner you feel that there is no breath left in you.[6] The 'cogitations' of the heart, by the Spirit of the Lord suddenly become very deep and real. Like Mary the mother of Jesus you begin to 'turn' (ponder) these things in your heart.[7] You think deeply as they are turned over and over, and these thoughts have to be put into action, as you utter what has been poured into you. What has been revealed takes away your breath because it is of such diversity, immensity and spirituality. Things you never knew are given to you at the precise moment of need. These pictures are not 'still slides', but pictures of action and moving things. Every time there is a manifestation of this gift, you know this is the hand of God; God has been at work. He buries His workmen but his work continues, as generation after generation are blessed with spiritual insights by the Spirit of the living God. Some things need unwrapping, and this is what the Spirit of the Lord does in revelation which is an unveiling, taking the cover off, revealing what is the true intent of the heart.

It is the *word of knowledge* that gives another aspect to that which is presented to you. You can see into a life from every angle, as if with a camera that presents the full picture to your spirit. Embedded within the gift is 'the truth, the whole truth and nothing but the truth', with the help of God. When there seems to be no answer, the answer is given as an echo from heaven, as the sound of a mighty rushing wind.[8] It is as if a fifth dimension has been added to the equation. That is why the prophets of the Old Testament and the apostles of the New Testament spoke with such conviction and clarity after the Lord had granted them an insight to challenge them. They saw the furrow and applied the plough to it.

Included in all the gifts of the Holy Spirit we have a casket of rare jewels. Each gift is a manifestation, a shining out of the power of God that reveals the glory of the Lord, just as the prisms of the diamond are revealed through light. Each gift brings some revelation of the unknown. The one who exercises such gifts knows nothing about the situation, except that which is revealed by the Spirit of God. There is no risk if the Lord has spoken. What you have received from God is able to detect folly. These gifts are not toys for well behaved children, they are weapons for soldiers. They are daggers for dangerous men, men who have hazarded their lives for the sake of the gospel.[9] They act as a gun rather than a baton. With them you can bring sin down from its dizzy flight to fall at the feet of the Lord. One man, while I was preaching in Canada, came to me and said, 'Has God given you this gift because of your faithfulness to Him?' The straight answer was 'the gifts are not given because of what we are but because God is a benevolent Father.' If we ask bread He will not give us a stone. If we ask for a fish, He will give us both rod and worm to catch the fish. The bones of the fish will not choke you as a tare in a field chokes the good corn. He will not give us a slithering, biting, poisonous serpent. What we ask for we receive, and when we do not receive we ask amiss, missing the mark we are aiming for.[10]

Much of my ministry has been centred in England, where I have pastored seven churches. On several occasions (by the grace of God) I have travelled to a number of areas in Canada. As I have been ministering to needy people as a needy person myself, seeking to be as an understudy to the Great Physician to apply medicine to the needy areas of the heart, the Lord has granted me many manifestations of the Spirit of God as defined in 1 Corinthians 12 and 14.

These gifts have been such a help as I have sought to help ministers, churches and individuals. The Lord has given me from His heart, in order so that I can pass on to others. These 'manifestations' of the *word of knowledge* are not crutches, but wings to help us to fly. Sometimes I have known about some things long before I went to Canada or to a church. Sometimes three weeks before a meeting, the Lord has slipped something into my heart as precious as the gold of Ophir and the rubies of the rich. I have been richer than a millionaire, being the son of my Heavenly Father who is rich above all abundance. I have said many times, 'Silver and gold have I none, but such as I have I give unto you.' I have witnessed much leaping, praising and dancing in the presence of the Almighty. This gift sets free, and 'whom the Son sets free is free indeed.'[11]

Sometimes, the *word of knowledge* has been manifested to encourage someone in great distress. There is nothing like a revelation from the Lord to wipe away tears, to heal the

15

heart and open the eyes to things that were hidden. On other occasions it has served to expound the human heart, and reveal to individuals and churches what has been in their heart and midst. The purpose of the gift has been that all who come under its influences and manifestations might be exhorted, comforted and encouraged. These gifts leave you with a sense that the Lord has been at work among His people.

There has to be great care, compassion and much prayer in exercising any of the gifts of the Holy Spirit. They are not part of the itinerant preacher's 'bag of tricks'. They are part of the gifts obtained by Christ and given to His church.[12] They are revealed to an individual, as they wait to hear what the Spirit is saying to the churches. He that has ears must use them! Great maturity has to be exercised, because the human element can become involved in what is defined as a gift of the Holy Spirit. No gift is a stage for the actor to perform on! That is why you would never give a child a machine gun! This does not mean that we mechanically, like robots, exercise spiritual gifts. God leaves room for you to express what He has revealed through your own personality. There is no one correct way of exhibiting a manifestation of the Spirit.[13] The Lord grants choice things, and then you have to choose.

The *word of knowledge* operates in different ways to different people. It is a manifestation, an outshining of the Spirit of God, but He does the outshining through human vessels. When Gideon's men shattered the vessels, the light inside was seen by others. Many vessels are made of different types of clay. Some are clay, brass, silver, glass, metal and gold. It is quite amazing that what you are and have, God takes and uses even through the gifts of the Holy Spirit. God will always use what we are, and give us what we have.

One great proof of the validity of gifts of the Spirit was illustrated when a man met me at the church door. He had a bad stammer, yet when he came to exercise a gift of the Spirit, there was no evidence of that stammer, only a flowing through him as if he had the silver tongue of an orator. I have heard people, so eloquent when exercising spiritual gifts, who normally could hardly put a sentence together in conversation, yet when touched by inspiration, it is as if they have found another source of blessing have said some beautiful things.

There is born within us as natural people that which the Lord will take and use for His glory. All you have ever met has become part of you. Life has touched you with a paint brush, and coloured your thinking. Experience has added line upon line to your life. You will use expressions and express yourself in a different way to another. That is what makes you so blessed, you came from your own mould, and when you were born the mould was broken.

For Moses it was a burning bush and a shepherd's crook that the Lord used. Amos sees things that are relative to his pruning and farm work. David expresses himself in warrior and work terms, through his music and his harp. He was a shepherd, and many of the figures he uses come from the sheepfold. Peter, being a fisherman, is used to fishing and boats, and it is that very thing that is taken and sanctified. Paul is a tent maker, and all his insights are taken and used. What nature put into these men and women the Lord takes and sanctifies to make them into vessels of honour. Nothing is wasted, and whatever experiences we have and are born with can be taken and used as we yield to the impressions and expressions of the Holy Spirit. 'All things' do work together for good to them that love God.

As nature declares His handiwork and everything He created declares His glory, so do the gifts of the Holy Spirit. Every mountain, every tree, every river and bird has something to say about God. Not every man will express himself in the same

17

way as others. Where we were born and the family we belong to will all influence us and colour our thinking. These things are vital when the Lord wants to speak to common people in a common language. We all understand the language of the heart. Heart language is what the Lord uses. He will take and use words, pictures, definitions and localities to express truth. When Jesus wanted to attract Mary's attention in the Garden of Gethsemane, He spoke to her in such a way that it appealed to her heart, and she knew it was the Lord.[14]

I am of a poetic nature. God takes that and by the Spirit of the Lord reveals pictures to me. I have to describe what I am seeing. When inspiration is let loose, those hearing what is said can be set free. Others are given a whole sentence from the Lord, and as they begin to speak the rest follows on. Others have just one word from the Lord. For some the gifts of the Spirit come in an overwhelming burden, and they feel if they do not say what the Lord is telling them they will burst as some dam of tremendous force. Some of the prophets had to act out the word of the Lord. For some, everything they had to say appeared on a scroll which they had to read. Even then, the language they choose was their own. That is why we do not want everything from God in the King James Version of the Scriptures! It is not given to us in just black and white. Sometimes it is seen as a sketch, and we have to complete the picture with colourful language. The thought, word or idea came from the Lord. If you have an English, Irish or Scottish accent, that is the accent the Inspirer will use. In Acts 2, Peter spoke to the hearers in the Galilean tongue when he preached. When they were anointed as a group of disciples by the Holy Spirit, the crowd said, 'How is it we hear every man speaking in our own language.' What you have to say under the anointing of God will have your accent as clear as any ringing tone from a bell.

When the *word of knowledge* is received it can be like reading the opening paragraph of a book. It is not word for word, exactly as the Lord has said. I do not say or repeat it all in the same way. I could draw the picture that has been received. If I was an artist this would be alright, but I am not. The best way I can explain the dramatic and enigmatic is through the emphatic. Words of description are abundant under the inspiration of the God who created speech. If we repeated word for word and dictum to dictum in a boring way then we would all be as wooden soldiers! We are sanctified saints. When it is received word for word, then the human element is introduced. God takes my vocabulary and sets it on fire like the burning bush or as the disciples gathered in the Upper Room when tongues of fire appeared on each one of them.[15]

To speak with other tongues is simple. When God anoints you there is a welling up within you of the Spirit of God that gushes out as a spiritual utterance in other tongues. This by-passes the mind and comes straight from your spirit as the Spirit of God plays upon it as a harp. Even within music there is room for expression. To be a good actor you have to make the part your own. If all you have to do is to read what the Spirit of God is revealing to you, then that is comparatively easy. When you have to describe what you are seeing, then you have to pray for great discernment, because you are human, and can easily colour what you are seeing. Some things are difficult to describe, while others are easy. What a torrid time John must have had when he wrote the Book of Revelation! The right description must be given to the right object, so that others might recognise what you are saying. To the Greek I want to speak in Greek, while to the German or Dutch I need to express myself in their language if I am ministering to them. You do not want to lead anyone 'up the garden path' when you should be leading them down by the river! The sun cannot be described as the moon for it is different. The same applies when describing trees or stars. Some seem to have little imagination until He who created imagination, (so that we might have roses at Christmas) comes upon them.

Let me illustrate further. The Lord reveals to me an aeroplane taking off from an airport. When I see things by the Spirit of the Lord, I begin to think that God is sending this person on a long journey. Is He calling them to a mission field? Are they being called as the apostle Paul was to go and help in Macedonia?[16] The answer is no. It might mean that the position they have applied for with the airline has been successful. It might mean that the Lord is calling them to train as a pilot. He might even be calling them to be an aeroplane mechanic! God reveals a tree, and you clearly see a man climbing that tree. Is the Lord saying that this person needs to climb up to new heights? The Almighty might be telling them that they are going to bear fruit, or in work he is going to become a gardener, maybe the head gardener because he is getting to the top of the tree. Has he been praying about such a thing for he desperately requires work? We need to ask God to sharpen our understanding, so that we see and say what He is telling us.

When God manifests Himself, He never takes the human element out of the gifts of the Spirit. We always keep our feet firmly on the ground. The Scriptures declare: 'The spirit of the prophets is subject to the prophets.'[17] It suggests that if anything is revealed to another who is sitting by, let him hold his peace and judge what the other is saying. 'Prove all things; hold fast to that which is true.' If in doubt, don't gallop into what you have seen like a horse without a bridle. With experience you learn to wait awhile until the full sentence, the complete paragraph, the whole picture is presented to you as if the artist has been painting the picture, and you are waiting for Him to complete it. The real picture appears when the paint is dry. Nothing is lost, everything is found, by waiting as the woman with the dough must wait for the leaven to spread throughout.[18] My friend, do not dive into the river bed unless there has been a great storm and there is plenty of water flowing. If you go too soon, the end will be disaster. If you tell people what is your interpretation rather than that given by God, you may ruin a good life and mislead many people, like the fox in one of Aesop's fables, who led them into his den to be devoured.

May the Lord give you understanding in all things. Be as children, but not childish. Be mature men in all things. Have I ever made any mistakes? Everyone who has been involved in Christian ministry, counselling or the gifts of the Spirit will hold up their hands as an acknowledgement that they have made mistakes. Have you ever made a mistake while preaching? If you hold up your hands in the shape of the cross as an acknowledgement of wrong, then everything will be dealt with by the blood of Jesus Christ. Mistakes do not prevent a scholar from qualifying. We can start the lesson again and again until we get it right. It is when your spirit is tuned to His Spirit that all is well and you become as ships sailing with the wind. As the pen requires to be dipped in ink so the computer requires a cartridge, and we need the flow of the Spirit. The student forgets the mistakes and makes sure he does not make them again. By gentle perseverance he gets the answer right. We always have God to help us, while we are waiting for the moment when we have his answer! Do not throw your pen away because you have misspelled a word. Wipe the pen clean, start again, dip it afresh into the fluid; hold it so the flow will come to the point, praying to do a better job as you listen to the voice of the Spirit.

Notes

1   1 Corinthians 12:8
2   James 1:17
3   Matthew 9:28
4   2 Corinthians 10:4
5   1 Corinthians 12:7
6   Daniel 2:1; 4:5; 7:15, 28
7   Luke 2:19
8   Acts 2:2
9   Acts 15:26 'Hazarded' means 'the throwing of the dice'.
10 James 4:3
11 John 8:32, 36
12 Ephesians 4:8
13 1 Corinthians 12:7
14 John 20:11–16
15 Acts 2:1–4
16 Acts 16:9–12
17 1 Corinthians 14:32
18 Luke 13:21

1

GOD SPEAKING TO US: THE WORD OF KNOWLEDGE DEFINED AND ILLUSTRATED

The *word of knowledge* is a gift of the Holy Spirit as found in the New Testament. (See 1 Corinthians 12:8; 14:6.) It is *knowledge* of a *word* from the Lord, as it is a *word* of His *knowledge*. It can be revealed in one word or in many. It is just a particle of the knowledge of the all-knowing, seeing, listening and loving God. This gift can be as a bright light on a dark night or as a beacon directing us through stormy weather. As each lighthouse has its own particular light, so each gift of the Spirit possesses and presents to us that light that comes from the nature of God. Thank God that no one needs to go to a 'fortune teller' or one who practises 'black magic', to consult with the 'stars' or signs of the zodiac, all of which is forbidden by Scripture. When people are involved with such things, then there is a lack of faith in the living Lord. Many try to discover things about their life, their past, present and future without the help of God, and what a mess they make of almost everything they do! They are like Aaron, the first priest of Israel who said, 'I threw this in and this came out' (Exodus 32:24).

The *word of knowledge* is not a *rhema word,* that can be written, spoken put into writing or given in a speech, but it can include it. (Matthew 12:36; 27:14. Ephesians 6:17.) The expression 'the *word of knowledge*' is not found many times in the Scriptures, but we need to remind ourselves that the word Trinity never appears in the Bible, yet we can prove its nature and existence by what the Scriptures reveal. The *word of knowledge* is made up of 'word' and 'knowledge'. It is something you 'know' and something you 'say'. This gift is insight and illumination.[1] It is 'insight and the power to express it' (a modern translation). It is different from that which is normally spoken; it comes from a higher level and takes you to a higher level because it is a gift of the Spirit. When the gift is in operation everyone acknowledges that the Lord has spoken. Some can say things that appeal to the intellect, but when this gift is manifested we know that our hearts and not our ears have been spoken to. Its source is more than poetic or artistic inspiration because it is inspired, owned and granted by the Holy Spirit.

It is the ability granted by the Spirit of God to see things from the God-aspect rather than a personal aspect. It given supernaturally about something on earth or in heaven. This gift brings the realisation that God knows all things and, therefore, can do all things as He reveals all things. Sometimes it is hearing, seeing and knowing what others do not know because you are engaged on a different channel to normal thinking. A *word of knowledge* can deal with the 'thought patterns' of a person. Jesus, when operating this gift, could tell what men were thinking before they ever said a word.

Logos translated 'word' is the expression of thought. Through this gift the thoughts or mind of the Lord can be expressed to another. That thought or word must be birthed in the Holy Spirit. It is not the mere name of an object. 'It is the embodiment of a conception or an idea. It is a saying or a statement. It can suggest a discourse, speech or instruction.' (*Vine's Expository Dictionary of New Testament Words*). These gifts are some of the splendours of the Spirit of the Lord.

When we don't know what to say, think, do or pray, this gift of the Spirit takes us into another realm where we do not have to grasp for words. That which is given is not too great for the curve of one's mind. We are exhorted to 'covet earnestly (with zeal) the best gifts'.[2] We are not left in the lurch grasping at straws or guessing what to do next. There is a voice that says, 'This is the way, walk in it!' Dealing with the Almighty there is no limit to what He can reveal to His servants. When we come to the end of our own speech, then we can begin to say what the Lord is commanding us to say. When He speaks it is like a rainbow after a stormy day. It is where midnight meets the dawn.

The *word of knowledge* is the gift of the Spirit that can work alongside the words of wisdom or prophecy. In fact these gifts do sometimes intertwine with each other, overlapping as waters of a sea. They are like the members of the human body assisting each other.[3] Operating this gift is having the ability through the Holy Spirit to see inside a situation, then to work from that inside to the outside. It is to see inside the closed door and to witness what no human being has said or suggested. It must be exercised without favour or fear. It was this gift in operation that pointed out the hypocrisy of Ananias and Sapphira in Acts chapter 5. You simply report what you have seen as the spies did as they went to spy out the land of Canaan.[4] It must not be simply an evil report that makes the heart of the person shrink or flow like water, it must also bring encouragement.

The *word of knowledge* is not a word passed on from someone else to you; it is passed on and directed from the throne of God. It is to have a listening ear and the spiritual insight containing the word of the King. It can be a healing word, a creative word, a comforting word or a word of hope and faith. Each time the Lord of Glory speaks, then glory should be seen and heard. It must promote others, to help them follow the Lord more nearly and love Him more dearly. When we are in doubt, here is the doubt remover. Sometimes each facet of what God is saying is opened up before you. A word of prophecy can tell you of the future, while a *word of knowledge* is the future in the present. These things are given so that you might 'know'. Once we 'know' then we need a word of wisdom to carry out the intentions of the Lord. What shall I do now that the Lord has spoken? The first thing is to listen.

There are different types of word in the New Testament but there is only one *word of knowledge* as a gift of the Holy Ghost. *Gnosis* is 'knowledge' suggesting to know, to recognise, to understand.[5] You may not understand another's situation but the Lord does. In a small way you are called to help. It is the understanding of the supernatural world that is revealed in a natural world, seeing with the eyes of the Spirit, who is full of eyes within and without, and understanding the mind of the Lord for a particular moment. In and by this gift we understand what the Lord is saying to others. We may not appreciate or understand its ramifications. You have to pass on what has been passed on to you as the disciples gave the broken and blessed bread to the five thousand gathered.[6] The outworking of that which is uttered is left with the Source, the Spirit of God. You can only give an utterance; it is left to the Lord to fulfil that which is spoken. If God gives a promise He will see that it is fulfilled to the last dot and comma. It is God who understands completely. When Noah was commanded to build the ark, Jehovah saw the finished article even before Noah commenced building. It is not the only word, it is part of the overall communication that the Lord is saying to the individual, company or church. It is to know in the sense of realising. It is after we have spoken through this gift that men perceive that of a truth God is in the midst.[7]

There is a relationship in the word *gnosis*, 'knowledge' between the person knowing and the object known. You have to hear what you say, or see it, and then pass it on. You cannot speak out of an empty heart. That heart must be filled with the Spirit. That which is known is of value to the one who knows, but it only becomes of value to another when it is passed on.

Human personality is allowed to be seen and heard through the *word of knowledge*. Ask any group of people to describe a painting, and listen to the different variations. Some will emphasise one colour or one object more than another. When an accident is witnessed, all see the same thing, yet because of humanity, upbringing and culture, the same accident is described in different ways. The main thread, the kernel, the heart of the story is not altered; it is the way it is expressed that is different. That is why when exercising the *word of knowledge* we are given words which are appropriate for us to articulate. I have heard the same things prophesied and the *word of knowledge* in action in different meetings and parts of the country, yet it has been the same word uttered in a different area through people with different accents, proving that the Lord is God above and over all.

It is knowledge that is approved. It can be tested as metal in a fire and found not to be wanting. It is the real thing. The word 'know' is used of God's knowledge of people in Amos 3:2. 'Such knowledge is obtained not by mere intellectual activity, but by operation of the Holy Spirit' (*Vine, on New Testament Words*). There is that which is a product of the natural mind and there is that which is a revelation of the mind of the Spirit. It is literally the reading of God's mind on a matter. What has the Lord to say? 'Have you any word from the Lord? Pass it on'

The Word of wisdom is different from the *word of knowledge* in its application but not its reception and inception, for it is 'by the same Spirit'. The *word of knowledge* means you know what you have received. You are more certain of the uncertain, and know more about the unknown by the Spirit of God than you can ever know by acquired knowledge or wisdom. This is not book learning or university education. Wisdom is how you apply what God has put within your heart. Wisdom can resolve what God has revealed. Neither gift has to do with intellectual attainment or academic acceptance. In a *word of knowledge* one has the knowledge, and in the other gift you have the wisdom to apply that knowledge. It is a picture of the blacksmith and the welder working together. It is the difference between receiving and understanding building plans. You can look at some things and they might seem to be written in Greek. You have the picture but it now needs application. The one who gives a *word of knowledge* has received it as a gift from the Lord, but it is the recipient who requires the wisdom to see it through to the end. These two gifts are illustrated in the screw and the screwdriver or the hammer and the nail. One helps the other to complete the task. You require the wisdom to put together that which you have seen. Wisdom works out that which is known by you. Inspiration produces the idea, and that idea or thought (knowledge) must be passed on to the one it was intended for, otherwise what has been revealed is wasted. Jesus commanded that the fragments must be gathered up into twelve baskets. God will let none of His 'words' fall to the ground as a ring slipping from the finger.[8]

The *word of knowledge* is illustrated both in the Old and New Testaments. Many times the *word of knowledge* is seen in the lives of the patriarchs as that which is given to them by God, the things they saw by faith which seemed to be afar off.[9] These things, these convictions of eternal realities, were brought near to them. What they saw they possessed. There was no thinking process involved in what God revealed to them by His Spirit. This gift shows something before it happens, and can describe the condition of the heart of any person. It is like the Word of God, as a discerner of the thoughts and intents of the heart, but that discernment must be put into words that people understand.[10] God speaks to us in the language of love, not just the language of learning. It is with 'tongues of men' that we speak to men. When you speak to angels, God will grant you the tongue to do so! The way in which He pulls on the heartstrings is by speaking to the heart. He uses another's heart to speak to your heart. He uses another voice to speak to you. There is a ring of truth and a recognition about what is said through the *word of knowledge*.

Moses on the mount and in the valley had revelations from the Lord, and was told to write down those revelations.[11] God showed him the tabernacle, how to make it and who should make it. He had lined up other men with other gifts to complete the task. Other gifts were added to help Moses accomplish what the Lord had revealed. We need a number of gifts of the Spirit because our God is a God of virtue and variety. If Moses wrote the books of the Pentateuch, then he must have seen all that took place in order to reveal it to others through his writings. Solomon had to build a temple, and the plan for it must come from the Lord. Abraham even 'saw' the Day of Christ.[12] Joshua received the plan of attack when facing the city of Jericho and Ai. Elijah and Elisha were both blessed with a *word of knowledge* for the occasion and the challenge that faced them. It is this gift that shows the way through and out. (1 Kings 21:20–29.) The Lord brought the words of judgement to Elijah, and he was able to describe the way in which Jezebel would die. Sometimes the *word of knowledge* is couched in the phrase 'The word of the Lord came unto Elijah'.[13] That phrase is used of Elijah and Jonah, Amos and Habakkuk, Micah and Obadiah.

Daniel was able to see an image of clay, iron and part silver, representing the world order that was to come. He then saw a stone made without hands smash it into fragments, signifying the end of one order and the commencement of another.[14] He was able to interpret the handwriting on the wall, because the Lord showed him that interpretation. He could tell Nebuchadnezzar what his dream meant, that he would be mad for a season and eat grass like an ox, with the dew of heaven wetting his hair.[15] Daniel saw the picture of a tree stump ringed with a steel band signifying the cutting off of Nebuchadnezzar's kingdom.

Samuel the prophet had a *word of knowledge* when he met with Saul who was seeking his father's asses. He told the servant to continue, while he told Saul what the Lord had to say, and that his father's donkeys had been found. (1 Samuel 9:6–20.)   (1 Samuel 8:7–18) The Lord told Samuel what manner of man the future king of Israel would be. The rejection of King Saul was revealed to Samuel the prophet.

(2 Kings 3:11–15) By the inspiration of music the Lord revealed to Elisha what would happen to Israel and their kings. From verse 16 Elisha had the revelation from the Lord by the *word of knowledge* to fill the valley full of ditches. Elisha knew who was under disguise for the Lord had revealed to him that it was the wife of Jeroboam. (1 Kings 14:2–6.)

Both Joseph and Daniel sought the Lord and were able by the *word of knowledge* to give interpretations to the dreams that others had dreamed. Joseph gives revelation in picture form to the baker and butler, and describes what was going to happen to them.[16] Concerning Pharaoh, he was able to give the interpretation of thin cows eating fat cows, and thin corn devouring good corn.[17] All was seen in picture form and described to those in need. A woman came to David and complimented him by telling him saying that nothing was 'hidden' from the king.[18]

The *word of knowledge* is much in evidence in the Book of Revelation. John describes many things in picture form and in the form of 'sound words'. The understanding of what John was saying is left with the reader of the Book of Revelation. 'May the Lord give you understanding in all things.'[19] The Book of Revelation abounds in metaphors that seem difficult to understand. The *word of knowledge* is less than Scripture, but the Scripture of Truth is awash with many manifestations of this gift. So much truth can be wrapped in a *word of knowledge*, and in each case there is the potential for miracles as much as when the lad presented his five loaves and two fish to Jesus Christ.

Jesus Christ exhibited the *word of knowledge* many times. All the gifts of the Holy Spirit are exhibited in His life except speaking in other tongues. He did not speak in other tongues because He was the Baptiser. The Spirit proceeded from the Father and the Son. He saw Nathaniel standing under the fig tree long before they met. Nathaniel naturally asked the question 'How do you know me?'[20] The *word of knowledge* can open the door of the heart and reveal what is inside. Jesus could tell Peter what sort of death he would die.[21] He told them of an ass tied up where the four roads met.[22] When Jesus required a place to eat the Last Supper, He sent His disciples and told them they would meet a man carrying a pitcher of water.[23] He told the woman of Samaria that the husband she had was not her true husband.[24] He saw Satan as a light falling from heaven.[25] Jesus saw the fish with a coin inside it long before He sent Peter to fish for it, and pay the temple taxes.[26] He knew where the fish were when Peter and the others had spent all night fishing and had caught nothing. Jesus was not a trained fisherman, but He was scholarly when it came to exercising the gifts of the Spirit. In looking we do not see, while through the gifts of the Holy Spirit we see without looking. With our eyes on another world we can receive something that will help and not hurt or hinder others. Something will be found in a *word of knowledge* that will not necessarily cause pain, but will be part of a plan, a plan written in the palm of His hand.

When we ask the Lord to use us in the gifts of the Holy Spirit, we require that gift from the Lord. To use the words of the apostle Paul, we must not be as a trumpet blower giving an 'uncertain' sound.[27] What is said can be judged, but if it is of the Lord then it will stand the test of time and trial. If we say what God has said, then we shall not be weighed in the balances and found wanting. We shall 'want for nothing'. That which is received can help others to go on with the Lord. That *word* given can strengthen your heart, another's heart, and help their hand to tighten its grip on spiritual things. It can present them with footsteps they can walk in, and help them to realise that they are going to follow the Lord to the end, because there is no ending in God, only new beginnings each day.

Notes

1 A T Robertson *Word Pictures in the New Testament*
2 1 Corinthians 12:31; 14:39
3 See 1 Corinthians 12:14–27
4 Joshua 2
5 Vine's Expository Dictionary
6 Mark 6:43
7 1 Corinthians 14:25

8   1 Samuel 3:19
9   John 8:56
10 Hebrews 4:12
11 Exodus 25:40
12 John 8:56
13 1 Kings 6:11; 13:1; 16:1; 17:2
14 Daniel 2:35
15 Daniel 4
16 Genesis 40
17 Genesis 41
18 2 Samuel 14:20
19 2 Timothy 2:7
20 John 1:48
21 John 21:18
22 Mark 11:2,4
23 Luke 22:10
24 John 4:18
25 Luke 10:18
26 Matthew 17:27
27 1 Corinthians 14:8

2

DISCERNING THE WILL OF GOD FOR YOUR LIFE

We had been at a particular church for a while, and I decided to spend a night in prayer, asking the Lord to show us the way forward. The work had been frustrating and unyielding. The church was small, rural and difficult with many traditions. I was only twenty-five years of age, and full of desire for the Lord. There was within me the longing to get out and tell the world of Jesus Christ. The church needed to grow into something good and glorious. I was like a man with a great thirst facing a river, but there was a chasm too wide to jump over between myself and that river, so I began to pray. Prayer would at least tell the Lord how I felt in this situation, and maybe some direction would be given. I would be pleased if there weren't four ways to choose from.

About 2 a.m. the Lord sent the answer. As I was praying there appeared an old, small door which had relatively new hinges. These hinges were black, different in colour to the rest of the door. They were wide at one end and narrow at the other. Rust could clearly be seen forming on the screws and on the large hinges. It looked as if the door had not been opened for a number of years. What did this mean? What should I do?

I stood before this small door with large hinges and looked at it, realising the door was not locked but shut tight. Not having been moved for a long time it was as if it had been left in history. It did not have a lock, so there was no need for a key. Time had visited the hinges and swept its ungainly hand across, seeking to paint them the colour of rust. What a great work time and tradition does to most things! This picture was peculiar in so far as there was no key, keyhole or lock.

Then, by the *word of knowledge* provided by the Spirit, I saw myself pushing the door, and as it was pushed from the inside the rust began to fall from the hinges. The door was opened and I stepped out into the world before me. I felt free after being in such a confined area as the small hut that was part of the door. These things were being revealed to my spirit. The Lord had spoken, and there was the conviction that we should resign from the church and move into another area. It was such a conviction that you could have travelled the world on it. God would lead the way, and He would meet the need. The drawback was large and foreboding. As with many ministers in those days of poverty and need, the house belonged to the church. My occupation was tied in with the pastorate. If we resigned the occupation, house and income would all be severed. I would be left to wander as lonely as a cloud. Nevertheless, the Lord had spoken and must be obeyed.

What the Almighty says makes it easier to do what you have to do. With the word of God as your guide you cannot walk in darkness, only in the light as He is in the light. It is still difficult, but the Lord lines all the burdens we are called to carry with grace, making it easier to accomplish the difficult or what might seem to be the impossible. There is great strength and capability in what the Lord says. It seemed to breathe fresh life into a dying lamb. There is 'comfort' (to make strong and brave) in the Holy Ghost. He is the Comforter. Wasn't I glad on this occasion that the real nature of the Holy Spirit was there to lift me up and put me down, to take me on and bring me through! With God as your guide you will walk the right way, the only way. The problem is that you don't always know what the other side is, or who or what is waiting for you there. God's appointments are His ointments, to heal and set free.

With no church, no job and no income what could we do? Two children had been born, and could not be fed simply with the wind of expectation. To beg I was ashamed. What would happen next? What did happen next? It is pleasurable to obey the promptings of the Spirit, but then you have to see revelation through to the end. Beginnings can be always beginnings, but there must be an ending, and an in-between stage where you need grace as large as the problem. The Lord who had revealed what I should do would grant us the grace and another revelation if it was needed before we moved on. We waited in hope, and we know that 'hope deferred' makes the heart sick (weak), (Proverbs 13:12). In my sickness I turned to the Great Physician,who has written prescriptions for everything in His rich, red blood.

Two weeks later, a minister from another local church dropped a card through our letterbox. Written on it was the fact that he had called to see us, but sadly, we were not at home. Would I make contact with him, for he had something to discuss with me that might be interesting. Contacting him by telephone, he revealed that he wanted a younger person to work alongside him in a large church. As we were thinking about this invitation, we travelled into Yorkshire to visit our in-laws. It was always good to do that; they had their own business, a large house, lovely garden with fountain and fish. The children loved it because they knew this was one place where we would be well fed. To them it was the Land of Kisses and Cuddles. Maybe we should come and live here? Knowing what the Spirit of God had revealed about our former church, I sat in the front lounge and began to meditate on the goodness of the Lord, praising Him for all that was past, and all that was to come. I knew He was the 'Steward of the Ages' (from Ephesians 1:10), but could He arrange our lives as He had arranged each flower?

There was a local church in need of a minister, but I felt that it was such a mature gathering they would never consider choosing me as that person. Men with great names and good ministries had graced their platform. As I meditated on these things the fire began to burn. My mind seemed to explode as I began to see outside of the house with my eyes closed. I could see the local church elder, George, walking up the driveway of the house. There was no mistaking his gait, for he was a portly man. I wondered what this sight of him could mean because I had not contacted the church or arranged an interview with any member of the parish. Each step he took brought him nearer to the house, and, as he approached, his face seemed to shine as the midday sun. He was a man on a mission and with a message. He came into the house as a bearer of good tidings and of great joy, an angel if ever I had seen one in human flesh.

The Lord began to interpret what had been received by a *word of knowledge*. He began to talk to my Spirit as a Father would speak to his lost child who did not know where to go. It seemed as if I had been lost on a dark night and suddenly, as the Spirit of God began to speak, the dawn appeared. It was as if midnight kissed midday.

The Lord said, 'The church elder you have seen coming up the driveway will invite you to speak at the church this Sunday.' That was a shock, such a shock as cold water being thrown into the face of one who had fainted. It was not what I expected. I thought if I were going to accept the oversight of another church, an invitation would come through the Royal Mail, or at least I could put my name on a list of those who were seeking to serve a church. Even another minister might recommend me to a church looking for a minister. These were the cogitations of my heart. God continued 'He will invite you to speak, but already they have had a meeting, and they want to see if you are the man they should invite to be their minister.' Could this be true? Was I hearing or even listening to what the Lord was saying? Was this the Lord sharing His heart with me? I did not know what to think say or do. All that had been my mind was being scattered to the four winds. I sat there in my seat as dumb as an ass. There seemed to be no more spirit in me. It was like seeing a robbery take place on the high street, you can't believe what you are seeing, and you console yourself by thinking 'It is just part of a film for some television programme.' If you pinch yourself you feel that you would come down from the seventh heaven with a loud bang that might addle your brain. You hold yourself steady, gripping your seat, as if that is your salvation.

Within the hour, gazing through the bay window which, in this large house seemed to give a kaleidoscope vision of the garden and pathway, the man who had been seen in that *word of knowledge* was walking, as I had seen him earlier. The strange thing about it was that he had a car, and he could have driven straight up the driveway to the house. He was walking, just as he had been seen earlier. He spoke to me in an enquiring manner, 'Are you out preaching on Sunday?' he asked. 'We would like you to come and preach all day on Sunday at our church.' I thought for a moment before I said anything. In spite of what I knew, I didn't feel ready to commit myself to going to that church on Sunday. When he saw me hesitate, he said with a twinkle in his eye and a red radiant face, 'If I were you I should think about it seriously.' He then left the house because he didn't want to open up the conversation in case I asked some embarrassing questions. He came at crawling pace, and left in a gallop!

I was left with the opportunity of contacting them that day if I was going to respond to his suggestion and invitation. Prayer became the order of the day. If eagerness took over my spirit it would not avail. That word from the Lord came to my heart, 'He who believes shall not make haste' (Isaiah 28:16). 'In quietness and confidence shall be your strength' (Isaiah 30:15). After thinking about it, there was nothing else for me to do but to accept the invitation, feeling that the hand of the Lord had arranged these things. We must always step into that provided by the hand of God. If the Lord was in this matter then it mattered. The decision which was made that day turned all my past, present and future upside down, inside out and the right way up.

The church had been visited. The message and meeting with the folk had gone well. Had I preached well enough? I wasn't there to prove anything, just to do what the Lord was revealing, feeling part of an ongoing revelation. We knew these people personally, and they were great folk. After the services that day, no one said anything to me, except the pianist who said, 'I have told people that we could do worse than invite you and your wife to become our ministers!' This woman did not know what the Lord had revealed. The lady was not part of the revelation, but obviously she was in tune with the Lord.

A couple of weeks went by and we had heard nothing. It was the longest period of my short life. It seemed like that described by John in Revelation 8:1, when in heaven there is no sound — just pure silence, as when all the clocks seem to stop ticking. I was in prayer at home when I saw the leadership in a car coming to where we lived, which was about fifty miles away. I knew immediately and instinctively that they were coming to see us in our home. They were coming to discuss the vacant pastorate. I said to Margaret, 'I think we should buy extra food, because the Lord has shown me that the oversight of the church we went to visit the other Sunday is coming to see us.' Dutifully she responded by buying the necessities ready for these lions of the tribe of Judah to descend on us. The Lord had shown me the day and the time they would arrive. Here we were waiting for something to happen that had been revealed by the Spirit of God. We waited and waited, the hours dragged by. It was the day time stood still. At 10 p.m., sadly, I drew the curtains over the day as tiredness began its ministry in my brain. They hadn't arrived! Was all this just a figment of my imagination? Was it a dream?

The church did invite us to be with them, working together to establish the kingdom of God. There was one burning question requiring an answer, it had stayed with me like the bush that burned perpetually that Moses saw when God was calling him. (Exodus 3:2–5.) What had happened on that day when they should have arrived at our house? Was there an explanation or had I been the victim of a strong delusion? When we were settled in the place and I felt at ease, I asked one of the elders about that day when the Lord had revealed to me that they were coming to our house. I knew the day and date for it was pencilled into my diary and had been written into my heart by the Spirit of the living God. The elder thought for a moment, and then said, 'Yes, we had arranged to come and see you on that date and day. My car was in the garage, and we had to borrow another car. It turned out to be a real 'banger'. We had just commenced our journey when it broke down, and we had to abandon our visit. We had not told you we were coming, so we felt that we were under no obligation to inform you what had happened to us. It saved our blushes, because most of us had cars but for one reason or another they were out of commission on that day.' God had given me the right word. What a relief! I had not been wrong was my song both day and night. What He had revealed was as true as pure gold, and as faithful as the hills. God had not failed, but the mechanical had. The will of God was fulfilled even when things seemed to go wrong. When one door closes, He opens another. When He opens many doors, be assured they will lead you into that one direction that He has chosen for you. If there are no doors to open, then He will lead you into pure pasture land, and you will be as happy as the grass is green.

3

THE EXPANSION OF A GROWING CHURCH

The building was too small to house the crowds. The church had moved from a small building to one of larger capacity a few years earlier. Occasionally, people looked at the building and wondered if it was too big. However the Lord would fill it. Eventually two services had to be arranged on Sunday mornings, with numerous activities in the building during the week, including a café called 'Daily Bread'. It was so full that private conversations were almost impossible; the people were so close to each other. Interviewing or counselling with anyone in the church had to be arranged by giving three weeks notice because somebody else would always be using the counselling room. It was rather like the woman with so many children that she did not know what to do. There was the desperation of Noah's ark about the place, with people in every area instead of animals. Queues and crowds were the order of the day. Large events had to be arranged in another building on the other side of the town.

There was a need to expand, to build a greater building, something that would be conducive to the needs of the people, and reflecting the heart of God and the vision of those in leadership. This would involve so many things. Many decisions would have to be made. It is through decisions that we are disciplined, we demonstrate our commitment. I was not involved in any of the decision making progress, but before those decisions were made God had revealed to me what was going to happen. It was as if I had a book on the history and future of the church as well as the present.

We prayed much about the new building. Week after week, fervent prayers had been offered with many tears. We expected the Lord to answer prayer. I sat about ten rows from the front, and as I prayed, the Lord poured into me a picture of Noah and the ark. Suddenly, without changing shape or recognition, the ark expanded as if built out of plastic. To alter the construction of that ark one would have to begin again. I saw Noah putting wood into the same ark he was sailing on. The windows and doors along with the different levels were expanding, not with the help of human hands but with the help and power of God. It seemed that the Lord was telling us that the church would remain where it was, but refurbishment would take place. It would not alter the outside of the building in a great way, but the heart of the old building would be taken out and changed dramatically. The emphasis was on the fact that the ark, the church, would stay where it was, and would not alter its shape. It would still be recognised for what it was. I saw the whole building enlarged as if it was being stretched into a new shape. The church oversight decided to refurbish the church building at great cost. They were assured that the need would be met and the alterations would take place. These alterations have now taken place and the heart of the building is of a different shape.

What happened to that 'ark' in the *word of knowledge* revealed to me meant that it could accommodate more occupants. It could accommodate more of those the Lord was calling to Himself. It was as if God was in the ark, and as He stretched himself inside that ark, so it grew and grew. The church is the body of Christ, and we see him at work in it.

The local church was in a prime position. Many other buildings had been considered, many suggestions made, before the decision was taken to alter the nature of the building that the church already occupied. The amazing thing is those who were making the decisions avoided many pitfalls and schemes that were not of the Lord but came from man's imagination. Plans were drawn up and prayed over. What had been revealed by the Lord showing me a picture of Noah and the ark was fulfilled. The ark was a bridge between one dispensation and another, a bridge between one world and another. It was a bridge that led deeper into grace as the Lord revealed Himself more fully to Noah. As building the ark was a place of trysting and training for further exploits, so changing the inside of this building became the same. Noah, within the ark, had to prepare those within it for a new world in God.

Once the building was complete, there was a need for office space, for in a church where the attendance numbered over 800 there is a lot of activity, as much as there is in any market place. Again, we had gathered to pray about a large garage that was next to the church. This garage had rented some ground from the church for a number of years. The garage was prosperous, in fact so prosperous it became too small for that type of operation. Like the church they lacked capacity. Cars were parked side by side like a pack of playing cards laid on a table.

We came to prayer believing that God would give us anything if it was going to promote the Kingdom. Privately as well as publicly, we were where prayer was 'required to be made.' God so prospered a garage business that it became too big for its premises and the firm had to move out to let the church come in! We knew none of these things at the time. Enquiries were made about the possibility of purchasing the garage to give the church greater facilities, in fact facilities fit for a King. The amazing thing was, after seeing so many cars of different colours and countries of origin at the garage, those same colours, in human form, eventually entered the church.

It was prayer time and all the faithful gathered. We began to pray about the possibility of the Lord giving us this garage. Some were bolder than others in their asking. Petitions large and small were offered. As I bowed low before the Lord God Almighty, with my eyes closed and my ears dull of hearing the noise around me, I suddenly saw to outside, where the garage was. The *word of knowledge* began to operate. At the time when I saw this by the Spirit of the Lord it was busy all day long, with cars coming and going in a seemingly endless shuttle service. As I was meditating, the garage seemed to have no cars in its car park. It was as deserted as a desert island. There was the silence of surety about the place. There were no cars in the showroom. The focus now was not on the cars in the past, but on the building which was empty. I had just walked by the garage to come into the meeting, and had seen it in all its commercial glory.

There was an eerie silence, as if some law had been made forbidding the silence to be broken. At one of the windows, the top of a small plant appeared. It slowly seemed to struggle for the light and the face of the sun to kiss its leaves. The congregation continued to pray; I continued to watch, as if I were watching a television screen or a film in a local cinema, but there was no darkness surrounding what was taking place. It was as if the light of day was attracting the growing plant. As it grew I began to look at the other windows in the building, and growing green plants were rising up, to fill each window, and then filling the rooms they were growing in. Each plant was growing stronger as it operated in the light around it, which seemed to be like the light of glory. It might have been one vine with many branches growing from it; I could not tell whether this was so, because I couldn't see into the building. I was watching it all happen from the outside. The Lord had given me a ringside view of what He was going to do.

There was a sudden crashing noise, and glass began to fly as if some bomb had exploded. Yet the glass did not fly everywhere as you would normally expect. It just disappeared as it broke into thin air. What was happening was that the plants I recognised as vines had filled the area they were planted in and smashed every window in that garage until the whole thing changed from a garage into something else. The vines were reaching out with strong stems, with leaves as hands, and were unceremoniously smashing the windows. They were not going from window to window, they were all smashed together as if under one command and were listening to one voice. The sweetness of light seemed to fill the air and float around what had been the garage area. The vine had conquered the garage, smashing every window. It was as if the Lord was pointing out that as the church adored Jesus Christ who is the Vine, He would fill all things with His presence. This entered my heart as easily as breath entering my lungs. I perceived that the Lord had just shown me that the garage would be bought and become part of the church. It would be part of a place where the young and the children could grow. It would be part of a place where all could grow up, and what the Vine had accomplished they would accomplish through the gospel of our Lord Jesus Christ. That night I returned home with the smell of the vine and the grapes upon me, not on my body but in my spirit. God had showed me something worth seeing. The eyes of my understanding had been opened.

Since that happened, the garage has accepted the church's offer and it is to become part of the church. Plans are being made to convert the garage into something useful to the church. God had revealed His will in a *word of knowledge,* telling of things that would happen before they happened, proving His diversity and faithfulness, and that He who begins a good work completes it until the Day of Jesus Christ.

4

THE HISTORY AND SPIRITUALITY OF A CHURCH

I should not have been in this particular church in downtown Montreal, Canada. The arrangements had been mixed up and they were not expecting me. My arrival had not been announced or prepared for. A message had been left on an answering machine which the church leader had never received. He agreed to have a meeting, but warned me that there would not be as many in attendance at this mid-week service as there would be on a Sunday. My coming had not been announced on the previous Sunday, so no one knew I was going to be there. Inspite of the frailty of human arrangements, if the Lord has something to say, and we are prepared to listen, then He will tell us His heart. When He does we are left aghast, realising that what we knew about the Lord being all-knowing, all-seeing and all-listening is true! No part of your history or spirituality is missing from His Book of Life! His line and voice go throughout the earth. Everything that ever happens has a voice, and that voice reports to the Lord God Almighty. We are vulnerable because we do not know. He is victorious because He is not vulnerable, only valiant.

Knowing nothing about this church, my mind was as open as

the heavens to what the Lord might reveal. Having never heard of the church before, nor seen it until I entered the building, a sense of ease filled my soul. There was no inkling or thought of what the Lord might reveal through a *word of knowledge*. The service commenced as normal until we were about three parts through the arranged worship. Then the Spirit of the Lord began to move upon my spirit, and I began to feel a holy glow filling my soul. My spirit was like a harp in the hands of a harpist. I was hoping that nothing out of the ordinary would take place, because I was a stranger in a strange place. At that moment, I felt as disjointed as an arm torn from its socket, yet God was here, and that was enough to comfort my spirit. What I felt would help me when the preaching commenced would be with clarity and conviction. Maybe the Lord would take hold of those who were astray and grant them a new beginning.

Suddenly, something in my mind exploded as if light had just appeared on the first day of creation. The Lord had said, 'Let there be light!' The light appeared. The *word of knowledge* kicked into operation, and the whole church was lit up before me. Different stages of this church's history began to appear, one after the other, in quick succession. There was barely time to grasp one scene before another appeared. Each picture was an attention grabbing headline! It was not an apocalypse that was being witnessed, but an evolution in reverse from one thing to another. The Lord was revealing by His Spirit what this church had been through, the many phases it had entered into, and where it was at this moment. Before entering the church it had been difficult not to see the faded photographs of the former grandees as ministers, and newspaper cuttings of the opening of their new building. This had meant nothing to me; I had only taken a briefly glance at what was pasted on the notice board that had all taken place so many years before. There was no need to have an archaeological dig into the history of the church. There might be so many skeletons in these cupboards that could haunt the members and me!

Things seemed to be in the distance as the Lord, by His Spirit, began to pour into me a *word of knowledge* about church, and picture after picture was seared onto my spirit. It was amazing! It was a war scene; I could see ships and aeroplanes. As quickly as one aeroplane landed on the deck of the aircraft carrier, another took off, as if there was no tomorrow, and the ship might have disappeared when an aeroplane came back and there would be nowhere to land. Movement and alacrity was the order of the day. What I was seeing was an aircraft carrier with many aeroplanes on its deck. Some of the metal birds of the sky were taking off as others were landing. It was a scene of absolute commitment and activity. Here was commitment to war as I have never seen it before. I had a bird's eye view such as any newspaper correspondent might have in the heart of a war zone. 'This is what the church used to be like,' the Lord was saying, 'strong, powerful and meaningful.' People came in and went out into spiritual warfare.

Missionaries in the past went from here as aeroplanes into all the countries of the world. This church had been a church of commission and opportunity. It had been the finest for missionary enterprise in its day. The ship, bristling with armaments, had been the finest thing for the finest day in their history. This had been their finest hour. It had lacked no good thing, it was not 'found wanting', only giving. It was the church where visions could be seen and fulfilled, not by warlords, but by workers together with Christ.

Quite suddenly, the picture altered, and what I was seeing suddenly appeared. One moment it was one thing, and then it was something else, just like the changing scenes of time and life. Nature seemed to be going through the seasons from summer to winter. It was no longer an aircraft carrier;

the scene now showing was as a man-o'-war with powerful guns. This was truly a battle carrier. It looked threatening but there was no landing and taking off on missions as it had been in the previous metaphor. This man-o'-war was sailing but the guns were not firing. It seemed as if sailors suddenly became seamen, and it would not be long before they became landlubbers. It was depending on the way it appeared in order to conquer that which surrounded it. Every gun was polished to perfection, yet where were the marks of war and conflict? There were no burn marks to show where the guns had been fired in anger.

Before I could get a further look at this different ship, (though still a warship), and before the details could be described or meditated on, another ship of less quality, meaning, and importance suddenly emerged, as that appearing out of a mist. Here was a frigate, one sent to patrol coastal waters and implement the laws of the nation it represented. It was doing a wonderful job as it sailed from area to area without docking or landing. Its work was simply to patrol and keep others under control. This vessel was for keeping law and order, yet it would conquer no nations. Larger ships would laugh and splash as they went by. No sooner had I seen this than something else began to emerge.

From this ship, as leaves appearing from a bud, emerged what could only be described as a cargo ship. It was filled to the Plimsoll line, carrying its cargo from country to country. It was more interested in trade and diplomacy than in winning a war. There was no picture here of war, simply a ship dealing with commerce and business, doing what it had been created to do. All this seemed a little too much for my spirit, and inwardly I began to cry, tears began to slide down the walls of my heart. My spirit began to shout, 'Why have these pictures changed?' What was it all about? Even as the crying commenced, the pictures continued as each ship was reflected in those tears. What had been so mighty had been reduced to the size of a human tear! Maritime had become playtime!

What a difference between the first ship and this one! The comparison was too great for my mind! I felt part of me was recoiling from what was being revealed. The succession of ships was going from bad to worse, and each one was of less value than the other. What they were seeking to accomplish was less and less. What did all this mean?

From the cargo ship appeared a fishing smack, going to face the dangers of the sea to catch fish. Nothing had been caught; the lines and nets were not in operation. It was as if they had just left port, everything looked fresh, as if the boat had been newly painted, was sailing as if it had a destination, but wasn't quite sure where that destination was. It seemed as if it would go to where it felt the fish would be, so rather than hunting it was chasing. As the boat sailed on its fishing mission, another boat was launched from it. I was expecting to see a lifeboat, thinking they were in trouble; maybe they had 'run aground' or were sinking. There seemed to be the appeal of intensity about the scene. Danger and need sounded out from it as if 'seven bells' were being rung all at once. The boat went up and down as if it was a cork in water.

To my amazement a rowing boat came over the side of the ship! It was the sort of boat that we see in England, when Cambridge and Oxford Universities meet together on the River Thames for their yearly race. 'Will the "blues" win this race,' I thought to myself, but there wasn't going to be a winner, because before the race had been under way for more than a few strokes of the oars, one of the ships went slowly under the waves. The blades began to 'feather' as they went deeper. They weren't supposed to go down, they should have gone onward and forward, but no one seemed to inform the crew.

That was short but not sweet. Still rowing, but sinking! What had been a rowing boat, suddenly, without warning or prior consultation, became a pleasure boat, the sort you can hire when on holiday, or which you want to row down the river on a Sunday afternoon. You can take your children because there is not much danger, only a lot of pleasure. It was as if time stood still. Nothing mattered any more. Those in this boat had no particular place to go, and had all weekend to do it in. There was no one commanding the boat — there didn't need to be, it was simply a pleasure boat, a boat that dealt with the senses rather than the sensible.

Then there appeared something quite ridiculous and I thought maybe there was the requirement of a brain operation to bring me to my senses! 'Pull yourself together, man,' I heard myself saying. As the words came from my lips, so another boat appeared, but it was made out of cardboard that could not hope to face even a duckpond. It certainly was not made for the wide, wet, open sea, which would cut it into shreds of paper before it even left the harbour. This boat began to sink. It was not built to last nor to face the blasts of the east wind.

Just as dramatically as before, the pictures were all reversed. What had been degeneration suddenly became evolution. From the lesser and the smaller came the great. What had been a sinking paper ship turned into a rowing boat, then a pleasure craft, on to a fishing boat, back into metal ships which I had seen before. It was now a cargo vessel, going from port to port and country to country. It became a frigate, then a battle ship, and finally an aircraft carrier.

What did all this mean? Through the *word of knowledge*, the Spirit of God in a few moments had taken me through the history and degeneration of this church. What had been depicted as going down and down was now going up and up, on and on. The Lord had seen it slowly decrease, refusing to comply with what He wanted the church to be. It had slowly become something less than He intended. At the end it had been in danger of being a ship in dry dock or as a show boat in a museum. The church had begun to realise this, and its new minister from France was beginning to realise this too. The church was moving back to where it should be, though it would be a long and arduous process, they were in the ascendancy as part of the resurrected life of Jesus Christ. It had not yet returned to being a man-o'-war; it would require time for this to happen. They had reached a certain stage in the process, and the Lord was leading them back to the original. Forwards for them would mean backwards.

It seemed as if the anaesthetic was wearing off. Had I been having an operation or a dream? A voice was mentioning my name. It was the interpreter, who was waiting to translate my English language into the French language, telling the people that I was going to bring to them the word of God. The first was for me to describe all that the Lord had revealed through the *word of knowledge*. I had no idea of the cross that had suddenly been placed on my translator, who had no knowledge of what I was going to say. I didn't have any idea either, when entering the church, what would be said. Taking a deep breath, and not knowing if they would even understand, I simply opened my mouth, and God filled it with the words that described what I had seen during the time allotted to worship.

5

A DISTORTED VISION

While travelling to Toronto, Canada, I felt weary as the aeroplane glided effortlessly through the afternoon sky. The trip had been a long one, and within the hour we should be landing. As others were fidgeting, as if the journey had been too long, I had a sense of well being, awareness of the Lordship of Christ mastered my spirit, and the feeling of completeness centred in my soul. As I began to think of the goodness of God, and the churches that were to be visited, a strange sense of the presence of God filled the aircraft. I had no idea if others felt as I felt, but I prayed that they might, because that would result in them all coming to accept Jesus Christ as their Saviour. Here was the presence of God, and it wasn't in a church or a cathedral! There was no altar, no incense, no sound or sight of a church or a choir singing; only the steady drone of the aeroplane's engines.

I began to pray. 'Lord, if I am going to help this church that is on my mind, and its minister and members, I need something from your heart that can be passed on to them.' I knew the church, and its leader, who was a fine woman of zeal and integrity, and a born worker. If a job had to be done, then this lady would climb the ladders, hold the trowel and cut the trees. To her it was all part of a calling and Kingdom building. This prayer was a talk between God and me. Here was I, telling the Lord things that He already knew, as if information was being imparted that He needed to know. How small was my theology! What was in my heart was only chaff, but what the Lord had to offer was corn.

The Spirit of God began to mingle with my spirit; the *word of knowledge* began to show me the church, its leader and members of the congregation. Maureen, the minister, stood on a well lit stage that was shaped like a half circle. This gave a panoramic view of what was happening. Tasteful clothes meant she was always well dressed, and although engaged in work it did not detract from her appearance. She was engaged in painting a mural which stretched round the stage from end to end. It gave a semi-circular view to the eye of the beholder. There was no shortage of paint or colours; there was now and again a backward glance at the congregation, seated behind. The painting made progress, as if the heart of the person was being painted. There was the manner and assurance in her demeanour of an artist who had a picture to paint.

Now and again there was a pause and a step backwards to see if the colours matched, and the pigmentation correct. What style was hers! What accomplishment via a thin brush with its long tail! Was there too much paint here, and too little there? Was there any place that had been missed? The examining of it led to expressions on her face, and then she would dip the brush into the paint. As she painted, when the paint became tacky and too thick she began to cry, but that was alright because the tears were added to the paint, and although it was oil paint it did not seem to matter. There was no wastage of paint. This was not painting for painting's sake. Here was someone who was painting what God had given to her, and she was expressing all her emotions, grief and love in each brush stroke. The thing was a riot of colour mixed together like a bouquet of flowers.

Tears flowed as she painted, not because she was sad —these were tears of joy. I don't know if this woman was a qualified artist. The scene reminded me of a programme on British television where artists are given a scene they have to paint. Then a famous painter comes to make judgement, and the best painting receives a prize.

The painting showed different scenes of church life. The beginning of the church had been painted, and then each step forward had been expressed in paint. The sad and bad times were painted in darker colours, the happy times in glorious green, pink, white and shades of red. Even the colour of glory was added. The time when the Holy Spirit had moved the church onto something new was depicted in the green of green pastures. The blue of royalty and dignity were much in evidence.

All this was acceptable until Maureen began to paint what was to come, and what they should do next, borrowed from the vision that the Lord had given to her in prayer. Now she required vibrant colours to express her deep convictions. The canvas was not just touched with paint, it was added without measure, so that she could express her treasure. These things received from the Lord were deeper than the bottom of her heart, and had to be expressed in a deeper red than blood red. When a colour could not be found or used, there was a deep sigh from the spirit of the person painting.

At times, weariness seemed to overcome the artist. It was then that a step backwards was taken and the brushes were laid on the palette. Then she took great strong breaths, as if receiving Divine life before she could continue. These were her times of prayer and seeking the wind of the Spirit. It was as if that which was being painted was too much for her to accept, but she had accepted it, and that is why it was being painted. It was not created to be put into an art gallery or some local art show. It was painted so that others could see what she had seen in the quiet place. This was not 'self expression' but Saviour expression; it was not modern art but moving heart, where the colours seem to creep into your heart. The work was being accomplished, so that it could bring to completion that which had been revealed. That which had been seen in the dark had to be shown in the splendid colours of the new nature in Jesus Christ. That which she had received through suffering, in the blackness of night, was to be expressed in diversity of colours.

As the paintbrush ceased its ministry of painting, a person from the congregation stepped forward to tell her that a better colour, a bigger colour, something more radiant, could be used. Another one came forward and took hold of the paintbrush and began to add to what already had been achieved. Instead of vibrant life colours being added, as I looked, I could see the blackness of hell being added to the painting.

Another came forward with a vessel full of what looked like sludge, and can only be described as when the apostle Paul said he 'counted all things as "dung"' (Philippians 3:8). This served to spoil the painting until it became unrecognisable. It appeared as if the glorious creation of God, when the light appeared, had moved back into the two opening verses of Genesis 1:1–2, where the earth was 'without form and void' and 'darkness was upon the face of the deep.' It became a pre-creation painting.

When you looked at what the person from the congregation had added, compared with what had already been accomplished, it looked like the scribblings of a child or the work of a lunatic. None of it fitted into the picture. It was like something imported from a foreign land, the land of the prodigal, as seen in Luke 15.

This person returned slowly to their place in the congregation, looking back as they went back admiring their 'slap dash'. The pastor might have painted one thing, they were seeing another. People only paint what they see. They were seeing it all in their colours as their painting. They wanted to dress the future as they saw it, and felt it had been snatched from them as a toy from a child. No sooner had one person sat down than another stood up and came forward — not to tell where things were wrong, it was with stronger motives than this. They had come to add colour where it never should have been. They were in danger of spoiling the whole effect. They would degrade this paining. With Maureen's name written on it as a signature, she would be ashamed to be identified with it if it were left as it was.

Another would-be artist stepped forward, as if he were going to paint the finest picture ever seen. There was that look of steel in his eyes. If determination could paint, then this would be a masterpiece. I could tell the way he walked forward that he felt he should have been a prime minister or a general! He carried a bucket that was so full the contents swept over the side as if they had outstayed their welcome. I was left wondering that he would add to this mural. Would he turn it into a miracle?

Where was his paintbrush? Instead of a paintbrush or a pallette of paint, he simply drew the bucket back, gave it an unceremonious swing from his thigh, and the contents splashed all over the painting. If he wanted to make a 'big splash' he had certainly done so. It now looked like one of those 'quick fix', do-it-yourself paintings, a 'painting by numbers', where you join up the dots and the picture is formed. First number one, number two, number three and so on, until all had drawn their convictions in paint. The numbers were not on the wall but in the number of people who stepped forward, willing to add their thoughts and ideas to that which they considered was not ideal or well thought through.

What colour had come from that bucket? I was like a man looking for colour where there was no colour. Had I become colour blind? It wasn't red, yellow or pink. It seemed as if it had contained the 'lukewarm water' that Jesus spoke of in Revelation 3:16, denoting a lukewarm person, neither hot or cold. These were the contents of his heart. It had the colour of pigswill that he had brought from the far country the prodigal son had visited in Luke 15. This man was neither hot nor cold, he had spewed this out of the vessel he was carrying, and I could detect that he was in that far country and a near relative of the prodigal. There was no 'many colours' found in the word 'manifold 'grace. The red rust of the steely law was not even added.

As this person without any artistic quality left the stage, another rose to take their place. I began to think and pray. Was there no end to this army with broomsticks instead of paintbrushes? The artist had used the slim type of paintbrush created by craftsmen to be used by those painting pictures. The brushes these people were going to use were broomsticks and yard brushes. If their suggestions were not acceptable they would brush everything away, to be seen no more. Have you ever tried brushing a wet painting with a yard brush? It doesn't improve, it rather gets worse! It wasn't the past they were trying to alter with their own paint and brushes, it was the future. They wanted to decide the direction of the church. They wanted others to see it in the colour of their hearts and personalities. Self expression can lead to self destruction and depression.

The next one to step forward came with a large tube of what

appeared at first glance to be paint. He ran towards the half finished mural, squeezed the tube, and the contents splashed all over the paining. To my amazement, what came out of the tube was not paint but glue. He was trying to make doubly sure that what had been suggested would not be altered. What the membership had added would remain permanently. This picture was in danger of becoming a farce. The problem was that the colours were now mixed together, and it wasn't a bit like Joseph's coat of many colours. It was as if two pages of painting had been stuck together in a child's painting book, then had been pulled apart with torn paper on some parts and paint peeled off in others.

A large, strong man came with a bucket filled with water. I did not realise that there was water in the bucket until he threw it over the picture, as if he thought the tide coming in would wash away the nation that occupied the land. Here was another King Canute! All the water did was to splash over the work accomplished, good and bad, and left it dripping wet. It was stagnant water: to avoid it was to live, but to drink it meant death, through poisoning. There is no colour in water. What sort of colour did he think this would add to the painting? If that bucket had been filled from his heart it would have been as dirty dishwater. If he had washed his hands in the bucket, then woe to anyone who followed to wash their hands!

The leader of the church fell to her knees, asking the Lord to remove all such evidence and the markings that had been added to what was so good, so clear, and so decisive. In her heart she had the feeling that all was marred, all was lost. No-one would ever be able to tell what her vision for the community was, because of those with long fingers like paintbrushes. As Maureen knelt down, and looked away from the painting, a Hand came from above, passed over what was a sorry mess, and wiped it clean. Amazingly, that completed by the pastor was left, and that added by others who were not artists was removed. It reminded me of the poet Alfred Lord Tennyson, who, when a person gave him a handkerchief with an ink spot on it, simply drew around the ink spot, turning it into a flower head, then added a stem to the lovely bluebell.

Any mistakes of colour or contour were made to look good. It was as if the Hand that came added the colour of glory to the painting. Each thing painted found its true form because of the Hand and the glory. That Hand had the ability to do what the leader or the people could not do. It added sheen to the painting like lacquer, ensuring it would shine in the darkness.

6

THE CHURCH ON THE MOVE

As the plane began to descend in Montreal, Canada, I felt weary because of the many miles that I had travelled, dragged through the air as Ezekiel had been dragged by his hair. (Ezekiel 3:14.) The weight of my body felt rather like an anchor to my spirit. I felt as if my body was closing down as if it had been a business that had been open twenty-four hours. The signs were tiredness and drooping eyelids, and as I thought about rest and sleep, there crept over me a consciousness of God's presence that only the Spirit of God can bring, and suddenly I felt as fresh as the daisy when it first pokes its head out of the soil in the meadow. I could now do all things through Christ who strengthens me. (Philippians 4:13.) I was ready for war, toil or torment.

I had visited this particular church some three years earlier, but since then there had been little contact between the leader and myself. One of the drawbacks was that I only spoke English, and he spoke French fluently but would stutter, stammer and guess when it came to speaking English.

Seven years earlier there had only been just fifteen people in attendance, yet the day that stands out in my memory there were approximately 450 adults attending, plus 130 children. The church was a hive of activity, with people praying, singing and radiating the presence of Christ. On the Sunday morning I was asked to place my hands on each child as they went by me. They lined up as an army of little people. It was a privilege indeed, but there was a need for Hur and Aaron to keep my hands lifted up, even as the hands of Moses, as Israel fought with the enemy. (Exodus 17:10–12.) As each head passed under my hand, the blessing of Abraham, Isaac and Jacob was pronounced upon them. They all looked delighted, as if somebody had mentioned taking them to Disneyland!

The *word of knowledge* had come into ministry as things were revealed to my heart for this church that had invited me. In my spirit I was in a large English country mansion with an open fire, and the minister of the church was standing before the fire in a room that was part of a country mansion. The grate and the surrounds were as if from Victorian era in the United Kingdom. Carvings of cherubim were on the outside of the fire surround, the mantle shelf was made of marble, yet there was nothing ornate on it. It was large, as if it belonged to a large house with many servants. Here was a sign of affluence and riches in the decor. The fire in the grate was burning hot and fierce, as if trying to keep people away rather than inviting them to come closer for warmth. The fire was so hot it reminded me of hell! The pastor could not get as close as he wanted. In his hands were tongs with long handles, the type used by servants in the Middle Ages in England. It was toilsome work trying to get close to that roaring fire.

To get to the fire to put on it the materials he had, the man was using fire tongs, which had metal fingers on the end to grab with. He was sweating profusely, the sweat coursing down his face and falling off the end of his chin. He placed the coal-like material on the fire, but, when the fire took hold of it, the material fell off because it was not the real thing, it was dross. There was no ready mix with the fire. It was not the fire that was false, it was the materials used. As soon as the fire engulfed it, there was the revelation of its true nature. As this happened time and time again, a worried look came on the face of the man with the tongs. Frustration seemed to be doing its best to hinder this beloved minister. He wanted the material to become part of his vision but it was failing to be combined with the rest of what was in the grate, burning merrily away. He didn't personally let these foreign coals fall off the fire into the hearth, it was the fire that was rejecting them. What a smell they made as they lay there smouldering. There had been such promise in what he thought was the right material, yet the fire was rejecting them with a definite 'no'.

The fire continued burning, and the man in the picture began to do what I thought was a stupid thing. He began forcing himself to get nearer to the fire. The tongs had been surrendered, now he was using his bare hands, yet flesh is no guard against a hot fire. Was he about to burn his fingers? Had he read 1 Corinthians 13, and was he about to give his body to be burned? Would he become the evangelist with no hands? He himself would be in need of healing. He was in danger of becoming the next man with a withered hand. I had heard of giving your all, but this seemed a little fanatical, but not half as fanatical as fire is when it hungrily and angrily feeds on fuel. There was attractiveness about the red flames, as if they were casting a spell. This person seemed to be dicing with death, trying to get nearer the fire as if he had some suicidal impulse. Without the rods of steel to help him, he would be burnt to a cinder! He was actually placing his hand under the grate, where the fire burned so fiercely, causing me to think that the hand, skin and bone would shrivel to be nothing. I was expecting him to recoil with pain, there seemed no other possibility. As his hand went under the grate, instead of it being burned it was lit up, and became a platform for other things. The glow of glory filled that hand, as it adopted the nature of the fire. From those burning coals drops of precious metal was falling through the flames, the hand miraculously catching them as they came from the fire. There were drops of silver, drops of gold, drops of other precious metals so rare that they could not be defined or recognised. He held his hand under the fire and I held my breath to see if it would disappear as the heat performed its evangelism.

Here were the coals on the fire being transformed into something neither expected nor explicable. Coal does not turn into silver and gold! By a process the coal might become a diamond if it was pressurised, but it would never turn into silver or gold. There is gold in the fire of God. A miracle being witnessed by the power of God. The greater miracle was yet to come. As each globule of silver and gold touched his hand, they went forth from the hand as if being set free. They had been the prisoners of fire long enough. Their term of sentence was over, and they had been the recipients of the King's pardon. No voice spoke; it was not a picture of words but of actions, of deeds and activity. This was like watching a 'silent movie'.

As each particle touched the hand of the minister, as he stirred the fire and put coals on, they flew from his hand through every window of the church (which were wide open). It was as if they had developed the wings of eagles. They went through every door of the church, and each door was wide open. They went through every orifice in that building. Where light could enter, they could get out. Where wind could blow, they would go. They had a compulsion to get out and go. As I looked through the church windows I could see them going along the streets and over the hills, through garden and vale on into the unknown. These silver and gold drops had become evangelists and missionaries to the world at large. Was the Lord revealing that this would be a missionary church? There was no looking back or tuning back, they went in a straight line, obeying their calling, on to their destination.

On the Sunday morning I was the speaker and, being invited into the pulpit, I stepped onto the platform. Then the pastor and his pretty wife were called out to the front of the church. They knelt on the floor as if waiting to be knighted. The Spirit of God began to flow, and I began to interpret to them in English what the Lord had revealed and what He was saying. It was the describing of a miracle. This was of Holy Ghost proportions. There was no groping or guessing, just a flow as the Spirit of the Lord began to move me to give the interpretation of what had been witnessed earlier.

The leader had tried to ordain men and women he thought could help with his evangelism. He was looking for those who would be true yokefellows (Philippians 4:3). All he had managed to do was to find a 'yoke' not a 'fellow,' somebody with the same vision that could plough the field with him. Using his natural powers he had made certain choices, but in doing so he had mistaken camels for horses.

This man had a heart of gold, the heart of an evangelist. His breathed-out prayer was that the lost might be found, and those perishing should be saved. He had chosen these so-called 'helpers', yet when the fire began to burn, when things began to get tough, like the dross seen in the *word of knowledge* they began to back off, and leave the church. We believe that when the going gets tough, the tough 'get going', but these were 'going' to leave the church. The fire had discovered the nature of those around the minister; as he ordained those pointed out to him by the Lord, the fire began to burn brightly. They were the ones transformed into globules of silver, gold and precious metals. They would go from the fire to his hand, and then into the world at large. These would go out of the church into the world to commence other churches, and lead many to know Jesus Christ as their Saviour. He would build on silver and gold as produced by the Lord. There would be no hay or stubble that could be burned as representative of self works. They had been born in the fire, and the fire would keep them as silver and gold, very precious, worth having and keeping.

It was in quiet conversation over a meal afterwards that the minister confirmed what was in his heart. He told me that all I had seen and said was true. He had tried to get others to help him but instead of being silver and gold they had become broken reeds, and when he had leaned on them they had failed him. He had gathered other men around him, and the Lord had given him a vision to go to another large township about sixty miles away, where he intended to commence a church. He had already pioneered a church that was 150 strong, which I visited from the Monday to the Wednesday of that week.

They were in the process of sending others out, and were to commence another church as soon as possible. I had given to him the silver and the gold. He wanted confirmation of the will of God, and the Lord had sent a man from England to confirm his dream, dreams that were about to become reality. Each word spoken had assured him that what he had was the plan of the Lord. He now believed that the Lord of the harvest would send out not only workers as sowers and servants, but as reapers into the harvest field which was all around them in that needy area. He had plans and the Lord had confirmed these plans, they were ready to move forward. In his mind he was thinking, as he prayed that day, 'Silver and gold have I none, but such as I have I give it unto You.' Whatever was given to God would become precious metal. When the Day of Judgment came it would not suffer through being tried by fire, but having been refined would stand the test of any examination and the trial of any fire.

7

TRYING TO ACCOMPLISH THE IMPOSSIBLE

John was a strong man, one of the strongest men I have met. Not a Samson or a David, but a Barzillai, a man of steel or steely man (2 Samuel 19). Here was one who, when Atlas was giving body parts to others to make them his disciples, had certainly been lavish with the doling out of muscles. He was physically strong, but not so strong spiritually. Looks can be deceiving, but they can also be dynamic! His hard eyes seemed to look straight through you as if he was looking to something that was beyond where you were standing. The marks of a tough life were part of his features, as if he had spent many hours working out in the open. It seemed as if nature had used him as a sketch board, and some of the best hours had been etched into the man's strong face. He was not only strong in face and features, but his body was well proportioned. He seemed to be a perfect match with all his parts fitting neatly together.

He was one of the elders of the church. On meeting him you knew you were meeting someone with a 'presence'; there would be no fooling around with him. If there was, his large hand would come upon yours and he would squeeze the life out of your little finger. If work needed to be done he was the man for the job. Built like a steel shovel, he could be used as such. He was gifted in so many areas. It was a pleasure to see his strong arms moving like tree trunks as he moved things around.

One morning, the Spirit of God moved upon this man and he began to cry like a baby. It was one of those rare occasions, rarer than a 'blue moon', orchestrated by the Spirit of the Lord. Unannounced, unexpected, the unction began to flow into his heart. As John's heart was stretched by the moving of the Holy Spirit, more room was being made for God and His influences in what had been a restricted heart, open to most things but closed to others. What was happening this Sunday morning was indeed making it a holy day, a Sabbath day, the day of the Lord. In it the Almighty was beginning to operate by the gifts of the Holy Spirit. What was revealed was universal in its application, for what the Lord does applies to one and all.

He came forward for prayer, as one who had been waiting a long time for this opportunity to listen to the Lord. He had been like the strong ass tied that the disciples were sent to loose and set free. That animal, having only burdens on its back, was to be the living throne of Jesus Christ as He went up into Jerusalem. (Mark 11:2.) Through the *word of knowledge* I saw through the man into the past, even as a present and a future in the Lord was revealed. Many times, the Almighty reveals people as they are, and then reveals all that they can be with His help. God doesn't tell us how splendid we are all the time; sometimes the gifts of the Holy Spirit are given for comfort, but not always.

John's strong arms were moving backwards and forwards. I wondered if he was swimming, or sawing a large log of wood, but on closer inspection, there appeared to be something in his hands. His grip was not that of a man holding the end of a roof, afraid of slipping off, it was the grip of a workman who meant business. If his arms had been wings, he would have taken off and flown away out of the church! He was part of something and here was the demonstration of his zeal for the Lord. Using his strength, he moved backwards and forwards. It almost seemed as if he might be in a gymnasium, involved in a workout. There was a need to know why he was moving as he was. The successive movements of his arms were attracting my attention, yet he stood still.

It was as if a camera had taken a close-up shot of his activities, but then, in a split second, the lens drew back, and the fuller picture of what the man was doing could be seen. I was amazed because there was before me a picture that would not have been found in my snapshot album. The picture revealed that this man was actually rowing a boat. He was in the boat alone. It was a small rowing boat that required no captain or crew; being such a strong man he was both. Where was he going? What was he doing? Was he about to take a trip abroad? Was John like the self styled seaman in an English seaside resort found drifting with the tide, out of control, with a 'road map' in his hands, trying to find his way through the swirling, boisterous sea with a map designed for roads?

All these mad thoughts rushed to my brain, and sent my head spinning for the moment. The Spirit of the Lord, who was the Author of what was being revealed, breathed His calmness into my spirit. The man might be rowing in troubled waters, but the calm of Jesus Who had said, 'Peace; be still' was at the centre and circumference of my soul. John might have been at the water's edge trying to get across to the other side. He certainly knew he had to row the boat using both oars to get there. Wasn't there a story of a drunk who got into a rowing boat and rowed all night, only to realise in the morning light that he had forgotten to raise the anchor and loose the rope that had berthed the ship.

Maybe the Lord wanted him to leave the boat and walk

on water? The sea of glass in the Book of Revelation was what he required, because despite his efforts the boat was not moving. He certainly knew how to row; it was as if he had trained as an Oxford blue. Maybe if I watched long enough he would turn out to be 'landlubber green'. What was he trying to pull away from? The arms and oars worked well together, though his arms must be aching ready to drop off. Was there the challenge here of a man entering into new depths, rowing the boat while it was calm, but needing to trust the Lord in the coming storm?

Then looking beyond the man's activity, beyond the boat and the oars towards the horizon, to my chagrin and disbelief, there was the realisation that became part of me that the way this man John was rowing was to no avail, for he did not sail. . . . Here was a lot of effort without any progress. Maybe his spirituality was like that? Was he full of good works but never able to accomplish anything, repeating the same old thing, day in and day out? With one oar marked 'grace' and another marked 'love,' or one marked 'faith' and the other marked 'works', he might move and arrive. If he continued his exercise he would require new oars and arms. He was ploughing and digging dust. It was flying everywhere, and as he kept rowing so the dust kept flying. What John did not realise was that beyond the cloud of dust, almost indicative of a coming sand storm, there stood a Figure; hidden by the dust stood the One that mattered. It was Jesus Christ with His hand outstretched, water pouring from the holes in those hands, water to satisfy John's thirst that had the grip of a fever upon him because of his worthless activity. When he stopped rowing, water began to stream from the hands, side and feet of Jesus Christ, creating enough water to row a boat in. If he continued to dig holes, the water would fill them.

It seemed as if a lifetime passed by, as the real import of what had been received and seen was given. Sense was put back into the sensible. The reason he was not making progress and had to row so hard was the fact that the boat was on a beach. John was in the wrong place at the wrong time. You do not row in sand! The oars will act simply as shovels, or ploughs to plough up the sand. The boat was surrounded by sand! There was no water for it to move through. The native and necessary element was missing. There would never be any movement until the man got into the water. It seemed to me as if more would have been accomplished if he dragged the boat with the oars inside of it to the nearest sea or lake. His future possibilities and the possibilities of the boat were in water, not in sand. Until John yielded to the Spirit of God he would make no progress. He could volunteer for many things, but he would become like a jumble sale, a mixture of unimportant things.

The oars might be stout and thick, well wooded and carved lovingly by a craftsman; the boat might be new from the boat yard, freshly caulked; yet without the water it can do nothing, go nowhere, and make no progress. His heart might have been as a maritime museum, but without water all was to no avail. Captain Blythe and Lord Nelson might have been distant relatives of his, but this would not take him to his destination. We need the Spirit of God as much as a boat or any fisherman needs water. The man would have been better if had made the sign of the cross with the oars for that is where God commands the blessing. What he needed to do was to take off his sweaty shirt, so wet with perspiration and desperation it would have rivalled Gideon's dewy fleece (Judges 6:38). He needed to place it on a pole as a sign of surrender and as a cry for help because he had been marooned.

Something, someone, had deceived this man. He had embraced a false doctrine or idea that sand was water; that being stationary meant he was moving. It was like the Electric

Bray, near Falkirk in Scotland, where if you park your car facing downhill, you get the illusion that the car is moving of its own accord back up the hill. It never moves from its place, yet there is the sensation that it is moving contrary to nature.

While he slept, someone had pulled the plug, and the sea had drained away. When he commenced rowing there had been plenty of sea, but now his sweat was more than the sea. He had been surrounded by the native element of the boat. When he awoke he was busy rowing, doing and helping, yet the waters were receding, the tide going out, and he would be left as high and as dry as those he was trying to assist. He had not been conscious of his position. While the water disappeared he was putting more effort into his activities to compensate for that disappearance. Here was a sailor without a sea and a boat without water. He would break no records, whether on land or sea. If this had been a famous painting, all who viewed it in the art gallery would have had a good laugh, because the vital ingredient had been left out of the picture.

The Spirit of the Lord would provide all that he required. There would be tide and movement in what the Lord would bring into this life. That move of God would bring the boat back into its area of trading. The native element would be restored. Stranded up a creek without a paddle, he would yet sail again. The lift he would receive would come through the waters swirling around him and his boat. He needed something to dip oars into, even as we all need the love of God. He was doing all the right things for all the right reasons, but reason had rejected him when he tried to row without water.

Like this man, many are good, Christian, religious and righteous, yet they lack the swirling waters. As the waters came so the rowing became easier. There was a movement in the boat that told John he was moving. The Almighty had given him an almighty push by sending water to help him. There are those who lack a move of the Spirit of God. You need water for eldership or any other gift. This man's talent would have been buried in the sand, for the boat was sinking lower and lower. He thought he was going somewhere, yet written in the sand as with a Divine finger were the words, 'The road to nowhere'. It was God who brought him back on course by supplying the water. He merrily sang as he now rowed away in the blessing of almighty God. He had learned the lesson that if you are to sail you need water, lots of water, and the larger the vessel the deeper the waters required.

Whenever the water level fell, then Jesus was seen standing near the boat, supplying the water from His wounds. The last time I saw John he was rowing, with a smile on his face, to a new destination in God. Maybe, just maybe, to a 'treasure island'.

8

THE SINGING TREE

The meeting had commenced with a sense of the Unknown being with us. What good things would the Lord do tonight? Here we were in Quebec City, Canada. Each time we had met in this particular Church, the meetings had gone on for hours because the people were so hungry for God. They clamoured for Christ. The meetings were always as well attended, as people sought bread to assuage their hunger. The Lord had been very gracious, revealing many things of an eternal nature. Truth had a banquet, as Jesus Christ, and Him crucified, was presented. Hearts had been emptied and then refilled by the Spirit of God. This church had become the workshop of Jesus of Nazareth, where many things were righted. It was time to pray for those who had responded to the invitation to come forward. As they approached, so the Spirit of the living God came down, and, as the two movements became one, Pentecost became the order of the day.

Sylvia had a confident look about her; she seemed to be at ease standing in front of a congregation; at the front of the church she was in her native element, without any fear of being in the public gaze. I was to find out why. As the Lord unlocked the secrets of her heart as through the Holy Spirit, the *word of knowledge* began to reveal the heart of God. What would I see? What would I say to this refined renegade? What was uttered came directly from the throne of heaven. Men in their wildest dreams cannot possibly dream the things that the Lord says to people.

I could see a tree, and you might think that there was nothing different about that because I was in the land of enormous trees; it being autumn, called the 'fall', every tree in this country was dressed in autumn glory, as the trees took on many different colours. Thousands of colours were seen, as if, in Creation, God had only one thing on His mind and that was colour.

The lady approached me, and I began to ask the Lord to reveal what He wanted me to say to her. It was to be a public word about the woman's private life. As I looked at the woman, looking to the Lord, the Spirit of God revealed the picture of a tree. The full tree in all the glory of nature appeared suddenly, as if it had been commanded to be planted right where I was standing. A poster which had caught my eye before I flew out of England had read, 'Plant a tree and save a nation.' This tree before me now would save a life by setting it free, as free as music from an instrument. You never know what music is going to do, and I had no idea what this tree might mean. It had many leaves on it, and was a mature tree when it appeared. It seemed as if nature had been in a good mood when this tree was dressed; in fact, by the number of leaves, it seemed as if it was overdressed. There was no sign or sound of birds singing in its branches. There were no feathered friends flying in and out of the tree. It stood motionless, as if waiting for something to happen, yet I had the feeling that if nothing happened then this tree would make it happen. It would be the evangelist and teacher of nature.

Suddenly, every leaf on the tree began to sing as if a

conductor had raised his baton. Each leaf was singing is if it had been filled with the Spirit of the Lord, and was 'making melody in its heart to the Lord with psalms, hymns and spiritual songs' (Ephesians 5:19). The Lord knows what He is doing. I cannot count the occasions during my ministry that the Almighty has spoken to people in a language they understood, or taken their profession to express some truth to their hearts. God takes what is familiar to tell unfamiliar stories. When He speaks in our mother tongue we listen with many ears. Jesus took the birds of the air, a woman baking bread, and a sower sowing seed, to tell parables the people could identify with. Here was the Creator of music, taking what He had created and using it for His glory.

The Lord does not always speak in high tones or a deep commanding voice. To youth He will speak in a youthful voice, not the voice of the Ancient of Days. He does not whistle to those who are deaf. He sings to those who need encouragement with the voice of the well Beloved. He is nature's favourite Musician, and the Leader of many orchestras. God will orchestrate a situation into that which sounds like music, when it was only expected to be a dull thud or the sound of a cymbal. He knows how to make music even out of cymbals! He knows that those things we do not understand can frighten us away, when His intention is always to draw us closer to Himself. You will catch more flies with honey than with vinegar. I have seen strong, steely men burst into tears as they listened to music. Music can hold the key to the heart, to open and break down resistance, until resistance becomes assistance.

As I looked, so I listened. What was the Lord revealing to my spirit? Voices singing as a choir were coming from the tree. This was no 'trumpet voluntary'. It seemed as if every branch was a baton, and the conductor of music had arrived at the podium. This was to be a night and day of music, yet there were no musicians and no orchestra. Maybe I was looking for 'wood instruments' because it was a tree. Where was the massed choir? None of these things were part of the tree. Miraculously, music was coming from every branch and leaf, vibrating as if each leaf sent rays of sunshine during the summer months. The whole tree was like a splendid orchestra on the opening night of the 'Proms'. The music was heavenly; it was the music of the spheres. There were no song sheets, time had not been given for practice; now was the time to play and make music. Nothing like this had ever been heard by me before this moment.

Here was a new creation in music, the creation of the world expressed in musical terms and notes. This music had been borrowed from the sons of the morning as they sang at creation (Job 38:7). Each song was as a star shining. Every voice, every rhythm was in tune, and all was as complete as any music could and should be. Every leaf was playing, singing its part. Oh, to belong to a church where every member operated as these leaves did, with full heart, voice and soul! This was their finest movement, expressing through music their dedication. Here was rhythm without the 'blues'. Here was music that could be listened to day and night. It was more than 'pop music'; it was more than 'classical'. It seemed to be opera music that was coming from the tree. If music in heaven is like this, then many treats wait those going there. I love music, and this music was 'the food of love'. Any wrangling that might have been in the human spirit would be released at this moment.

When heaven's music comes to earth, as it did at the birth of Jesus Christ, the whole hillside stops and listens, as if their life depended on what they were hearing. (Luke 2:13.) It was instigating and inspiring, the sort of music that brought refreshment to the heart, mind and spirit. All fighting armies have their own music to breathe fresh inspiration into the troops before and after battle. You could fight any battle and win with a line from one of the songs coming from the tree. It was of the same nature as that played by David on his harp when King Saul was depressed. (1 Samuel 16:23; 18:10; 19:9.) It soothed away sorrow and promised a brighter tomorrow. If only that tree, or a tree like this, could be planted in my own garden in England. Then the words of the poet Robert Browning would mean something quite different when he wrote, 'Oh, to be in England now that April's there.' Oh, to be in England now that this tree has been planted there! My heart was comforted. Things that could never be in my country could be in my heart.

The strange thing about this music and the tree was that every leaf was singing a different song, as if each one was a soloist, although together it seemed as if they were singing the same song. Then, when a leaf fell to the ground, it seemed to the listener that it was a different song coming from every leaf. Each leaf had been trained in music, trained by the highest realm known to man. Here was a college of music, beautiful and complete. To remove one leaf would spoil the whole music and singing. With these beautiful sounds in my ears I could have climbed Mount Everest, Ben Nevis, and the whole of Snowdonia and Kilimanjaro in one step! There was in the music that which swept away every discordant sound my ears had ever heard. If I had been ill, that music would have healed me. From it was coming a therapeutic wave to wave goodbye to every malady. Here was music that could soothe a spirit, open a blind eye and set the cripple walking, leaping and praising God.

It reminded me of a time in an English Bible college when the students were to speak in a church. They travelled in the college people carrier, and as they did so the Holy Spirit entered the vehicle, and they began to sing in tongues. There was nothing unusual about that, for Pentecostal people sing with the Spirit and with the understanding. (1 Corinthians 14:15.) What was remarkable was that they were all singing yet it was the same tongue they were singing in. That was more than unison. They were singing in a language they had never learned, the same language for all to express their worship to the Lord.

The Scriptures speak of 'making melody in your heart unto the Lord', and my heart wanted these songs that the tree was singing. (Ephesians 5:19.) They were not there for my purpose. This must not become self-indulgence. These things were being revealed through the *word of knowledge* for someone else. I was hearing songs that must be passed on. The music was meant for another. They were not necessarily spiritual songs, nor were they the latest release of a chorus or a hymn. It was as if they were being created as a testimony to the musical ability of the Writer. This musical 'score' had 'scored'. My grandchildren must be sent to this Author for music lessons!

The leaves were singing as if they were worshipping as in the Christmas story, Luke 2, presenting gold, frankincense and myrrh through music. The trees' national anthem was being expressed through many songs and voices. It was so great that it could not be expressed in one song, it needed many. The song was their signature. Tongues of men and of angels, tongues known and unknown, give glory to the Lord. This song was no 'swan song', no funeral lament, or reveille call for soldiers to arise and put their armour on. It seemed as if the Lord had done the impossible by putting a rainbow into music. It was more colourful than colour; it sounded like something never heard before. Were angels with angelic voices hiding among the branches? It seemed as if every leaf was a harp, being made to play and sing.

The leaves of this large tree were not perennial, not green in colour as one might have expected. They were too numerous to count, but they had turned brown, as if they had gone through their youth, beyond maturity, and degeneration had become part of them. Who had coated these leaves with degeneration? I felt in my spirit that at some time each leaf had been silver or gold in colour. Each leaf had been willing to play its part by singing sweet music, but was Sylvia standing before me willing to play her part? Did the colour of the leaves depict her state of heart? Was there part of her repertoire that was missing? Was there something that she would not sing for the Lord?

Part of what I have written here was said to this large lady standing before me. As soon as I mentioned singing, she fell to the floor as if she had been shot, not to die but to live. Tears became too many to count; her sobs were the sobs of the prodigal as he returned home and fell on his father's neck, a father who, when he went looking for his son, carried with him shoes to put on his feet. Here was the music that the elder brother heard while he was out in the field. (Luke 15.) The words spoken to Sylvia were, 'There is music in you. I can see a tree with many leaves, and each leaf is singing a different song. There is lots of music in you.' It was at that moment that she was reduced to a crumbled, crying heap on the floor. Why was she so upset when music was mentioned? This should have revived this fainting lady.

After a while, the lady composed herself, and said she wanted to speak to me. 'I have never heard anything like that before,' she said. 'I am an opera singer, and I have just completed a tour of Europe. This is my first day back, and since I left town I have not visited a church. My heart has been growing cold towards the Lord. The songs of Zion and the song of a soul set free have not been part of me. There were plenty of other songs to sing, but the Lord has found that my living has been 'off key' and I have been hitting the wrong notes. I realise He wants my life to be like a melody. I am returning to Him, to let him retune my life so that I can sing for Him, and glorify the Lord wherever I am.' Praying for her was easy, as easy as those leaves that were singing their joyful songs. Sylvia was there as an instrument waiting and wanting to be retuned by the Master's touch. Music had found a musician and she came back to the Lord. She was as an instrument put into the hands of one with a ready spirit waiting to express their deepest feelings through music. Music had done its work of stirring the spirit and bringing back fond memories of former days.

9

DEALING WITH CULTURAL DIFFERENCES

The church had just a few members. Ruth and her husband were invited to accept the pastorate. What could they do among a few old women? Preaching and serving God in Manchester, England, was tough — as tough as an elephant's hide. With the fire of God burning in her heart, Ruth decided to make a go of it, and applied herself diligently to the work that was presented to her. Like many in the Scriptures, this woman had a mind to work, and loving the Lord with all her strength meant serving Him to the best of her ability, and beyond. There was such a strong conviction within Ruth's heart that all things could be done through Jesus Christ who strengthened her. She was simply a woman, but she was all woman, and 'all for God' was her motto. He was her rising thought, her sleeping dream. Her life was a circle, the circle of the crown that He wore when in her spirit there was that witness of His presence helping, chiding, loving and gracing all her being. This was a romance with Jesus Christ that had been established between her soul and the Lord of Glory.

As this spirit prevailed in the community, with many outreach projects the work began to grow. It was hard work which took many hours from what seemed to be a short life. The work for Him must be deep; His love must be poured through that work, whether it was in the pulpit, in prayer or in passion as she worshipped. All were tokens of her love for Him, and were part of that love that had been poured into her soul when forgiveness was introduced into her heart. The church began to fill, and very soon there was a need to extend the building. If anyone could have merited heaven by prayers being answered it was this couple who pleaded with the Lord until something happened. The barren wilderness began to blossom with roses and all manner of flowers. As the congregation grew, many different ethnic origins were added. Anyone looking for a multicultural society had only to come to this church and witness what the Lord had done. It seemed as if a little bit of heaven had come to earth, because the congregation were made up of people from every tongue, tribe and nation. What can be described as a 'massed band' was seen in the different coloured faces as they met together Sunday by Sunday.

Each one made their own contribution to the church as they met together. They expressed their love for the Lord in many different ways, but the end result and the statement of faith were always the same. One worshipped using an instrument, another with a loud voice, others as a massed choir echoing the praises of the Majesty on high. Others were more vocal in their worship. There were those who worshipped as if they were instruments of worship, with a Divine hand moving swiftly but gently over the strings of the 'string section' of an orchestra. All resulted in a true symphony of worship. The grand conclusion was that Jesus was Lord over all. He was Lord not only above every sunset sky, the glittering stars, the moon or sun, but in the hearts of these who gathered to worship Him.

I could hear Ruth weeping as prayer was offered for these

new ebony, yellow, white and brown converts, these different nationalities that were in the church. How could she, a mere human and a woman, bind them together? Many times they had been placed together, brick upon brick, but they had fallen down when the wind blew upon them. Ruth understood how Nehemiah must have felt when he was taunted by Sanballat who said of the work of God, 'If a fox hits the wall with its tail it will fall down' (Nehemiah 4:3). He was really saying, 'You haven't heard from God at all. You require a new building manager and a new building plan. You have lost the plot.'

Ruth tried every method in the book she was reading, the Bible. None of what she had learned in remedial classes or the training on how to counsel seemed to blend these people together. Her own soul seemed to be in need of a counsellor at this moment. Maybe if an outing was arranged everything would gel? Many activities were suggested, and Ruth exhausted herself trying to promote them. When anything was arranged, each segment appeared to migrate to its own breed and nation. They were as different as the proverbial chalk and cheese. Who can get oil and water to mix? There was a feeling of desperation such as must have been in the heart of Aaron when he reported to Moses. 'I threw this in and this came out' (Exodus 32:24). He was speaking as if it couldn't be helped, and what would be would be.

This could not be allowed to happen. Ruth must work on these unpromising and uncompromising materials. It did not matter that it would take minutes, hours, days, months and years. Ruth was determined to see it work, to bring these people together to sit at the feet of Jesus where cultural differences did not matter. When people are taken up with Jesus, they forget they have differences, culture is turned into character. Eternally, character, not culture, will be the deciding factor. Ruth's brain became heavy with torment; it seemed as if condemnation was awaiting her, as a judge with a black cap, as she sought to find a way through. Each time the thought of winning came into her heart, it was overtaken by thoughts of losing and destroying. Losing and binding, instead of people being set free. 'Where, oh where, is the theology that deals with separation, and nation speaking peace to nation?' Ruth cried. She was aware that, in the natural, if you force people to forget their differences and come together you drive them further apart.

I saw Ruth through the *word of knowledge*, standing alone with all these different threads in her hand. At first it seemed as if she was a weaver and had gathered the many strands together. As they were placed in her hand, the colours were mixed up. Some of the threads were torn apart, and it was her ministry to join them together. As they were knotted together, the wrong colour was united to another. Some threads were shorter than others, and that presented another problem. Maybe a pair of scissors could clip the ends, and then they would all be of the same length. Each thread seemed to be of a different material, which was so unusual. Was this worker and prayer making a new dress out of old pieces? Unlikely, because the dresses she wore were beautiful and plentiful. As she walked among the people, ministering to them, there was the appearance of the Queen of Sheba as a flower, adding décor, brightness and colour into drab situations. If she had attended a flower show, the first prize would have been hers.

The threads were fed through her hands, each one gazed at lovingly. If only there had been the heart and ability of one who could change things here, then from each thread a flower would have been produced. There was a longing that meant if it was possible, then it would have been accomplished long ago.

What was needed was not pushed to the back of Ruth's mind

it was part of her, mind, body and soul. These threads were part of her ministry, and there must be a way to transform them into a Scotsman's kilt or a Persian rug with its usual knot, telling where it came from. 'Maybe pictures of seraphim and cherubim with angels could be printed on them when they were joined together, Just like it was in the Old Testament tabernacle,' she thought. If thoughts and prayers could have brought about the transformation, then it would have happened long ago. There needed to be another creation, but where was the pattern to come from? Ruth knew that we are His 'workmanship', and it is from this word that we obtain the English word 'poetry'. (Ephesians 2:10.) What was needed was something or someone to turn these people who were like words that would not stand on the same page and form a sentence together, to take this alphabet of different colours, and make sense of it all. Where was the word of wisdom?

As each thread like a bit of old rag or something that a cat had chewed passed through her hands, it fell to the floor. Ruth picked up each piece and dusted it down as if it had been the first present she had received on her birthday as a child. There was more love in her heart for them than for herself. Like the prodigal son there was the knowledge that in father's house there was bread enough and to spare. (Luke 15.) It was required here and now.

As Ruth was busy engaging in her thoughts, looking for a vision to unite these people together, there was a Man standing by her side. For a long time He had been there. I knew, because He had grown a beard while He was waiting. There was no look of weariness on His face, it was the face of a Winner and Worker combined. Here was the Man with the face of eternity, wanting to help, but in the confusion He had been seen as one of the threads that needed to be brought together.

The Man called Christ Jesus smiled and held out His hands,

which seemed to say, 'You can trust Me with those things I have trusted you with.' As He held out his hands, so as not to appear as a figure, a voice spoke to Ruth by name. 'Ruth'— and immediately she realised He knew her name, and there was a ready response. Instead of these threads tangled around her, binding her hand and foot, she passed them towards the open hands of the Saviour, and waited with bated breath to see what the Man of Galilee would do. Would He throw them away and give her new pieces of cloth? Would he reject the miscut and misplaced threads? Would He accept from her what seemed like the contents of a stall at a jumble sale?

Then an amazing thing happened, so amazing that she remembers it to this day. As the number of threads grew, so the arm of the Recipient lengthened to reach to where Ruth was, and the hand grew large enough to take hold of all these threads. He first wound them around His fingers, like she did as a child, tying a piece of cotton or a shoelace around her finger to remind her not to forget. As the hand of the Saviour closed upon those threads, it seemed to squeeze them, not with the squeeze of restriction but with a gentle squeeze, the squeeze of a mould that was saying, 'I can transform these things if you will give them to Me.' Each thread seemed to disappear, but then it came from His other hand. The threads had kept their colours, but had become one, they had twisted together to form a cord of colour. It reminded Ruth of that text on the approach to Cliff College, Derbyshire, where local preachers and ministers were trained for the Methodist church, and read: 'All one in Christ Jesus.'

Each length of material entered that hand as different entities, but they seemed to come out of the fingers as one. The threads were coiled together as young lovers taking their place in society, no longer as different tribes seeking their own with a nationalistic spirit, but ready and eager to serve the Spirit of the living God. Each finger made its own contribution as if representing a ministry gift as found in Ephesians 4. They were heralds of a new era, suggesting that the five-fold gifts of pastor, teacher, apostle, prophet and evangelist, if used together, could produce colourful and meaningful unity, as part of the expression of the love of God.

All the threads were now made of silk, bound together as one length of silken cord, not separated and apart but suddenly part of the whole. Each thread, mattered because it made up the whole cord. Here was diversity, colour and strength in unity, made strong in the power of that Hand. Now gold as a colour along with the white, the black, the brown, the pink and the yellow were all part of one cord. Along the cord, as it came from His hand was writing which read: 'The cord of love.' Here was racial harmony and a rainbow army, for it contained the colours of the rainbow. It had been made into one without any loss of identity. By being part of something bigger it would be useful.

Ruth took up the challenge as she accepted this cord of mixtures that became as one in the love of God. That unity could be a wonderful force for good. Whenever she prayed, this cord would be used to bind the strong man, or trip up those who were chasing the saints into fear. It could bind anything and any influence that came against this church. This red cord had a mixture of gold and red in it as part of the many colours. The Deity and blood of Christ held them together. Ruth would take the cord and put it around those who were weak and infirm; those who were suffering temptation above what they were able to bear would be surrounded by it. If it was placed strategically it could take hold of straying sheep. Next time she met someone who needed Christ she would simply and yet profoundly say to them, 'Take hold of this!' As they took hold of the cord marked with the words 'The cord of Love' it would wind itself around their heart until they were bound closely in the bundle of life with their Lord. With it she could climb every mountain and ford every stream, follow every rainbow, for she had found her dream and received the answer to a long-standing prayer. Fibres had become one in Christ Jesus. This would be their battle cry and strength during a time of storm, for any ship being pulled out to sea and danger could be secured by this cord.

10

SAND, SWEAT AND STONES

The work Malcolm was engaged in had been so difficult. He had never realised that to work for the Lion of the tribe of Judah meant he had to be lionhearted. He must be as Caleb, whose name suggests a lion's whelp. The dogged nature possessed by Caleb had to be on standby 24/7. There was a 'rough and tumble' about church life in Manchester, England, that he had never calculated. The church he was invited to shepherd was so small that if another member left he would have to conduct the funeral of a church! Even those who had been added in the past had come and gone, as if there was nothing stable about their relationships. As something stuck on, they kept dropping off.

Slowly and surely, as the mills of God grind, so the work began to grow. God began to widen and broaden the hopes and hearts of those to whom he ministered. The numbers began to increase, numbers that would bring a smile to a bank manger's sallow face! Sadly there was a realisation that numbers did not mean growth. Here was quantity, but where was the quality? It might impress, but would it last? There were those who had been added to the work, but Malcolm was unsure of their commitment. As he preached the gospel of Jesus Christ, they had responded, and were added to the church. It was all a matter of sowing and reaping, being faithful and following. He could now put all the spare chairs out, and did not have to strategically place them in an empty hall, so that to the casual glance or to the visitor it looked as if they had more people than they could seat. Would they stay, or would they become as fond memories of the past? He longed to build people together for a habitation of the Spirit of God, but they were like grains of sand thrown together by a wild storm. Who can build on shifting sands? They were of the same nature, but the only thing he could build with them was sand pies and sandcastles! Maybe they would become part of the stained glass window of a historical church. He would have to pastor a church at the seaside for anything to happen of an Eternal and valuable nature.

Could Jesus Christ build a church out of sand? That which was rough, raw, ready to disappear, could it become malleable? Could God work ropes out of sand? He had witnessed the incoming tide do some strange things with the sand. Children gladly see it as a friend. He saw himself on a desert island with sand and sea on all sides, but no material with which to build a shelter. The answer to his many questions was a resounding yes! Whatever the question, no matter how thick the book of questions is, God's Book, the Bible, has all the answers. He had said, 'Before you call I will answer.' (Isaiah 65:24.) 'Before the dawn and before the tide comes in I will answer.' God would step in before the first twinkle of the new dawn. God has more ways to answer prayer than there are grains of sand on the edge of the sea. These thoughts were like the pools of water among the sand that crabs and small fish live in. Jehovah had said to Abraham that his seed would be as plentiful as the sand by the seashore. (Genesis 22:17; 32:12.) Malcolm knew there was sand along the shores of all countries whose bounds are the sea. There would be those who would belong to the Lord from every tongue, tribe and nation. He protested, 'Lord, I have never heard You call me to the seaside. Sand was not in my dreams when I came to this place.' Meditation (like a cow chewing the cud) was the order of the day, as past, present and the future were considered in prayer.

The church had invited a preacher named Terry Atkinson for the weekend, not knowing if the Lord would help in any way. It might be just another preaching weekend that would not bring with it a ray of light. They might be left as they were found. Anything was worth a try. Malcolm had marshalled his people together when the preacher arrived. The last time this speaker had been to this church, the fire engine had to be called out, because there was something wrong with the fire alarm system! What a testimony, a preacher had to have a fire engine to put the fire out! Maybe this time the fire would start in the hearts of those around him, and would spread out into the community like a prairie flame. The church needed to be something wild and unexpected, as 'suddenly' as the fire of Pentecost in Acts 2 fell on the early disciples. One of the publishing firms in the 1940s had as their emblem a spreading flame, which was a token of the nature of the church.

The preliminaries were over, the musicians seeming to disband while the last song was still floating in the air. Everyone went to their own place as if they were pigeon-holed. One moment they were vigorously playing their instruments and singing lustily as they led the people through song and dance, but now the curtain had come down on that part of the church order. It seemed as if they were about to move into another era. They had played their part in the worship with *fortissimo*.

A new order was about to begin as the speaker and teacher

was invited to come into the pulpit, or should I say on to the platform. The message was preached, the appeal given. A number responded to what had obviously convicted them. The word had entered their spirit like the flesh hook entered into the flesh of the Old Testament offering. When Peter preached in Acts 2, they were 'pricked' in their heart.

After the visiting minister had prayed for many people, the pastor and his wife came to the front. They knew that the beast that treads out the corn is also a sharer of the spoils. (1 Timothy 5:18.) The mouth of the ox should not be muzzled; even petrol is put into a tractor. One can guess that after the miracle of the feeding of the five thousand the disciples enjoyed a good meal from the spoils of the miracle. This dedicated couple, like Elijah, would go on in the strength of the memory of that meal for many days. (1 Kings 19:8.) Each time they had a hunger in their soul, they simply remembered what the Lord had done, and were as well fed with the manna, the living bread, as the children of Israel were. Taking hold of the leader's hands, I thought: 'These are praying, working, anointed hands that God is using. God, enlarge these hands and make them as large as the moon. Give this couple hands and heart as large as a banqueting table, then they will feed many.'

Immediately I began to think like that, and wondered what to say, as the *word of knowledge* began to reveal the man's heart. He was standing by a pile of scattered sand, as if there had been a sandstorm that had all been swept by nature into a sand dune. Was he in the Sahara desert? No; we were standing in the local church at 12.15 p.m. Where did all the sand come from? What was seen, and what would be said, was not part of the script, for without knowing what was said, the man's deepest thoughts were being exposed. This sand was a picture of the people around him. Every grain mattered to the Lord. Even wild nature paints some lovely pictures in sand.

Around part of the sand was a wall built from house bricks. The wall did not seem very strong, and on closer inspection the reason became apparent. The bricks only had sand between them, there was nothing of substance to hold them together. They lacked grip and grasp. There were only a few bricks, because if they had been built any higher they would have fallen over. What was being revealed could never be described as a Babel tower that reached to the sky. This man was trying to create a method of building, but what was built was not cemented together. I thought this was strange because one member of his family actually had his own building firm.

The people that he had gathered together were as shifting and swirling sands. The leader was tired of counting the bricks, seeing his vision for building the church of Jesus Christ thwarted by lack of adhesion. When the storm came, great would be the fall of it. (Luke 6:45–48.) There was too much individualism in this church for it to be strong and powerful. Joseph's branch would never go over the wall. (Genesis 49:22.) No matter how high or low he built, there was always the danger of collapse. How could he build in this desert wilderness? Noah had built an ark in a place where there was no water; here there was nothing for each brick to hold on to. If only they could have been as the soldiers of Sparta where every one was described as a 'brick'. Maybe he was using the wrong materials? He was certainly preaching the right message. He required that which was hot in the Holy Ghost to lift people out of the burning fires of passion, addiction and hell.

Then I heard the voice of the Lord telling him to stop simply seeing the sand as sand, and begin believing that in Jehovah it could become something else. The bigger picture was being presented to him. He was to stop counting the bricks, for the materials that he would use would be provided by the Almighty, just as He had provided through ravens for Elijah. (1 Kings 17.) God wanted him to see something different. Commanded to look elsewhere, he felt that what he was about to see would be an oasis in the desert, or maybe a paradise island. None of these things was revealed. God was not taking him to another area to work, but he had to see the potential where he was. Like Isaac, he had to sow in the land until he became very great. (Genesis 26:12.) There was no call for him to build on sand or with these bricks. He must not build, he must dig.

Suddenly, as he listened to the voice of the Lord, he began to get on his knees and started moving the sand. It seemed he wasn't used to digging. At first he was like a large turtle seeking to bury its eggs in a shallow grave. As he progressed, however, it became easier. The only moisture was that coming from him in beads of sweat. His back felt disjointed. As he went down into the sand, he wondered if he was digging his own grave. Was this a prophecy foretelling his demise? Malcolm began to feel strange objects buried in the sand. Was this the place where treasure had been buried after a town had been attacked and conquered? Was an Aladdin's cave under this sand? He did not know what he might find, but he knew that in seeking, digging and sweating he had such a large desire for the things of God, a desire to build the church of Jesus Christ where he was. If only every grain of sand was a precious jewel won to Jesus Christ.

As he dug deeper and deeper, the thoughts became to his mind as a balance to a weight scale, to keep equilibrium in this heat that was slowly frying him in his own fat! He felt first one shape and then another, one object and another, and began to lift those shapes to the surface, away from the sand. There were large rocks placed there by nature. Israel had to do this as they crossed the River Jordan into the Promised Land. (Joshua 4:5.) He took the rocks and began to brush the sand from each one as if adding refreshing strokes with a paintbrush to a masterpiece. No archaeologist had ever been as careful when raising an artefact as Malcolm was as he lovingly embraced these misshapen rocks. He treated them as if they were long lost children who were as dear to him as eggs are to a broody hen.

Malcolm began to worship God, as he scattered the sand everywhere, discovering more and more pieces of rock. Here he was discovering the pattern for building the church of Jesus Christ. It was in sand, and if you draw a pattern and the wind blows it away it is lost forever. It seemed as if the Lord was drawing a plan in sand, not to be washed away when the tide came in, or to be covered when the wind began to blow. Here was the conviction of Pilate who put the accusation of Jesus on top of the Cross in three languages: 'What I have written, I have written,' he said to those who wanted him to alter the writing. (John 19:22.) God was writing in those sands, 'Not by might, not by strength but by My Spirit,' says the Lord. An awesome sense of the presence of God filled his heart. Conviction, like grains of sand, seemed to have entered into his spirit, and he felt convicted. He had been doing things his way, not God's way. Wasn't it from sand getting between your toes that our English word 'scruples' was developed? There would be some chaffing, but also there would be much building and blessing. This pastor would build much higher than he had ever built before.

He would build far higher, after digging deep into these shifting sands. The deeper the hole dug, the more rocks as materials were discovered to build with. These were pearls from the sand. These sands embodied the character of the people he was ministering to. He had been building out of well-shaped, organised, coloured and squared house bricks with nothing but sand to hold them together. These people had lacked deeper teaching from the word of God. Malcolm must take these rough, unshaped stones in order to build the church. The materials were in the sand. God would by-pass the clay, and supply that which was from the area around.

This fitted in well with the area around the church, which was notorious for crime, prostitution and drugs. He could see sand dunes in the sins of the people. The Cross must be drawn by the finger of God in every sand dune. Where the mark of the cross was drawn, so underneath were the stones required. As the Roman conquerors had sent their standard bearer to plant the sign of Rome on the seashore of a country about to be conquered, Malcolm must do the same with the cross of our Lord Jesus Christ. Right here was the material that would bring glory to God. 'Use what the Lord provides and you will discover Jehovah Jireh' was the message to the messenger. Lordship seen and realised meant that there is nothing on earth, under the earth, or in heaven, that can measure the influence of the Lordship of Jesus Christ. In his heart this man had been trying to build on the respectable, now the Lord was telling him to go for the worse, and by doing so God would build them together into a place for His habitation. Those in darkness, buried or thrown away, as onto a rubbish heap, must be rescued. As with Nehemiah, the stones of the new city must be uncovered before he could value them. Lost, they were valueless, but when found, then the hand that touched them added value and dignity to them. In the plan there was a place for every stone to find its proper order.

Whenever he knelt to pray and sweat in prayer, as Jesus did in Gethsemane, there would be a ready response and recognition from the Lord. God, in His wisdom and knowledge, knew where these stones — elect and precious — were. Malcolm must not use man's wisdom. It seemed impossible that rocks should be found hidden under sand. If he was prepared to get rid of that which was blowing in the wind, and all that was shallow, then all would be well. Sand can be blown away by every wind of doctrine. These rocks were here to stay, and would be unearthed as Malcolm sought the Lord. What had been written in sand to disappear would be written into rock with a pen of iron, using one of the nails from the Cross of Christ. He would give hope and acceptance to that which was buried in darkness. A resurrection would take place, and he would see many being built together, until that which was built would become a Bethany, where Jesus loved to stay with the small family of Mary, Martha and Lazarus. (John 11.)

11

THE SOUND OF MANY WATERS

The church was not difficult to find, although it was situated in one of the suburbs of Manchester. It stood in the centre of a square surrounded by shops. It was here that market stalls were erected on market day. The church had great opportunity and responsibility. They had not far to go to touch the world around them, because the world was on their doorstep. The church had an appropriate Pentecostal name, and was housed in a modern, well furnished building with all 'mod cons'.

The people were bright and lively, rejoicing in God's presence as a strong man ready to run a race. It was here that they witnessed the power of God moving from seat to seat and soul to soul, tremendous times of truth coming into hearts by the front door, error leaving by the back, as they listened to the Word of the Lord being expounded. The atmosphere was so good you felt that whatever you believed for, you would receive, bringing to mind the words of the apostle Peter who said, 'Lord, it is good for us to be here.' (Mark 9:5.) The Lordship of Christ was crystallised into character, as it became part of their charter. You could not leave that church as you entered. It was in an atmosphere like this that the prodigal was changed into poet and priest. A dog could be miraculously turned into a lamb. Conversion was the hallmark of this gathering, part of the 'standing orders' of the day. One would be quickened, another set free. Others were so blessed that their cups were full and 'running over' (meaning 'pleasant places', Psalm 23:5). In the services, the Good Shepherd was ministering to His sheep. Some required feeding, tending, leading, rescuing; all were part of the meaning of the name Shepherd. As they worshipped, the glory of God was birthed, and began to shine forth as it did on the bleak hills of Bethlehem, so long ago. (Luke 2:9.)

Psalm 23 was being expounded to them, and it was so real you could smell and see the blades of grass. The words 'I shall not want' brought peace into their inner beings. They were being coaxed into Bible truths as new and green pastures, the gentle waters coursing over and restoring the soul. The Bible was suddenly a living book, like the 'pop up' books you can buy for a child, where the picture suddenly comes out of the page. Every head was anointed with oil from the Shepherd's cruse. What did they care about 'the valley of the shadow of death' while He was so close that you could reach out and touch Him? Vows were renewed to follow Him all the days of their life into that forever land of Glory. Oh, this was so great! There couldn't be a hell while you were in such a heavenly atmosphere as this. The only sound heard was the sound of worship, of falling tears, the sound of tissues crumpling as those tears were wiped away. The Spirit of God moved from heart to heart from one life to another as they were all baptized into one body.

They were brought to reality as the preacher made an appeal for people to step forward to be prayed for. Not that anything required adding to this atmosphere, for perfection cannot be added to. What the speaker would seek to do would be to plant the seed deeper into the soil (soul) until it stayed with them even in difficult times. Some of these had been straying sheep; they were being transformed into loving and following sheep. The hard times were melting away like winter snow, as summer sun began to shine into souls. The 'goodness and mercy' of the Lord was acting as a fence for the sheep.

An elderly gentleman stepped forward to be prayed for, one of the church elders. His hair was white as snow, and he looked as if he had spent many years toiling. The moment I placed my hand on his head, he collapsed, and fell to the floor as if a rifle shot had found its target. As he landed there was a certain amount of dust that was displaced.

As he fell, the Spirit of God began to show me a fountain. The fountain was empty and dry. It was not a modern fountain with a slab floor, but one that had been cut out of deep rock. There were dust particles in the basin which should have contained precious water for all to slake their thirst. Here was an object that was not functioning as it had been created to do. It was just an ornament, an empty ceremony with no content. The man fell backwards as if he believed that the open arms of Jesus would catch him before he hit the floor. These strong and Eternal Arms would throw him back onto his feet. Of course this did not happen, and as he fell on the floor he began to cry out to the living God. The only water in the fountain was his tears of grief.

The fountain bed was as empty and as dry as ever that was in 1 Kings 17, where Elijah taunted the prophets of Baal to bring fire down upon the altar, and barrels of water collected from the nearby sea were emptied around the trough of the altar. That altar was so dry that a spark from rock might have created a fire, yet the prophet of God did not need any such assistance from the natural world. If fire was to fall it would fall with the help of Jehovah, where the water was flowing.

Elijah seemed as if he was trying to make it impossible for God to answer his prayer. In spite of what we 'are', what we 'do', and what we 'say', the Lord God will still come in and intervene. Just to make sure the rays of the sun did not kindle even a twig, Elijah commanded that water should be poured all around the sacrifice. This life, this man before me, was a dry old stick that needed refreshing water from under the throne of God such as Ezekiel saw in Ezekiel 47:1. Whatsoever that water touched, lived. The flow of life needed to come back into this empty, dry vessel.

As the man fell backwards I saw that he landed in the base of the dry fountain, that had seen neither rain nor dew for many years. His head struck the part of the fountain which was the inlet for the water, yet he was not injured. A soft landing for the man was provided by the Spirit of God, coming between him and the landing. The natives of Africa, when gathering coconuts, throw a piece of sacking to the very place where the coconut will land, and it is not broken or bruised. If the water had been turned off, and the fountain was dry, it was suddenly turned on; suddenly there was a gushing sound, and hidden water spouts came forth as if the fountains of the deep had broken. (Genesis 7:11.) The fountain was awash with water. He was a man lying in the water, not attempting to move, but content to let it gently lap over him. There was healing and restitution in these waters. All his past, all his rebellion, was being washed away. He would come from those waters as a child freshly bathed in God's love.

I have heard the voice of a cataract; I have been to Niagara Falls in Canada, and heard its thunderous roar. In the countryside there is often sweet music as the stream gently flows, sending out musical chimes as it meanders along. Never has the human ear heard sounds as clear and challenging as when that water began to flow, for as it flowed it spoke to the man. There was a human voice expressing itself through water. Here was the silver tongue of the orator. Every gurgle, drop and gush was turned into a human voice.

It was one voice with many things to say to this Christian brother. God spoke to Balaam through an ass. Jesus spoke to Peter through the crowing of a cock, and I knew that God can take anything and use it for a purpose it was not created for. That is when a miracle happens.

Jesus Christ, with a voice as the sound of many waters, was speaking, and the man needed to listen to what the Lord was saying. (Revelation 1:15.) This church was close to Strangeways prison in Manchester, and what was happening reminded me of the meaning of the name 'Strangeways'—the 'gathering together of many different waters'. Here was Jesus Christ ready to re-direct those waters, each to its natural source and resource. Whichever way the life of this person had flowed, the Lord in multiplied water like grace was seeking to re-direct his life back to the source he had abandoned. That which had been flowing away from the Almighty was now made to flow towards Him. He had so much to say to this repentant person that He chose water — lots of water — to speak through. Such a natural thing, but God was speaking through it. In the future this brother would have to go with the flow.

When the Lord needs to speak He can do it in silence, in a gentle flowing way, or with a great gush of inspiration. Now and again He uses many waters to speak to us. The voice that spoke as the waters gushed out was not something spoken in a foreign language. Here was an English voice speaking to an English man in a language that he fully understood. God was moving as close to humanity and human understanding as He could without becoming incarnate. These were not just words, they were Divine words. God had bypassed the voice of the preacher, He was taking over, and as a teacher might teach a scholar using language to do it, so the Lord was doing the same for this Christian. It brought to my mind the time in the temple that Jesus took the scroll and read from Isaiah and, when He sat down, the eyes of all those in the synagogue were on Him. (Luke 4:20.)

The man did not open his mouth to reply to this voice from the waters. If he did it would have been many voices against his one voice, many words that would defeat his words. They came out of the water as short sentences one after the other, as marshalled troops ready for peace or war. The answers to his prayers were heard in what was said, and all his conundrums were solved. This voice was as quickening and refreshing as cold water on a hot day. It was not questioning the one in the fountain; it was simply soothing and inspiring. Something, Someone, had to inspire this man to get out of the fountain, take those words with him into the world around. The beautiful thing was that this voice was many voices, yet they were all saying the same thing. It seemed as if a crowd was speaking all at once, there was no accent to be discovered, all blended together. It was a sort of Babel without the lack of understanding or the confusion. (Genesis 11:9.) Many voices had been turned into one, suggesting that the voice of the Lord was above all other voices, and what God had to say was far more important than all the voices he had ever heard during his life. What was said must be acted upon as a soldier would act on a command.

How many times the Almighty had spoken to him in the past I do not know. Maybe God was reminding the servant of the many times throughout the years He had spoken to him; each voice as one required attention and surrender. Jehovah having spoken often meant that this convert's memory would be refreshed and conviction quickened when those voices were heard. These were not bubbles or waves, they were voices, and he could hear plainly what God was saying in a torrent of words. He remembered voices and something God had said in his youth. Then, as a teenager, God had spoken once, twice, three times, many times that were without number, and that is why many voices were speaking. God was taking a voice from each stage of his life to remind him of what had been said. These voices were not clamouring for attention, they were as one on a mission that must be fulfilled. This same voice had said, 'Let there be light', and light appeared. (Genesis 1:3.) It had commanded, 'Darkness disappear,' and it went out as if blown out by the light. He could not help but listen, for he had fallen into the fountain. God had brought him close to the fountain head, that he might not miss one word. His head and ears were close to the source of the water, so that he caught clearly the meaning of what was said as the voice sounded out of that water.

As the man listened, his face began to beam as if painted with glory. Here was a voice and a language he understood. It was the language of love and the voice of virtue speaking to him. It seemed to be a combination of all the pleasant words he had ever heard. The words spoken were as new wine poured into his arid spirit.

The days of seeking, of emptiness, and of the barren wilderness, were over. He no longer needed to be told about a fountain of love, he had been pushed into one, to live where the flow was forever. As these waters flowed in different directions, if he obeyed, then there would be many new avenues of service that would open up to him. Each service demanded a calling and a voice. He could take one of these voices and go through pain. He could take another with him through a long, dark night. If ever he feared, one of these voices would be as a rod and a staff to comfort him. He must now live a life as an echo of what was heard. The opportunities would increase, would be as many as the words spoken through the moving, living, surrounding and flooding water. The words and promises of the Bible had been found in a fountain and in flowing water.

This was water worth having. He had not got to carry it, or seek for it, this was where he was. As he obeyed the voice of the Lord, then all would be well. Thirst banished forever! The days of dryness were history. As a dry and thirsty man he had found that which would assuage his thirst and meet his deepest longing as a spiritual order had been poured around him. As the waters were speaking, he drank as if he was drinking the words of the Father to a son. The more he drank, the more he required. As he spoke, those things that had entered into him in the water were poured out as the Word of God was ministered. This was no ritual, it was rich in content because it was all part of the plan of God for a life. He would never again just 'talk his noise', what he had to say would be 'water words' that had a depth and a life in them.

12

RESIST THE DEVIL AND HE WILL FLEE FROM YOU

To look at the man you would have thought he was strong. He was built like an elephant, but looks can be deceiving and what is inside of the shell can be so debilitating. The man looked as if he might have been another 'Mr. Universe'. When he came for prayer, the *word of knowledge* opened up a life from top to bottom, inside and out, in the twinkling of an eye.

Robert was a family man with responsibilities, but was not as strong as he appeared. Although six feet tall, there was part of a pygmy dynasty in him. Spiritually, he was a dwarf. Physically he dwarfed others, but evil influences affected him, turning the man into a shadow. He had fought day and night to keep those things at bay which troubled him, but the time had arrived for him to trouble, trouble.

The problem was Robert could not fight these influences with his bare hands or feet. If he had trained as a soldier for the British Army he would have still been defenceless because he was as weak as water, defined in the name Reuben (as weak as water), one of the sons of Jacob.

The difficulty was one that had been in existence and operation for many years, and needed to be dealt with. If there is one thing that Robert illustrated more than anything else it was if you don't deal with the matter of temptation, it will deal with you.

It reminded me of Samson, who took hold of a lion and tore it in two with his bare hands. (Judges 14:5.) Later, within the carcass of the lion he found honey that he could feed on. (Judges 14:6.) Honey that would enlighten his eyes, and restore his strength, honey that would help him to be cognizant of the way he was travelling.

The *word of knowledge* showed me that Robert was in a large, stone built house with many windows. These windows had never been bricked up. Anything was free to fly in. Centuries ago in England taxes had to be paid on glass, and the way round the tax law was to brick up the windows, despite a loss of light and the disservice done to the architect and builder of the property. Robert would have had to pay many taxes had he lived in those days!

The doors of the property were nowhere to be found. I looked again and again in the Spirit of God, but there were no doors in the house, just gaping holes providing free entry into the home. There was no notice saying, 'Do not enter!' All and sundry were invited to come right in and make it their home, and that is what was happening.

I saw Robert in the *word of knowledge*: he was tired, out of breath and 'out of sorts', running frantically from room to room and window to window, as if it was a matter of life and death that he went to each opening to be as a guard outside Buckingham Palace. He was in a race he could never win. He was moving but going nowhere; doing something, yet doing nothing. His ample activity was not achieving anything. Here was an athlete with no prizes. He was footsore and soul weary because he was chasing that elusive thing that was chasing him. He turned this way and that, like a corkscrew. Here was a man in a fight that he couldn't hope to win, because he had no strategy, no plan of attack.

He was fighting alone. Where were the rest of his family? I knew he was married with children. There was no prayer uttered, no promise quoted, no other member of the human race standing with him. As in many trials, the problem is not the trial itself but the loneliness of it all. It seemed as if nobody cared a fig for this father. Where was the man's faith and ability to resist? It seemed as if it had abdicated long ago, and here he was facing onslaught and might in his own strength, a strength that was too small to overcome any opposition.

It was a war of attrition. First at one window and then at another, running from floor to floor, up one flight of stairs and then another not staying long enough in one place to either conquer or slay the opposition. Swiftly as any bird flying, there was movement between the attic and the cellar. He ran rather flew, as fast as his feet would carry him, from door to door. It seemed as if his feet were on fire; wherever he went, that which was troubling him went alongside, never to depart, seeming to declare 'Lo, I am with you always.' Only the devil could twist the words of Jesus, and apply them to temptation. I heard a sob come from his lips as he grew wearier, as the battle was fought and lost. If respite was not found, then all would be lost to a 'lost cause'.

The things causing Robert trouble were the window frames without windows, the door frames without doors. You might have thought that common sense would have prevailed, and instead of being of ant proportions he would grow into a giant, but this man had lost all sense and all sense of direction; there seemed to be nothing to fight for, nothing to live for. Raising his arms above his head to beat off the attackers, weariness entered his spirit. He raised his hands, stretching out his arms horizontally, making the sign of the cross, which seemed to lessen the attacks and give time to breathe.

Robert was troubled by large birds that were swooping from the heavens, trying one after the other to enter the open doors and windows, using their beaks as spears to injure him. These birds were free, while Robert was a prisoner in his own home. That which was of his own making was his ruination. The birds swooped this way and that, inflicting punishment with their razor bills. They were not coloured but were all black. They had many wings, these multi-winged creatures of the sky. They had not come to pick his bones clean or tear his flesh into ribbons, they simply wanted to make that home their abode. The birds had made a claim on Robert's property and private possessions, wanted to build nests and breed their young. They had no leader. They possessed only one thought, and one thought possessed them: how to gain access into the house, and in doing so they would kill the man at the doors and windows.

It would be easy, for it was one human being against many flying creatures, and he had no hope of being at every window and door. These birds were many in number, and together they made what they lacked in size count. Swooping here and there, turning and twisting as if they were vultures, the smell of decaying carcase filled the air.

What was revealed reminded me of the parable in Matthew 13, when Jesus told of the birds of the air swooping and snatching away the seed corn before it had time to germinate. The birds in the parable were robbing the seed of a future. Future growth, and what nature had determined them to be, was being snatched away and gobbled up. These birds had great hunger, far more hunger than the seeds had to take root and grow. The life of each seed had been a short one. Those birds were there as a figure of temptation.

Robert was surrounded by dark temptations great and

small, not worming their way in from under the ground, but flying in the light of day through open doors and windows. There was nothing to stop them. There was no scarecrow in the garden that looked like an unploughed field. To blow the trumpet in Zion would have been as useless as trying to blow through a stick from a tree, and expect the walls of Jericho to fall down. These birds, these temptations, were on a mission. That mission was being fulfilled as they entered through every window and open door. There was no moat around this house as there would have been around a castle to keep it safe. Birds fly over water when migrating, and these were migrating birds. Robert's only protection was the hand of God.

They were there to withdraw from Robert that which was precious. It was the story of Naboth and his vineyard that wicked Jezebel took from him, to give as a present to Ahab. (1 Kings 21.) There would be nothing left to pass on to others if these birds were to wing their way into the home. It was Robert's inheritance in Christ that they were seeking to snatch away. They had come to occupy, not to feed and drink. They would become his eyes, his ears, his hands and feet, mouth and tongue. They were there for a conversion to evil. They had not come for carrion but for character, to peck to pieces the character of the heart, to take over a life, then a home. Jesus said that the kingdom was like a tree full of birds. (Matthew 13:32.)

Having entered, would they alter the whole contour of the house? What had been a dwelling for humans would become a cage for birds, a cage without bars, for they would have access every moment of every day, free to come and go at leisure. They were coming in to eat Robert out of house and home, taking his food if they were not dealt with. Sparse would become the order of the day. They would occupy pride of place. They would never surrender to become parrots or canaries in a cage, singing merrily on a perch. They would spend his money, eating him out of purse and pleasure, they would be in the beds and on the chairs, and no room in the home would be sacred. I thought, yes, temptation is like that, it occupies every part; wherever you go, it is there. If you sleep or eat, pray or watch, temptation is there. When you lie down and when you get up it is still there. If you are not careful it takes the place of the Presence of God Who has said, 'Lo, I am with you always, even to the closing of the age.' If only God would zip up the age in which Robert lived, then all would be well.

It would have been more acceptable if, when one bird entered the house, it decreased their number, but it did not. As one bird disappeared inside, another two came to take its place. If was if they were being bred out of one another. All temptation is like that. There is not one single temptation; they are all married with large families! Read about it in the Book of Job, or my book entitled *In Sickness and in Health*, dealing with the temptation of Job.

The birds that appeared as others disappeared were not smaller or larger, yet they all seemed to have the same mission. They were 'dive bombing' Robert. In his mind here was another Pearl Harbour, where the Japanese bombed the American fleet in the bay. Would there never be an end to this constant harassment and destruction? This was highway robbery under another guise. The thief had come to destroy kill, and maim. They were claiming and taking what did not belong to them. They were taking 'squatter's rights' with no intention of being squatters, they wanted sole ownership. These birds in flight would not be put off. They were as missiles that had 'homed in' on a target, and that target was this man's home and moral fibre. They knew what they wanted, and he knew what they must not be allowed to take. These were thieves and robbers coming in some 'other way'.

As suddenly as the birds appeared, so they began to disappear when a Presence came to stand by Robert, as he made the sign of the cross by raising his arms to heaven. It was as if a man with a shotgun had appeared, and the birds recognised the danger. They did not disappear into thin air, but fell to the ground, as if a farmer had taken aim with a doubled barrelled shotgun hitting the target every time. They were soundly beaten. It was another Man with shining garments and the tools of a carpenter in His hands that came to Robert's aid. As the Stranger stood, each empty space was filled with His presence, and that Presence formed a door, filling the gap and keeping the birds at bay. Any birds that made it to the door fell on the step, as that door became a trap of death. They were like flies throwing themselves onto a fly catcher. It was at the door that their history was terminated by the Exterminator. He was as a door to repel those birds trying to enter. His was the message that He was the Door, Way, Truth and Life. As that Presence filled the door frames, so He began to speak the Word of God, and as He spoke, then each window frame received a sheet of glass. It was clear glass, as clear as the sky is blue without a cloud. It was as if the Stranger had taken sand into His hand and blown upon it. This was not ordinary glass, nor that taken from the sea of glass in the Book of Revelation. (Revelation 4:6; 15:2; 21:8.) It was glass created in fresh air. It did not seem to be there, and yet it was. What the voice was speaking was a revelation of light, and that light filled the window frames. As the birds tried to fly into the house, they were killed when they hit what they thought was an empty space. They were flying into the revelation of the Lord, the revelation of light filling those empty frames. A revelation could and did resist all evil.

The Presence went from door to door. Filling those door frames with a shape, it entered into every room of the house.

This was the place of the Lord. In that home, Christ would be the unseen Guest. Christ would be Lord in the home and in every thought, He would reign supreme. This home would become a Bethany where Jesus dwelt, with his Name on the doorpost: 'Jehovah Shamma' — the Lord is here.

God was saying to Robert that the carpenter of Nazareth had become the door, or many doors, for him, to help to resist and overcome all temptations. The words He spoke and the promises He had given were large and plentiful enough to outnumber temptation, whatever its size or number. The door and the revelation were too much for the birds, but enough for Robert, for as he believed the Lord, and took to his heart the whole armour of God, and the whole ability of Christ, he would resist any temptation trying to get into his house. The door of Jesus' Divinity and the fullness of revelation are far too much for the forces of evil. He is Light that cannot be penetrated. He is resistance that cannot be resisted.

13

CARDBOARD CHRISTIANITY

Thomas was not feeling very well. He had suffered a number of serious illnesses; he was feeling weak at the knees, his hands hanging down. He was so discouraged, low in spirit, that he could tie his shoelaces without bending. Throughout his life he had to 'tough it out' when things were tough. The years were taking their toll, and what a toll they had exacted from him, leaving him as one robbed of much, with little left to give. He was on the verge of giving up, of leaving the work to someone else. After all, he had been training a younger man and his wife for a number of years. Would it be too soon to leave it to Samuel and Sarah? He did not want to step backwards or downwards too early or too late. All these things were in the mind of Thomas as he entered the church that day. He knew Scripture, and that he ought to enter God's house with thanksgiving and praise, yet he was filled with discouragement and doubts about the future of the church. In Thomas's life there had been so much giving and there was so little left to give. He had given his all, there was nothing left.

Thomas was working for the Lord in this needy area, a suburb of Bolton, Lancashire, England. This area presented unique problems with its drug addiction and high divorce rate. He mulled these thoughts of the needs of this area over and over, trying like a boat with a leak to go over each wave, expecting the next one to sink him. He was approached by a man who wanted to pray for him. He himself had that morning been praying for different ones, asking the Lord to encourage them, but the underlying need was in his own heart. While God was blessing them, his silent prayer was that some of that blessing might come as an overflow into his own heart.

He gladly acceded to the man's request to pray for him. He was in need of a word of prayer from somebody who might understand his situation. What had he to lose? What had he to gain? For surely there was no more pain or discouragement to come. It could not be midnight in his heart forever. He wished that maybe someone from Japan, the 'Land of the Rising Sun' would utter a passionate prayer for him. It would have been so acceptable if a Joshua could put his arm around him and stop the sun from going down while it was still day, but in the man who came was what he desired and needed. He knew, when God sends, he sends the right one at the right time, to speak, to do, and to bring the right thing.

A *word of knowledge* had been revealed to the man next to him, and as he placed his hands in the hands of the local minister, he began to tell him what he was seeing and hearing. Thomas, doubting Thomas, was amazed, because he was describing just how he felt. He said he could see Thomas with a cardboard box. It was a large box with no address on it, so Thomas was not posting it to a needy area of the world. It was going nowhere, and being carried by no one. There were many things in this large box, and it seemed as if some of them had been inside it for many years. Each gift and object represented ministry and the years of working for the Master. It was full of the latest gadgets and all manner of gifts that would be helpful. Looking at these gifts so rare and lovely, the word 'helps' seemed to adequately describe their function, for they covered every aspect of service. They had not just been thrown into the box; they had been neatly placed there when they were needed. In the past, Thomas kept filling it with good things as the years went by. Even now, after such a long time, there was still room in this cardboard container.

There were many gifts around Thomas on the floor, and it seemed as if these gifts were for teenage people. Why weren't they in the box? They were not the sort of gifts you would give to a child. These abilities needed to be activated with thought. You might presume that these gifts should be put into the box because of its capacity. They were lying there with a pleading look on their face as if asking, 'Will nobody help us, and lift us into the box?'

The gifts were not made of cheap material; not glued together, having the appearance of something that 'Jack built', thrown together and hoping for the best. There was no stamp on them telling of the country of origin. These had not been produced by 'slave labour' but by a 'labour of love'. They could be described as 'the best of British', hand crafted gifts made from the materials of the heart. Someone had cared enough to use their creative ability. This was no jumble sale stall! It was not just odd things gathered together to be thrown away or given to the next garbage cart that appeared. That which had cost nothing would not be given to the Lord or to the Lord's people. They had lovingly been chosen; they were part of the man. Each item was the shape of his heart of love for the people. There were still plenty of gifts on the floor, as if this number went beyond mathematical ability. There was still more to do and more to give. The box could take more if more was put inside it. Each gift had a place and a function of its own.

The cardboard square represented the heart of the people that Thomas had ministered to over the years. There had been many gifts and many years. He had given his best in so many different ways. Trying to do secular work and the work of pastoring a church had been no easy thing. To this dedicated man it had been rather like trying to climb Mount Everest while eating lunch! Thomas looked at the gifts on the floor, and then at those in the box filled with his intentions. In his lowness of spirit he felt that if he had found a flag he would wave it in glad surrender. A yellow duster would have sufficed, but he was no coward. His spirit had become like a flag at half mast, even though the King was in residence. There had not been any abdication by the King, only by His servant, Thomas.

The room itself was empty but for the box and the articles in it and those items left on the floor. There were no other workers standing with the man. He was alone, what he was passing through was lonely, yet it could be a lovely thing, because the Lord was here to help. If God was a very present help in trouble, more present than the trouble, why did he feel like this? A recent illness had left him bleeding and dying on the Jericho Road. There was so much to do and so little time to do it in. The years of waiting, praying, various methods of outreach, had taken Thomas as a reluctant prisoner to this place of misgiving. Who knew? Who cared? With whom could he share his heart? If only these gifts could be plugged in or wound up, then they could march into the container by themselves, and all would be well. Thomas knew that life was not on automatic pilot, that there are some things we must do to achieve our goal.

Those gifts on the floor still required to be put into people, and so he must add them to the box. Thomas had been called into the ministry for such a time as this, but it seemed as if opportunity was a door closed and sealed with seven seals.

Those things from the Lord had been given as gifts to be passed on to young folk. There were so many gifts, more than the stars that could be counted. Their variety matched the abundance of them. Who can count variety or colour? The man's heart ached, his back and limbs, also seemed to be aching, but he was forcing himself to go on, do a little more. Maybe tomorrow would be a better day?

The strange thing, stranger than fiction, was that instead of Thomas picking up the gifts and putting them neatly into the box, as neatly as tucking a child up in bed, he was actually closing the lid of the box! I thought in my deranged mind: An enemy has done this. His mind is out of kilter. The work is not finished, and he is closing the box, not to post it to a needy part of the world, but to leave it there incomplete. It would become a testimony of a work that was not finished. What Jesus said would come to pass: he had not calculated the cost, and men would laugh at him as he left this as some half finished building. (Luke 14:28.) The project must be projected. I never heard the whistle blow for full time, but Thomas was listening to something else, something telling him it was time to 'shut up shop' and go home. His ministry was finished, he had had enough. He had a large roll of tape, and he was going to spend and be spent as he applied it to the flaps of this box.

Suddenly a new zeal, more relish, entered into his spirit. It was not what I thought it would be. It was the desire to close down, not to open up. It was the desire to go to sleep, the sleep of death, and let things drift idly by. The man's work was not complete, but he was going to let it come to a grinding halt. At all cost and with all effort he must close the box. He seemed to be wrestling with the flaps and the tape held in his other hand. He was as clumsy as an elephant trying to get into a tin bath.

If only he could put as much zeal into his ministry as he was putting into closing that box! As he pressed the lid down, it seemed as if he was trying to parcel resurrection life, because the lid kept coming back to leave the box open. He was 'losing a fighting battle'! Thomas was sweating with anxiety as he struggled to close cardboard flaps that should have been inanimate, but were proving that they were alive, were fighting back as if they knew more about the will of God than he did. They knew what position they should be in.

It was a reminder of the man in the New Testament who went to bury his talents, Matthew 25. In burying them he dug the deepest hole he had ever dug. If he had put as much enthusiasm into his ministry of trading his talents as he was putting into burying them, they would have never been buried. The question must be asked of Thomas, 'Why had he developed a taste for waste? Why all this expansion of energy, when it could be put to better use to fill the box and obey what you know to be the will of God? Still Thomas struggled as if, like Samson, the Philistines were upon him.

As he struggled to close the flaps of the box, they kept opening and created a wind. It was a stronger wind than any cardboard could create. Something miraculous was happening. Here was a rare moment to be savoured. It was a wind that cleared the atmosphere and the head of the one who was trying to close the lid, as he breathed in the wind that came into the room, sweeping away the anxiety and sweat. The wind was bringing with it new visions of the world outside and its needs. Suddenly, Thomas felt invigorated, as new strength entered into him, yet he still could not close the flaps of the cardboard box. New strength was his, but instead of him closing the lids, in this new found strength he began to make sure it stayed open. He threw the tape to one side, knowing he would never again require it. With new strength he began to pick up the gifts on the floor with a sense of purpose and love in his heart. This was no more of a chore than laughing was. As he picked up the gifts, a sense of destiny gripped him.

As he lifted the gifts, he muttered, 'Well, there will not be much room for many more, so I might as well fill the box.' Taking each gift from the floor he began to lift them into the box, as lovingly as a mother putting her twins into a pram. That container had seemed as if it was almost filled, but as he began to put more in, it began to expand. Room was made for every addition. There was no cramming of style. 'The grace of God is like this', every gift lifted from the floor seemed to whisper into his heart. This was a box that was blessed, because it grew with the gifts that were put into it. The more gifts he put in, the larger it grew. The box expanded with the gift that was put into it. It was like the sky that seems large enough to contain all the stars with every cloud, plus the sun and the moon.

God was saying to Thomas, 'A man's gift makes room for him' (Proverbs 18:16.). 'As you work, and put what you have and what I have made you into the lives of others, there will always be room for more. Your ministry has not finished, you need to continue. The grace that has been brought into your life, and has brought life into you, is still expanding, reaching, teaching, praying, touching. This box, and the opportunities for you, will never cease to grow. The door will always be open; you must not try to close it yourself. Self-closing boxes become trap doors, and people are locked behind them.' God knows when the final day, hour and moment have come. He opens a door that no man can close, and closes a door that no man can open. 'I have set before you an open door.' 'Do not close the box. When the day comes when you are of no more use, I will close the lids of the box, but then there will be something new of another dimension for you.' Leave the parcels of life to the delivery of God. Do not step in and trip up when there is no need; God wants to give you greater capacity and, by the wind of the Spirit, He will enable you to fulfil your calling and to reach your destiny in God.

Your style will not be cramped or stuffed into a box with four sides, will not become square, old fashioned and limited. What goes into the box, as on Christmas Day will come out of the box. What was ministry in you passed on to others will become their ministry. You have given them a start using your gifts; they will continue to make progress in the work that you have begun. In those gifts inside the cardboard were faith, love, hope, everlasting life, peace and joy. Thomas began to cry, and there was no handkerchief large enough to wipe away those tears, for from his face they went into his heart, washing away the discouragement as if it had never existed, each tear drop glistening with hope, and he knew that all would be well.

14

THE SINKING ARK

There were so many problems in the church of which he was the leader that he did not know what to do. As one was solved then another appeared from nowhere. He felt that if he had been a social worker he could have done better. Here he was the 'Jack-of-all–trades and master of none! His domestic life was also in tatters. His wife had a long standing illness, and added to all that he suffered at home was what he had to endure in the church. His wife had not only been 'at death's door', she had seen inside that door. There had been terrible tragedy in his life, and both he and Mary, his wife, had found it very difficult to cope with everything that had been thrown at them. They had not only been bowled over, but had been knocked flat. In 2 Corinthians 4:9, Paul says he was 'knocked down but not knocked out' (a modern translation). This couple, however had been both knocked 'down' and knocked 'out' for the count.

His life was irreproachable, but what he had to suffer from many church members was diabolic. If it wasn't one moaning it was another groaning, if it wasn't one clamouring for attention it was someone else commanding he should come, and now!

Timothy knew that 'all things work together to them that love God', but why did the reverse feel true? In this instance things seemed to fall apart because Timothy loved God. Everything seemed to work against the good that he was doing. Romans 7:24 states that when he would do good, evil was present. Who would deliver him from this body of death? His good was not only spoken of in an evil way; it was being turned into evil. Life for them was like an over ripe fig that had fallen from the tree. Who would take and scatter the seeds of his suffering? He had just come into this situation. He knew the way in, but he had to guess the way out.

If there were a thousand ways of doing a thing, and every one was the correct way, he still seemed to choose the wrong way. This was not going with the tide, it wasn't even going against the tide, and it was sinking into what was around him. Timothy was tired of being the builder's 'hod carrier', tired of being an errand boy at everyone's beck and call. His heart was beating faster and faster, his head was swimming, even before he had reached the water's edge.

He felt like Jacob, the father of Joseph, who on being told of the death of his son, and the evil things that followed, exclaimed, 'All these things are against me!' (Genesis 42:36). Was there any suffering as deep and as costly that Timothy and his wife had not yet passed through? He knew the meaning of the verse 'Deep calls unto deep' (Psalm 42:7), and 'All Thy billows have gone over me' (Jonah 2:3). If only he had the faith of Moses, whose name means 'drawn from many waters'. They were in the deep, not only for a night and a day as the apostle Paul when he was shipwrecked; they were in 'outer darkness' all the time. They had experienced the wailing and gnashing of teeth as the screw turned more and more, reminding them of the tales of torture during the Spanish Inquisition.

Timothy had prayed, searched, called and sought, but there

seemed to be no help. When the hand of God was outstretched towards him, just as he was touching the fingers of the Hand, the Hand closed before he felt he was able to take light from it. Whatever he touched turned to water. He felt he was in the ark without Noah; but Noah's God had not deserted him. They always seemed to be short by a metre. They felt that Jonah was their neighbour, brother, uncle and father! They were trying to make the best out of a bad job. Here they were in a situation they had no control over; everything around seemed to control them. Fatalism had cast its awful spell; they were constantly told that they were doomed. They were as clay in the kiln that should have been turned into brick, yet the result was ashes! The curse of Cain seemed to be their curse. Where and when would they find a way out of this dilemma?

A friend had been invited to minister that Sunday. Maybe the Lord would send them a word that they could lean on and rest in. It would have to contain light. It must be a healing, helping, guiding word, because anything less would not be acceptable. They were praying for light in a dark situation. They wanted, they needed, an outshining of the Spirit of God as seen in the gifts as revealed in the New Testament. (1 Corinthians 12 and 14.) They required an 'unveiling', to ensure that the cloud and darkness they were under would be destroyed forever. Timothy knew it was always darkest before the dawn, but this night of darkness had lasted, it seemed, longer than eternity. An answer from the Eternal was needed to solve the problems surrounding them, squeezing them to death. The disciples of Jesus had toiled all night, but refreshment came when Jesus appeared. Would Jesus do something like this for them?

The speaker stood to his feet and began to describe what the Spirit of God was revealing to him. He could see Timothy and his wife in an ark, Noah's ark. They were not in it for a pleasure cruise. They were not visitors, as some were to the

'Ark Royal', part of the English fleet, which people paid to look around it when it was in dock. They were as hemmed in as Noah and his wife had been when they sailed with their family in the ark. There were animals everywhere, with little room for manoeuvre or self expression. Timothy lacked sleep and comfort; even the comforts of married life had forsaken him. This ark was like the 'Black Hole of Calcutta', where so many had perished years ago.

Timothy was running around like a headless chicken. He was not like the ostrich with his head in the sand; his head was in water! There was no sense of direction or calling. He was on automatic pilot, coming and going, never ending. The more he did, the more there was for him to do. He was carrying a bag of tools on his back; in his hand were pieces of broken wood that he was trying to nail to the inside of the ark. The ark had sprung some leaks, and Timothy was doing a foolish thing by nailing the wood over the area where the water was coming into the boat. His theology on carpentry was all wrong. The boat was filling with water, yet he was creating more holes in it. This man was not a carpenter; he was just an 'odd job man'. He found himself, as another in the Scriptures, in 'jeopardy'. (2 Samuel 23:17.) Drowning, they say you only go down three times, but the times Timothy and his wife had gone up and down were numberless.

First one person called him, then another and another. Each 'animal' had a voice that was calling for his attention. The boat was still sinking. He did not know how to swim or to organise people into a lifeboat, for the ark had no lifeboat. The more he responded, the more they cried for attention. He became like a nurse without qualification on night duty during an epidemic. Every person wanted the wood and the nails to be applied to stop the leaks, but this was not the way to do it. He was running out of wood, the hammer was being worn out, even as he was. If the wood ceased, he would have to use the hammer shaft to help him cover the leaks. There seemed no way out. If only a larger hole would appear, then he could get through it into the water, where all his worries and fears would be washed away. The way out, however was not to take the first opportunity and swim to safety, it was to stay with the vessel, because so many were depending on him. If he swam through a hole he would be in a sea without navigation, and with no paradise island in sight! If he swam to safety, where would he swim to? These were shark infested waters. The ark was lurching from side to side, making him feel sick.

He decided that the next hole which appeared in the vessel he would try to get through and swim away into oblivion. A new opportunity would meet his need, a change of scenery; maybe another ark would serve him better. The first boat he saw he would board, and live 'happily ever after'. Why didn't they just throw him overboard and get rid of him forever? His hands were marked with hard work. The hammer had been used so much it felt as weighty as a sheet anchor. His arms were like lead, and he had to force them to work in conjunction with his body, they seemed disjointed and were acting independently from the rest of his body. They were not tied to his will.

It seemed that wherever he went, whatever he did, was not bettered. Like the woman in the New Testament with the issue of blood, she and he were not bettered by what they did, but were made worse. (Mark 5:26.) Could anything be worse than this: being in a storm, with the waters from outside lapping the inside of the boat, trying to plug the holes with nails! There was so much to do, so many calls for his attention, that he did not know where to turn to next. As soon as he had been to one place where the waters were coming into the ark, another leak sprang through the wood in another area. Here was a work that could never be finished. The only thing to be finished would be

Timothy. In these conditions he was expected to be a plumber, farmer, shepherd, carpenter, organiser and manager. Only Jesus Christ could be all things to all men.

A large hole appeared, created by a wave, and the impact swept Timothy off his feet, onto his back. Looking upward he saw a Man. Kindness seemed to ooze from Him. Here was help. He seemed to be made conscious of another deeper, larger, healing world. Here was Someone who had not been on the ark, and Timothy was staring at him. The Man seemed to have gentle and understanding eyes. The Man reached out His hands and took the hammer and pieces of wood from the hands of Timothy. Immediately the blisters and the blood disappeared from Timothy's hands. Timothy felt that he was dreaming, that this Man of Galilee was going from hole to hole, and instead of using wood, He was taking something from His hands and applying it to the point of entrance, so that wood was made whole. The holes in the wood were sealed as the Man lifted His hand over each one. Timothy thought to himself, 'How easy it seems to be to Him; He is an expert at what He is doing. He is plugging the holes like a plumber, yet has the appearance of a Carpenter.' As He worked, there was no clamouring for attention. The lion and the lamb were quiet as they lay together. There was a picture of peace in that ark with this Man on board. No hole was too great, no wood too broken for Him to fix.

The Man was spreading something from his hands that was red in colour. Was it pitch that had sealed the boat? The word in the Old Testament has the thought of atonement in it. (Genesis 6:14, Hebrew *Kaphar*.) Timothy, as he watched the Lord of the ark at work, could have stayed there forever. It was like living in Psalm 23, with the Book of Ephesians being poured into his spirit. He felt like the disciple who said, 'Lord, it is good for us to be here' (Matthew 17:4). If only life could be like this, someone else dealing with the leaks in the ark, that they would not become as a leaking vessel (in Hebrews 2:1 margin), or as a drifting vessel (in that same chapter). He could turn the leaks into fountains if He was left to do His work.

Timothy began to interpret what he was seeing. There were so many problems in the church that he was constantly running to help this one and that, yet he was never able to solve the problems, they just kept appearing. As soon as he resolved one difficulty, another appeared. It was like cutting down weeds: when it rains, more appear. Timothy had taken on himself the work of the Carpenter. He was doing things he had not been called to do. He had moved out of his depth, as a man stepping off dry land into a deep sea. He was using broken wood, broken bits, and broken experiences, to try and patch up other people's lives. He was using the wrong substance. What he needed to do was to believe that 'the blood of God's Son Jesus Christ cleanses (keeps cleansing) from all sin' (1 John 1:7). That which was necessary to meet the needs came from the hands of Jesus, His rich, red blood can heal any situation, but Timothy must take a step backwards, to lay down as he seemed to be doing at the moment, and let God do His work, while Timothy did what the Lord had called him to do. No problem is solved by another taking on a role different from that which he has been called to do. Do your best, the message seemed to be, and let the Lord do His work in His own way. You can never have success by doing the Lord's work in your own way, for His ways are above our ways — as far above as heaven is from earth, and the east is from the west. His ways are so far away from our ways as the beginning of eternal life is from the end of it! You are son, He is Father. Never exchange roles or get them mixed up, for if you do, the ark will surely sink. You will have to swim for it, and you will never arrive at Mount Ararat, and a new country of opportunity.

Timothy had been listening to all this. He seemed to have fainted, and, while in the faint, had received the plan of God that would deal with the past, the present and any future exploit. Whether the plan revealed would work or the ship would sink was left to Timothy's application. If the plan was enacted, then Jesus could sleep in the boat as He slept during the storm. (Matthew 8:24.) This boat could yet be a Bethany and not a bedlam.

Suddenly, the ark surged forward as if engulfed by a strong wind, the sort described in Acts 2:2. It had been sealed, and the holes were no longer evidences of calamity, stress and worry. They were evidence of what had been accomplished in God. Timothy reminded himself that expert craftsmen built the 'Titanic' which sank, but a humble man, under God, built an 'ark', and that ark would not sink because it was the church of Jesus Christ. Before his eyes, the Scripture and the promise had been fulfilled: 'I will build my church'. The work had been complete, the ark was sailing, moving merrily along to its next destination. Now, Timothy could relax and take it easy, the strain and the struggle had been taken out of sailing. Where the boat was, where it was going, and when it would arrive, was left to the Man who had appeared to him when he was unable to help himself.

15

THE MINISTRY OF HELPS

God had great plans for her life, but Margaret struggled between what she felt she was and what the Lord had designated her to be. If she had to describe her life it would be as quicksand not quartz, as pebble quality rather than what her name Margaret suggested: pearl. As a mother and housewife, she was quite content to fulfil this role to the best of her ability. It was expected that she should be the mother of the family, nothing more and nothing less. Who made such a command? Who uttered such an edict? Was there a tyrant alongside her, or some important secretary writing these things onto her heart? It certainly couldn't be found in the Bible. If there was a move outside her 'comfort zone', then she believed the referee, as in a football game, would blow the whistle and she would be sent off into dark oblivion. Maybe she belonged in the 'sin bin'.

Faithfully, week by week, she laboured alongside her husband. Margaret was up with the sun and went to bed with the setting moon, reliable in her dedication to her husband and family. Her husband was a strong man with deep convictions concerning the role of a woman in the church. His theology was 'women should be heard and not seen.' To him a woman was simply a woman, but the Lord was calling this woman to be more than the man expected of her. The dwarf must grow into a giant, even if the giants did not like it or appreciate what would happen. Margaret had accepted her lesser role alongside her husband. His theology became hers, as faithfully she stood by his side and sought to help the church forward into a new blaze of glory. There was dignity and assurance with obedience in what she attempted and accomplished.

There were precious gifts in Margaret that were as dormant as the dormouse during winter. There was a stirring in her heart when the visiting speaker ministered the word of God. He was ministering on 'strong drink' that was poured on the sacrifices offered in the Old Testament. (Numbers 28:1–15.) This, he said, was a type of our zeal for the Lord. As each offering was put on the altar, depending which sacrifice was offered, the wine that was poured on top was measured. One sacrifice demanded one measure of wine, another demanded a greater measure. It is only through zeal that we accomplish things for the Lord. The larger the sacrifice, the greater the measure of wine was poured onto the offering. This wine was not like water to put the fire out or even to create steam, it caused the flames to burn brighter and greater, and sacrifice with zeal always does that in the Kingdom of Jesus Christ.

The speaker had called Margaret and her husband to the front of the church. Margaret stood with Colin, wondering what the Lord would say. Margaret knew that the Lord had said if you ask for bread, He will not give you a stone, and if you ask for a fish, He would not give you a serpent. They believed that their prayers would be answered, as the day follows night. It would be a 'sure' word, a 'pure' word, and a 'cure' word.

After her husband had been spoken to through a *word of knowledge*, the visiting speaker turned to Margaret, and placed his soft, sure hands on her hands. As he did so it seemed as if she was passing from the present into the future, from time into eternity. He took hold of her hands as if he were a weaver of silk, taking threads of silk to include in a pattern. It was as if eternity was in those hands. Her destiny was about to be revealed.

He could see Margaret in the shadows. Her demeanour was as someone rather withdrawn. The final curtain had been drawn across her life as if the play had finished. The end had come before it had really begun. As she stood in the shadows, a voice was calling her forward to stand in the front line. She had been called into the Battle of Life. To win she must fight, and there must be a step forward. God was going to use her in prophecy, and where, in the past, there had been contentment in the heart to let the men do all the ministering; the Lord was reminding this woman of the calling that was in her life. Suddenly that call was heard again, as clear as any trumpet call on the still morning in an army encampment. 'Those who are going to become great must commence that greatness in small ways. They do not grow great all at once. It happens little by little, as every experience is added to by the Spirit of God,' so said the Spirit of God through His servant. What Margaret had expected to become by herself would be erased, the Lord would re-draw her life in His rich, red blood. He would continue adding to what was given, until small became great, and nothing became everything.

Margaret had felt isolated, had the feeling of being cut off. When the Lord used others, she had felt that the blessing should stop with them. It seemed as if she was at the end of the queue, and the queue was never ending. Others were more gifted than she was, and more available. It was only right that she should know her place as a woman, and should never compete with men. How could she fulfil what the Lord was saying to her? God would not mock her; He would make her into a glorious example of faith and good works. The words were entering into her heart as rays of light at the beginning of a new day. In the past this mother had tried to exercise ministry, but there had been no one to encourage or help her. When help was required, it always seemed to have been refused, and she was pushed back into the role of sister, mother, parent or friend. It never went any deeper, wider or longer than this. Who would set her free? Here was a woman with potential, but that potential had been squeezed into another mould.

Margaret, by the word of the Lord, was now being set free to become what she had been called to be. To her heart the Lord was saying, 'Woman, worker and soul winner, be free!' It was a message that was for no one else. It was as if this lady had a private audience with the King. He spoke as if she was the only person in the universe who mattered; other ears would not hear what the Almighty was whispering to her heart. It was for her ears alone. What the Almighty created must fulfil its role in nature. He had arranged a mould for her, and when she was born, that mould was broken. There would be no one like her from this time forward and forever. There had to be faith to accept what He was saying, and what He was prepared to do. Margaret must not interfere with what the Lord was doing. If she did, it would be as if adding darkness to light, or letting a child throw mud over a masterpiece. Margaret was not prepared to let that happen. What God said in Genesis: 'Let there be light,' and there was light, would happen in her heart. Her character and charter would be the command of the Lord. This woman would be prepared to be full of the word of the Lord in action. In Jesus Christ, the Word became flesh, and in this lady the flesh would become full of the word. Her life would no longer be held as a Bible verse between two dark covers. What God said and commanded would stand forever and a day. This was the day, and the forever would follow as she surrendered. She never realised that surrendering to God could be so sweet, inspiring or heart warming. The Lord of the universe seemed to be putting the universe into her heart.

In the past, when this lady had wanted to fulfil her calling it seemed as if no one wanted to help. Whatever source she turned to, that source became a dry well. It seemed as if her abilities were so restricted they never got off the ground. Everything she attempted resulted in frustration. This mother had many children, and it seemed in her spirituality as if there were not enough clothes to clothe them, not enough food to feed them. There never seemed to be enough of what was needed. Her hand was always empty, her arm was always outstretched, it never caught hold of that which was passing by. Would this just be another of those experiences that passed her, as a ship in the night? The frustration would bend her lower until she was walking on her knees. She had prayed, 'Dear, Lord and Father . . . be kind in helping your handmaiden.' Would God answer this prayer or would it be like words that disappear as the morning mist?

If Eve had fallen by listening to Satan, then this lady would be successful, and resist all temptation by listening to the voice of the Lord. Margaret was willing to be an echo of that Voice. Whatever the Voice said, so she would do. One word would be her command.

The speaker could see Margaret reaching out for help, but each time the hand that was extended was slapped, and it was quickly removed. This was proving to be a ministry into misery, as help was denied. The hand was always as empty as the hand of a beggar begging from others. Skin and bone was offered in an outstretched hand, and skin and bone returned. Margaret needed to receive from the Lord what the man at the Gate Beautiful received from Peter and John in Acts 3. Not silver or gold, they were not her heart's riches. It was 'such as He had' that she needed, for that would make her richer than a millionaire. Then she could 'spend and be spent'. (2 Corinthians 12:15.) Margaret had been going to the wrong source for help. The help, and the 'helps' that were required for her to fulfil what the Lord had promised, was in those around her. God had brought help, but that help could not be seen because dull eyes were peering into the dark to find it.

Huddled as a crumbled heap in her small corner, Margaret was knitting. You could hear the clicking of the long needles as she laboured hour after hour. The ball of wool was so large, as large as the sun in the sky. Was it a grape from Eshcol that was being used? (Numbers 13:23.) As time went by, the ball of wool became smaller and smaller until it disappeared, to re-appear in the pattern she was knitting. On that pattern was a picture of the Lord Jesus Christ. The church could be seen in the background. In that church the congregation could be heard praising God from whom all blessings flow. The knitting pattern was only half finished, and unless more wool was obtained there would be no hope of it being completed.

A hand took hold of Margaret's hand, placing it on the back of the sheep that she had seen grazing as she pondered on what to do. It was a firm hand that did not lack conviction or direction. It was not a hand waving freely in the air, nor a hand giving a signal for a race to commence. It was a hand with a mission, about to take the hand of this mother to her mission field. It reminded me of the Hand in the Book of Daniel. (Daniel 5:5.) Should she leave this pattern never to be finished? Should she make it into something less than it was intended to be? It would make a shawl or two, to keep those in cold climates warm for winter. It would make a nice cloak for the apostle Paul, who requested Carpus to bring him one in the New Testament. (2 Timothy 4:13.) The Hand took her hand and put it on the back of the sheep, and Margaret began to realise what must be done, as the light of revelation broke into her imprisoned spirit. The people who were gathered around her had been placed there by the Lord to help her. These sheep were not marble sheep or statues, not part of a painting; they were part of her life, gathered around her to help in a time of need. These were clumps of soft wool. The need would be met through the sheep that gathered. Margaret had always ministered to them, giving to them and never taking anything from them in return. The Lord was telling her that it was 'pay back time'. These around her would supply what was required in the work of God. They were the source of inspiration that would enlarge her heart and vision. Sheep must be more than those shepherded.

As her hand rested on the back of first one sheep and then another, Margaret began to feel soft wool in her hands, and she touched it as treasure. As the woman touched the wool on the back of each sheep, it came off with such ease. Before long her hands were filled with wool, wool that would become a help from the 'helps' that God had provided. All help did not come from human sources, for the Lord had more resources than the number of stars in the sky. The sheep were not there just to follow, graze and give birth to lambs; they were there to provide wool for the pattern of the life that this woman was designing. They were not there to be butchered, they were there as 'helps' to further her ministry. What the sheep and lambs had would help Margaret complete the picture of Jesus Christ and the church as revealed in the pattern that was being produced.

Much wool was taken. Each piece, after being spun, was used to enlarge what was a representative of Jesus Christ in the pattern on the wool. There was no end to the supply, for there were many sheep. Each sheep would turn occasionally and look at the figure of Christ on the pattern that this mother was knitting. As Margaret reached out, the picture began to grow, as the church grew to its full capacity. All this would happen because what had been grazing, and gazing sheep had to be seen as a factory where wool was grown, developed, taken and used. There is potential in sheep, as there is in people. All the help she required was in those around her. When they fail and falter, then the Lord will step in and help. He presents to all, in our need, the wool that is part of the Lamb of God that takes away the sins of the world. It is from faith in Christ that we see the image of God in Jesus Christ. (Hebrews 1:1–3.) Through Him, the church is built — is made stronger. All growth grows with the wool from the Lamb of God. As the vision of Him grows larger, so also those things we deal with become larger and greater.

16

THE BURDEN BEARER

I did not realise until after she had been prayed for that Mavis was the minister's wife. She had a forlorn look, as if there was something or someone missing, and despite years of searching, whatever was missing had never been found. There was an emptiness about her, lines of anxiety etched across her face, as if it had been a page from an artist's sketch book. Life had left its imprint upon her face, not to disfigure her but to add to it, making it more appealing. There was a maturity in her openness. She felt as if the race was long and her legs were short, but she would never give in or stop. Would the end of the race ever come? When would this day be closed down? 'Every dog has its day', and this had certainly been the day that had 'had her'. There were many burdens in her heart, which Mavis could tell to no one but the Lord. A burden shared is a burden halved. The half being carried on her back was heavier than the whole burden. Often the Scripture had come to her ,'Cast all your care on Him, because it matters to Him about you' (1 Peter 5:7, modern translation). The 'casting' was alright; it was the letting go of the burden that held the great weight. If only that could be let go that had become part of an every day ritual.

The person praying with Mavis knew none of these things. With eyes closed, the prayer was made to the Lord to bless, help and keep. Suddenly a desert appeared, as the Sahara with all its sand. The picture was of many dimensions, totally uninhabited. Nothing grew; no animals had made it their habitat. It was as if time had deserted this flat pack of sand. Not even the wind was blowing. The only sand that was moving was under the feet of an ass, as it travelled along. This ass was not part of a desert caravan; it was a lonely figure, and the only figure in this terrible wasted wilderness.

As the animal came closer, it looked as if it could have been the donkey that Joseph and Mary travelled on to Bethlehem. (Luke 2:4.) I looked for the star of Bethlehem. It was high noon, with the sun beating down mercilessly. Although the sand was golden, it held no appeal; to think of it as gold would have resulted in a grasping of 'fools' gold'. Maybe this was the Damascus Road that the apostle Paul travelled along, or it could have been the journey from Jerusalem to Jericho.

Why wasn't this animal part of a company of desert traders? Why did it travel alone, with no hope of continuing for long, because there was no water, and certainly no oasis to spread green foliage to the right and to the left? These and many more questions would be answered by the Holy Spirit through a *word of knowledge*, as He began to clarify the picture into the spirit of the one who was ministering.

The ass had begun its journey at the far end of the desert. It was an outstanding picture. Apart from the sand, the ass was the only thing worth looking at. As it walked closer, it kept stopping, and as it stopped more burdens were placed on its back. Each stop meant another burden added. I could not see where the burdens were coming from, they just arrived. There were far too many to count, and the ass's back was too short to carry what was being loaded on to it. It seemed as if the beast had no choice in the matter. Would the next burden received become the proverbial straw that broke the camel's back? Every time it paused, either to paw the sand as if looking for a hidden spring, or to raise its head to see if there was the scent of water in the wind, another parcel of what seemed like sand was loaded onto it. Why didn't someone set it free by lifting the burdens from it?

As the ass came closer, its colour matched the colour of the sand, a reddish brown. As each burden was put on it, a remarkable thing began to happen; it began to sink slowly into the sand. It was as if someone or something was hammering the legs of the donkey into the sand. The further it went, the deeper it went. I thought to myself, 'If this continues, there will be no legs left for the donkey to make any progress.' The fool donkey was allowing itself to have its progress impeded by others. Why didn't it refuse to take any more packs onto its back? The answer was in the nature of the beast, for it had been raised and trained to carry burdens. No one seemed to care that it was carrying far too many, and was slowly being killed by the burdens it carried. The life was being squeezed out of it by these mill stones.

On closer inspection it was actually unclear as to what sort of animal it was. It might have been a camel, an ass or a donkey. The packs were gathered around it until the colour and nature of the animal was hidden. It wasn't being allowed to express itself in the way it had been born to do. If anything is added above what we are able to bear, there comes a breaking point, and this beast had reached its sinking point. Slowly, it began to disappear as if it was being rubbed out. There was no one to help, no one who seemed to care. 'What can be done?' I thought. 'Shall I take hold of some of the burdens and throw them from its back, and bury them in the sand, never to be remembered anymore?' I knew if this was done, the donkey, by virtue of its nature would search for them, and would find the hole they had been buried in.

Maybe the R.S.P.C.A. or a dog patrol dealing with animal cruelty should be contacted? How would they find this wandering beast in such a large area of sand? While pondering these imponderables, another beast appeared on the horizon. Was this another stupid beast doing the same thing? Would these donkeys never learn? I knew they had not much sense, because often you could see donkeys at the seaside, going forward and carrying children on their back. They went one way, returning the same way, just walking backwards and forwards all day, until the tide came in and washed their footprints away, as if all they did was of no consequence. They were just a plaything, a living toy for tiny tots to take and use.

The donkey had so many burdens on its back, its stomach had reached the ground. It could not lift its legs because the burdens had thrust it into the deep sand. This sand was not soft and yielding, it was hard sand, baked by the sun, but the burdens were stronger and more demanding than the sun or sand. Those burdens were weighty. If they had been filled with heavy rocks they could not have pushed the donkey any farther down, because the limit of depth had been reached. If it stayed where it was it would die and become a table prepared in the wilderness for vultures and any other marauding beast of prey.

When all seemed lost in the hopelessness of the situation, another donkey appeared slowly over the horizon. It carried no burdens, and seemed to be free to come and go at leisure, moving at a leisurely pace, as if it had never heard the word hurry; this animal seemed to be on a mission. This second donkey was white, and did not stumble, or walk as if lost. It walked straight and true, as if it following an unseen leader. It seemed to hold back until the first donkey could go no further, waiting until it sank to its belly and began to bray, and then it quickened its steps until it came to where the sunken donkey was. How could this beast help with the burdens of the other donkey? Would there be someone to transfer the burden from one to the other? If they both had the same amount of burdens then all would be lost, both would sink into a grave of sand with nothing to commemorate the work they had accomplished. No one would know where they were buried.

As the white donkey came alongside the donkey in the sand, it seemed to have an understanding of it. The donkey in the sand began to receive help. As if by an invisible hand, the burdens on the dying beast were transferred to the back of the other one. As each burden was transferred to the other, the back of the second donkey began to grow larger and larger. The more packages that were added, the larger the back became, until it grew large enough to take every package that came from the back of the one and was put on the other. If there had been mountains, streams and planets to be added, it seemed to me as if the back of the white donkey would have been large enough to carry these. These packages of all sizes and weight did not need any string or straps to fasten them; they lay as if they were children in a pram or resting in the arms of the mother.

As the burdens were removed, so the donkey that had been buried in sand began to climb out of the hole it had been forced into. In fact, 'climb' is the wrong word, because the sides of the hole became level with the rest of the desert sands, and the beast of burden had only to walk forward. It was now light; it could travel as far as it needed to go on this road that was seemingly leading to nowhere. New life entered into the one that had been buried. It seemed to scent water, for it began to go forward at a quick pace. The animal did not run away, but walked behind the white donkey, for the donkey knew where it was going. Then they walked side by side. The reddish brown animal that had been in the hole glanced backwards, and to its amazement its eyes were filled with a miracle. Where they had walked, there were no hoof prints left behind. It was as if they had never been, as if the wind had taken a large broom and swept everything clean. This had become the Land of forgetfulness. In it was the message: what is forgiven is forgotten! All mistakes had been cleared away. No one would follow the hoof marks to the hole that the reddish brown donkey had gone into. All evidence of its failure was covered. The remnants of the hole and the marks of walking donkeys had all been removed, yet here were many prints ahead of them. It suddenly dawned on the donkey that this must have happened many times before. Mavis was not the only one to experience this sort of problem with burdens. It reminded Mavis of the Lord Jesus Christ, and the many people He had brought out of holes made of sand into which they had sunk, as she had, when the burdens in the heat of the day had become too much.

As they walked together, or rather as the first donkey followed the second, the way opened up, and instead of sand there was a beautiful oasis with grass as green as that in Psalm 23. It seemed in my mind's eye as if each burden carried by the second donkey was turned into grass, with trees on either side of a pool of water, a fountain in the middle, and all manner of fruits, with as much pleasure as any beast could desire. All the delights of a donkey were seen in that oasis. Life could be different. It would be different as the first beast followed the second, step by step, to waters that had turned brown sand into green verdant pastures. Life from now on, especially now the burdens had been lifted and given to another, could be different — as different as desert sands are to that in the full flush of green, with plenty to eat and drink, and no burdens to be found anywhere.

This dear sister had taken the burdens of others upon herself, and had found them too much. She was only small in stature, she had a large heart, and what was asked of her and thrust upon her was too much. Mavis was the first donkey; the second 'donkey' signified the Lord Jesus Christ, Who had said, 'All you are weary and heavy laden, come unto Me and rest, take My yoke upon you, for My burden is light and My yoke is easy' (well fitting). (Matthew 11:28.) It was Christ who was drawing alongside her. He would take the burdens, and as Mavis followed Him, He would break those packages open. Inside of each one there was that to bless and nurture her. (Psalm 55:22) 'Cast your burden on the Lord.' The margin of the King James translated 'burden' as 'gift'. A transformation would take place if every burden was let go, and each one could be as a drop of water in a pool that would slake her thirst, would become fruit on a tree to feed her hunger.

Following Him meant treading on firm ground. There would be no occasion when the burdens would force her into the ground, or force her to come to a stop by having to carry more than she had been designed to do. When the reddish brown donkey moved slowly, so did the white steed. Jesus Christ knew where He was going, even as the white donkey did. His back is large enough, and if necessary He will increase to a size that is able to deal with every burden. The donkey's back grew, but the breast of Jesus grows larger as weary heads are placed on it. There is room for many more to come and rest and gaze into His eyes, as the apostle John did in John 13:25. Jesus was always big enough to deal with every thing; He had all capacity that would deal with Mavis's incapacity. Failure and sinking would be a thing of the past. That golden brown desert could be turned into the wilderness that blossoms as the rose, for here was the One to help her see it come to pass.

He had appeared as a beast of burden, He came as the same nature as she was, like a donkey in the desert, travelling the same way, and enduring the same conditions. Mavis could not help but trust Him. He did not come as a man with a whip in His hand or as a stranger, but as one of what she was, a 'burden bearer', even as she herself was. He was made in the 'likeness of sinful flesh' so that the flesh with its weariness might be overcome. Appearing as a donkey, He knew how a donkey thinks, acts, and what its nature demands. An angel would have been no use here! Jesus had not appeared as a bird, a dove, fox or rabbit, because none of these would have been able to help. An ostrich would have been of little use, putting its head into the hole she was buried in. He came to Mavis as she was, and what He was became that which helped her out of a mess. A rabbit or fox would have made the hole larger, and Mavis would have sunk deeper.

A radiant smile appeared on the face of Mavis, as if it belonged there but had been absent without leave. There was glory painting that face before my eyes. As I gazed at her, I could not help but wonder if this was the same person who came forward for prayer a few moments earlier. It was, but what a difference. There were no hunched shoulders, only a bright smile that would light up any dark room.

17

THE RESCUE MISSION

The area of Manchester where they were to commence their work for the Lord was one of the most notorious regions. Drug addiction, divorce, gang warfare, cheating, stealing and prostitution were some of the highest in the borough. It was a place where you either robbed others or they would rob you. Many had tried to do a work for God here, but they had failed spectacularly. It was both a graveyard and a mortuary. Jean and Ron had been called to the area, and tonight was their Induction Service. They faced the future with faith. There were no clouds, only rainbows provided by the promises of God. They were ready to do battle, to see converts yielding to Jesus Christ.

Their earlier years had been a preparation. They had operated as a double act in the clubs and pubs around Manchester, and had often been in touch with those whose needs were as deep as any well, and as high as the sky. Consequently they had great compassion for those in need. This couple were the social conscience of the area. In love with God, they could not help loving those that life had dealt a 'bad hand'. These modern missionaries had seen God perform a miracle in their own daughter. Sheila had been 'stone deaf', so deaf that the television in her bedroom had to be turned to its full volume. Often she had to go to the children's hospital to have treatment.

Sheila had been prayed for, and the one who prayed believed that God would heal her. She could hear plainly, even better than those who had no history of deafness. Everything was as clear as a drum. When she returned home, the parents, Jean and Ron, wondered if deafness would be turned into delight. The family returned home when Shelia, as was her custom, went to her bedroom to watch the television. To the amazement of her parents they could not hear any sound coming from the television, which normally would have filled the house. The next thing was even more amazing; Sheila asked if they would turn the volume of the downstairs set lower, because it was too loud for her, she could hear it in her bedroom!

This couple who wanted to serve the Lord in such adverse circumstances had experienced the *word of knowledge* at work in their lives. It had been such a happening that brought Ron to know the Lord as his Saviour. They had been travelling on holiday from the Manchester area to Wales when their car developed a fault. It kept jumping out of fourth gear. Ron knew there was no way that the car, which was towing a caravan, would ever get them to their destination. The only sea he expected to see was floods of tears from his wife and daughter as frustration crept into their heart. The only sand that would be trodden was their broken expectations as they became exceedingly smaller.

Jean had returned to the Lord after backsliding, and had tried her best to convince Ron that there was a God, and that He could be a personal God. The atheistic spirit in Ron ruled supreme from within. He thought it was all in the mind. If there was a God, He would have to prove it to Ron with undeniable evidence. He thought he would barter with God, so he prayed a simple prayer: 'Lord, if you exist and you are God, help me to get this car and caravan where we want to go, and I will serve you all my life.' The prayer was simple, sure and to the point, as if a little child was asking its father for assistance to tie a shoelace. I don't know if Ron really believed that the Lord would hear or answer that prayer, because, after all had been said and done, he had thought there was no God. The Lord answered that weak prayer in power and strength, in spectacular fashion. Suddenly the miles seemed to fly by, and they were where they wanted to be. To add to the confusion they ran out of petrol, and it was in the days when garages rarely opened on a Sunday. However the petrol was obtained and the car arrived with caravan and occupants intact at their destination. What was Ron going to do now? Would he simply submit to Christ as part of his bargaining? Certainly not. They had arrived, and his prayer was soon forgotten as they prepared a meal.

The following day they attended a local church, and mingled with the crowd. There was a visiting speaker, a well dressed lady, who from her speech and the way in which she conducted herself gave the impression that she was in touch with God. As she rose to speak, she hesitated because the *word of knowledge* was beginning to operate. The woman said, 'There is a couple who have arrived at this church who are on holiday, and they have a young child with them. The man has been bartering with God. He has had trouble with his car, and he has told the Lord that if He fixed it, he will serve Him. God wants you to know, whoever you are, that you cannot barter with God.' The woman continued to mention other things she could never have known, even if she had been reading from Ron's diary. Ron began to slip further and further down in his seat, trying to hide. He did not want those around him to know that he was the person that the woman was describing in fine detail. He felt like being a mouse, and wanted to find the nearest and smallest hole to run into.

After the meeting, he rushed away with his wife and daughter back to the caravan. How did the woman know all about him? He had never heard, witnessed or experienced anything like this before. It opened up a new world to him, the world of the spiritual, and a God who can be so intimate that He knows your thoughts in the bedroom and in a caravan. There he surrendered to Jesus Christ. He had been weighed in the balances and found wanting. He had been found out. 'There is nothing to hide from a Jesus that knew everything,' he muttered within himself.

Time moved quickly, and they were now being inducted into this area as minister and wife to serve the people. God began to speak to them through a *word of knowledge*. He had called them into the kingdom for such a time as this. The area they were now in was like an island. They had to learn to build bridges; to learn to walk on water; to learn to keep the beaches clean, making sure that the sea did not flood the island, because if it did all would be lost. As a couple and as a church they were like an island. God had set them as a lighthouse to warn all who entered these waters of the hidden rocks, reefs and sharks that awaited them if they did not take care.

The sea around them was filled with man-eating sharks. Anyone who tried to get near the island would be destroyed if they did not receive assistance. They were surrounded by needy people who were being destroyed by debt sharks and of other things. People were deliberately coming to these waters, and diving in, even though they could not swim. They were committing suicide. The work of this couple was to rescue the perishing and care for the dying. As they fell into the water, shark's fins appeared above the water line, and then disappeared to attack their prey. As they fell overboard sometimes, they grabbed an oar to beat off their attackers, but this was to no avail. There were parts of the water where murder had been committed, and the water ran red with blood. You could see the evil in the eyes of the sharks as they came to attack. I saw the hatred of a thousand years in their eyes. Those eyes were as metal eyes that had been cast into steel. They were as something possessed, and there was always an urgency about what they did as they threshed the foaming water.

Some of the people were sinking slowly, drowned as water entered into their lungs. Others were dying immediately they entered the water, because the sharks were waiting as an army, ready equipped with razor sharp teeth. They were torn to pieces. This couple loved every piece of humanity, torn or whole. Jean and Ron were going to the edge of the water, praying for the victims as they plunged beneath the waters to enter a watery grave. Their prayers were to no avail, the people were screaming, and their cries lingered longer than the tide remained in.

This couple had to be prepared to get their feet wet. They had to enter into the waters. They had no time to get the correct swimming equipment. The need of the moment was to dash and dare, and to enter the waters — whether to die or live did not matter. There was such a compulsion about the situation. They were surrounded by people who were dying, who were dragged under the waters by sharks, crying for help, waving in desperation, waving as if it was their final wave, waving goodbye to this world. The only thing was for this couple to challenge the thinking of this estate — to enter the waters, to tie a rope around them to secure one by one from the waves, and pull them away. One stood with a rope round the waist while the other went into the deep, murky waters. Darkness descended on island and sea. When one returned from the inky sea, the other went into the waters. The rope represented the prayers that each would offer for the other as they ventured into shark infested waters red with the blood of the victims.

This was not a rescue with a net, it was one to one. As one was rescued, another had to be rescued, but how many could they save? The water was cold, but the love of the Lord in their heart kept them warm. I don't even know if naturally either of them could swim! Spiritually, they had to enter the school of Christ and learn very quickly, because the future of the people living in that area depended on them. What they could not do before, they were doing as if they had done it all their lives. They had to be lifeboat and lifeguard all in one. They would never hover over the situation like a helicopter. When one was rescued, another sent out a cry, which grew ever more faint as they were dragged under the water. The command of this couple to go in and rescue would not be found or heard in a promise from God; the cry of the people became their call to action. The distress signal was in the tears that they wept as they fought a losing battle. There was no choice to win or lose if the Almighty did not step in and help. They had to be quicker and cleverer than all the sharks put together. They had to look and see where the next victim might enter the waters. The sooner they knew, the more likelihood there was of a rescue.

This was not going to be an ordinary pastorate, where a vicar daintily drinks tea with parishioners. There was no Psalm 23 theology here! Gentle flowing streams with tender grass would never be seen in this place. This was no slipper, rocking chair and sweetmeats theology. This was risk and return, do or dare, extend and extricate. It would be a matter of dash and dare, entering into unknown situations dragging people out of those areas in their lives that would sink them into oblivion. There would be no time to dress in the latest fashion. The need was desperate; they must be as desperate people meeting a desperate need. Even as they were thinking, souls were sinking. The only plan they required was the plan of the swimmer: to go into the waters, making the sign of the Cross in the breaststroke, and win many from the deep. Sharks and other evil influences they represented would be denied power. The plug would be pulled out of the waters, making every shark vulnerable. The plan was not to capture sharks, but to save the people who were perishing. The sign of the early church was the sign of the fish, which contained a message, and this mission would operate as a rescue mission.

They prayed and breathed deeply as they thought of what had to be done. There would be those who would readily cling to them for safety in these shark infested waters. It was important that they should be empowered by the strength of the Holy Spirit as they began to rescue those in the waters of death. They were not there to tell the victims of the seventy ways of swimming to safety, there was not time for that. They were there to convince those struggling because of influences surrounding them how to surrender. They knew that unless they repented there would be no forgiveness. This was where and when Bible promises were turned into flesh and blood in order to rescue people. The promises in the word of God had to become larger than this sea, higher than these waves, and stronger than many sharks. Each shaft of light from a promise would shatter a shark. As they surrendered, they were taken from the deep sea onto the island, into the church that had been set up to become a paradise island. It was the only place of refuge in the sea that surrounded it.

Ron and Jean had to stand up for these people. None of them could swim, and none had learned the secret of evading sharks that would attack. They thought the louder they shouted, the more noise they made, the safer they would be. The opposite was the truth. When drunk and shouting at others they simply attracted the predators that would destroy them forever. These two workers were to become as mediators between the sharks and the people. Their vision was their mission to rescue men and women from the foul influences around them, and bring them into a haven of heaven. Some were bleeding, some had torn flesh and torn hearts, and the local church must become an army garrison, a hospital, a lifeboat house, and a pot of ointment. It was in this church that they would receive healing from helping hands. All their hurts would be washed away by the blood of Jesus Christ. In this church were members acting as Florence Nightingale, Doctor James Simpson and Alexander Fleming, for all made great discoveries throughout the centuries, that helped to heal the sick and the dying. This had to be like the inn to which the Good Samaritan delivered the victim. (Luke 10:30–36.) They had to believe God, and as they trusted, so they would triumph, for faith was stronger and larger than sharks and oceans of water. These waters must be turned into a 'Pacific' (meaning peace).

The larger the island grew, an island that represented the church, the less water there would be surrounding it, and the number of sharks would diminish. The island needed to grow so large that there would be no more sea, Heaven will be like that. (Revelation 4:6; 21:1.) This was to be their vision, revealing their calling into crisis for such a time as this.

18

THE POWER OF THE CROSS OF JESUS CHRIST

He was not a weak man, he was strong and resolute. His face shone, as the Holy Spirit began to move upon him. He seemed to shiver from head to foot as if he was a tree, marked with a cross, and the lumberjack was applying an axe to the trunk after cutting it with an electric saw. This happening was electric; it was dynamic, for the Lord was speaking to His servant. Samuel had listening ears, and feet ready to respond to what the Lord was saying through the man of God. A *word of knowledge* was revealing the heart and purposes of this local pastor, as if an artist was panting on a canvas.

Samuel was in a boat, and it was a boat that was covered. It had a number of decks, and a captain, if he could be called that, because he did not seem to be in control; events were controlling him, as a leaf blowing in the wind. Samuel was not giving his attention to where the ship was sailing. He was not looking out for rock or reef. Certain waves were not called 'breakers' for nothing. He was busy going from place to place, from trouble to trouble and trying to sort it out. The striking thing was that there did not seem to be any crew aboard this ship, only the captain as the man to steer it on a straight course.

The captain was sweating, and I could see by his bulging eyes that he was under pressure. I was wondering if his eyes would pop out! His teeth were gripped together like a vice, and it was impossible for him to smile or to speak. He had the concentration of a bar of steel. He was running around in ever decreasing circles, and was quite dizzy and unable to focus properly. There were so many things to do, and he had such small ability when dealing with them. They were too big for him. He was swaying and I thought he would pass out. There were many needs, and no one was helping him to meet those needs. He was not only standing alone, but working alone. I have heard of the 'one man band', but I have never heard of a 'one man ship'. He ran around so quickly, he was in danger of colliding with himself.

The ship was lurching forward, listing to starboard as if in danger of sinking. Although there was no crew, there were passengers who were crying out for attention; every one of them was panicking. I did not see any lifejackets, nor even a lifeboat on this ship. It could only go one way, and that would be down to Davy Jones' locker. The passengers would get off at the first opportunity, using the captain as a footbridge as they rushed and trampled on him to get away. For those who were praying, the opportunity was now or never. The ship seemed to be going in only one direction, which was not south, east, west or north. Unless the captain received help from someone, he was as doomed to a watery grave as the rest of his passengers. He had taken every job on himself, and was fast becoming the 'Jack-of-all Trades' and the Master of none. 'Wild' and 'disorganised' did not explain what was happening.

Samuel had picked up pieces of wood that were scattered everywhere, as if they had been blown about by a strong wind. Some had come from the ship itself, other pieces were driftwood he had taken out of the sea. There were people among those on board who could help, but they were all taken up with their own distress and failure to float if the boat sank. I dare not let the people hear me think that word 'sank', for if they did, this would have increased concern and turned into panic. Thought would have become anxiety. Samuel was holding broken bits of wood which suggested that every crew member was like a piece of broken wood. He could build no ship out of this mess. The captain was running from one gaping hole in the side of the vessel, to another, and as often as he moved, so another hole appeared. Where, oh where, was there someone who would take hold of a hammer and the pieces of wood! He could do with a gifted carpenter to stop this ship from sinking.

Samuel, foolishly I thought, was trying to patch up the holes in the vessel with pieces of wood that were of many different shapes and sizes. None of the broken bits in his hands seemed to fit the holes; they were either too large or too small. I thought, 'the only thing he can do with that wood is make a good bonfire, and commence cooking.' The ship would become a fire ship, and building a fire would hasten its demise! Then I checked myself because I realised that if a bonfire had to be kindled it would be Samuel who would have to do it as the lone worker. If cooking commenced, he would also have to be the cook, the candlestick maker and the baker, for there was no one apart from himself, and he was a slave to frustration.

The reality of the situation was that Samuel could not mend the holes by using mastic to seal the wood at each opening. These openings were as windows with funny shaped frames with jagged edges, but instead of light streaming through, water was gushing in and flooding the ship, waters which were spelling the words 'end' and 'doom'. Samuel was trying to stretch each broken plank into the shape of the hole, but it was labour in vain. The wood resisted his many attempts to change it. What to him seemed to be a labour of love became love's labours lost. The problem was that the wood could not be bent to the shape of the holes. He had neither the knowledge nor the strength to bend those broken pieces into shape that would fill the holes and stop the vessel from sinking. He was a man with many tools, but no materials that met the need. He tried first one piece and then another, one shape and then another. He had a plan, but the plan was an impossible one to fulfil. He might as well have been using straw, for the wood was not much better at filling the gaps that had arisen because of the storm. This that he was doing was like you putting your fist into the air, and expecting it to fill the sky!

On the floor was a cross, not a special cross, just one made out of wood that might be seen on any sailing vessel. It had been thrown to one side in the confusion. There it lay, forsaken and forgotten. As Samuel gazed at the fallen cross, it seemed to speak to him. It had a message, and it was saying, 'Take me and use me!' 'How can I do that?' thought Samuel, the lonely captain of a sinking vessel. He dropped the pieces of broken wood, and taking hold of the cross advanced towards the next hole with water streaming in.

'What shall I do with this small cross?' thought Samuel, as he went towards the gaping hole that looked like a shark's mouth with serrated teeth. 'Shall I commence praying? I cannot do that, because the ship is sinking and I need to keep it afloat.' The voice coming from the cross was louder than the creaking timbers of the ship, or the cries of the people destined to be doomed. The noise of the gushing water seemed to quieten when the cross was speaking. 'Put me in the holes where the wood is broken!'

Samuel thought, 'Well, nobody is looking; everybody is trying to save themselves. I might as well have a go and see what happens.' The cross looked so small and insignificant compared with the holes, the roaring sea and the lurching vessel. Its smallness seemed even more diminutive as he placed it at the centre of the first hole, and the waters began to cover the cross. Suddenly that small cross began to grow, and fill the empty, broken space. It continued to grow until it grew into the shape of the hole created by the smashed wood. This was not timber added; the cross was growing to the size of the need, stretching to each fragmented piece, from the side to the centre. The small cross was taking on new dimensions. He was witnessing the power of the cross that had been lacking in his ministry.

There were certain people among his congregation whom he had been trying to get to help him to further the cause of Christ. He had approached one and then another, but each had seemed reluctant to help. What others would not do, and in some cases could not do, the cross would do. That sign of a death, the cross of our Lord Jesus Christ, could expand to any size, could fill the deepest hurts, hurts as deep as hell and as wide as the sea. Wherever there were jagged edges, the cross filled each one to the smoothness of planed wood. There were no joints or splinters to be seen. If the hole was wide or long, then the cross was able to fill it. The cross became as the wood of the vessel, so that not a drop of water came through. The power of the wooden sign seemed to be flung to the far corners of what had been ruined — making the broken vessel whole, as if it had never been changed. The whole thing was made complete with a completeness that complemented every part.

Samuel had not realised the power of the cross of Christ. What others failed miserably to do, the symbol of death and crucifixion would accomplish. The wood he had taken hold of was old wood, and the Lord was telling His servant that old methods were not the best methods. The oldest method of all was the plan of God that would meet the need. It is the cross that stretches from broken piece to broken piece and heals all distortions. There was still more power if he could believe that the Lord was able. The power of God was not in strong and resisting men, but in an old symbol of suffering. The cross was able to fill the holes because One had suffered on it. It was the achiever in all things, and would cover the emptiness with a fulness that could not be measured by the metre or mile. That which had been torn to shreds was put back together never to be torn apart again.

When the holes were filled, it meant the ship could sail on. It could collect others and make them part of the endeavour. There was now no in-pouring of water, drowning everything before it, treating one and all as matchsticks. That which had been sinking and listing suddenly began to gain power, as if the power of that cross had not only gone to the holes but also right into the heart of the ship, putting new zest into it.

There was no fear now from those gaping wounds. Samuel's concentration could be on other things. He had been taken back to fundamentals, the cross, and whatever dimensions of need, the cross could be used to form the shape, to dry the water and seal the timber. A holy glow came upon Samuel's face, for he had been brought back to the centre of Christianity, the cross of Jesus Christ. It was not as if new pieces of wood had been added what was missing was supplied. This was a Day of Jubilee when everything returned to its rightful owner.

When the cross had completed its work of healing, the holes — those that had been part of the moaning, groaning and grousing number — stepped forward as if they had been lying in wait to effect an ambush. These were strong, able bodied men who came from behind the cross. They had hands as large as dinner plates. The thought passed across the surface of my mind: during the feeding of the five thousand, they would not have required baskets if these men had been there! Their hands were large enough to collect much miracle bread and fish. These were men whose faces had been tanned bronze by the sun, who had travelled and seen a thing or two, for it seemed as if the sun had etched a map of the world onto their faces. They, without a word from the captain, went to their stations on the ship. Every man had work to do, and would do it from the rising of the sun to the going down of the same. As they worked, pulling, tugging, straining and stretching, they appeared as those in worship letting their hands and arms rise and fall together.

Samuel began to realise, as if a fresh spring day had come into a dark December, that if he had nothing, in the cross he had all things. It could heal hurts, and provide men, seamen, of quality and destiny out of ordinary people. The tools and weapons for building and winning were in that small object that had been thrown on one side like a crumpled piece of paper. From that one piece of wood, a sign of Jesus' death and suffering, had come pieces of wood of all shapes and sizes that had slotted into place like the pieces of a puzzle that had been missing. The men had appeared as those who would work with the captain as 'salts' of the sea.

The only piece of wood that God required and recognised was not obtained from builders' merchants. It was not even in a fine oak tree. It was in the piece of wood that represented the truth, the whole truth and nothing but the truth of God. The men had been there all the time in the congregation, but they did not rise to the occasion or accept their responsibilities until the cross of Jesus Christ began to reveal its true nature and power. In the day of His power they had become willing.

19

MRS NOAH

It was good to be in a church where the congregation contained people of every age group. The minister was an older man helping this pioneer work to come from puberty to maturity. He had worked hard and long, and the Lord had added those who were being saved to the number. Part of the congregation was made up of young people, and I was to discover that some of them attended a local college of further education. As I gazed over the congregation on this summer's day, it looked like a field of flowers. There were colours and shapes of all descriptions. It reminded me of the New Testament where the people were guided into groups and there was much grass in that place. (Mark 6:39; John 6:10.) The word for 'companies' is 'florets', a small bunch of flowers arranged by the gardener to show his handiwork. The word 'etiquette' suggests the same, seen in a border of flowers around a lawn. A 'privet hedge is a 'private' hedge around a house. These borders are added to bring beauty and diversity. When God brings a congregation together, He has all these things in mind. He plants, He waters and He plans. The word 'novice' suggests 'one newly planted'. (1 Timothy 3:6.) According to Psalm 1, every believer should be as a tree planted at the side of a stream, whose leaves do not wither.

We were in the Yorkshire Dales, but as quickly as winking I clearly saw Spalding in Lincolnshire, England, where tulips and daffodils abound in the warming spring sun. These people, as they worshipped, were as flowers blown by a strong wind. The sight and the sound of the songs were beautiful, not only in the eye of the beholder but in the heart of the worshipper. Spalding has the nickname of 'little Holland' because of the many flowers grown there; it is reminiscent of Holland where, in the fields around Amsterdam, tulips and daffodils are so abundant there are more than can be gathered in.

I was reminded in my spirit, by the Spirit of the Lord, of Doctor Banardo, the English philanthropist working among children and adults, who named all his almshouses after the names of flowers. He did this so those entering into them could live lives like flowers, full of colour and perfume, and always following the light.

I thought of Lydia (see Acts 16:14), whose heart the Lord opened, as a flower opening up its petals as the warm sun shone onto it. Then a reminder and a rebuff came in the thought of the English crocus, and how it survives a cold January day, but closing its petals to the weather; yet when the sun shines, it traps the sun within its petals that keeps it warm. Would the Lord open hearts this morning, as the sun in springtime opens up the buds to adorn the trees? I could feel that spring was in the air, the time of the birthing and skipping of lambs had arrived. Enough of my dreaming, for people were coming to the front of the church to be prayed for!

Among those who came forward was a pretty young girl. As Petula came shyly forward, I could distinctly hear animal noises. Was I on Macdonald's farm? There seemed to be a menagerie within the four walls of the church. There was the growl of a bear, the roar of a lion and the bleating of sheep, muffled by the neighing of a horse. They were all together, and one was left asking whether the millennium had arrived, where lion and lamb will lie down together. Now, I know and you know, that God's saints have been called to be sheep, but that was taking the figure a little too far. Was there something in the background of this young girl that meant she had been raised on a farm? There was no smell of animals about her; she had obviously used perfume before coming to the church, and her face was shining like a red apple hanging from the branch of a tree. Was there turmoil in her life, with many things suggested by the beast nature? I need not have feared, for the Lord had everything under His command.

Following the scent of the animals came a picture where all manner of animals were forming a circle, and the young Petula was at the centre. She seemed to be the queen of the beasts. Wasn't the lion supposed to be king of the jungle? Was the Lord calling her to be a lion tamer or a farm worker? It was important that the interpretation of this *word of knowledge* was correct. Here was a young lady associated with animals. Around us was a farming community, and it was in this area that James Herriot had written his books about the work of vets. English television had made a series of films of the books: *All Creatures Great and Small*.

As she stepped forward with modesty and humility, I distinctly heard the words 'Mrs Noah', spoken in a voice of authority. The voice seemed to be placing her in history. It was the same voice that called Peter and John from their fishing to follow Jesus. It sounded like the voice in Genesis that had said, 'Let there be light' and light appeared (Genesis 1:3). What was said surprised me, because for the moment my mind was dull, and the animals in the picture were not being associated with Noah's wife. Would the Lord promote

Petula as He had promoted Noah's wife? When they entered the ark, Noah's wife was placed last in the list, but when they came out, she was mentioned before the sons of Noah. (See Genesis 7:7, 13; 8:15–16) How could this young woman be associated with Mrs Noah? Here was a conundrum to which there was no answer. It was as if a mathematical proposition had been set down for me to remedy, and I did not know the answer. My brain was being stretched beyond my skin. I felt as if Samson should have been standing here, and he would have given the interpretation to this riddle. (Judges 14.) Even Daniel could have interpreted these hard things. Joseph would have been most welcome, with his wisdom in interpreting the dreams from another world that had relevance in this one. However, we were part of another generation, a generation which requires answers to the things that trouble them.

Just to say, 'Mrs Noah' was not enough to meet the need. That alone would have left the young lady hanging by a thread when it was a cord of love that was required. There had to be a further explanation. All things must be explained so that the mind can regulate what has been said, either by accepting it or rejecting after the first and second admonition. (Titus 3:10.)

I spoke with an anointed voice, loud and clear. The words that flooded my heart as the pictures had been deposited in my spirit were clear as a moonlit night. 'Hello, Mrs Noah,' I said. As those words were uttered, it was as if the young woman had been hit by a hammer. She fell to the floor and began to sob as if every tear contained her whole heart. Every time Petula was seen that day after this encounter, she was crying. Who had upset this young woman? What had I said that had made her cry as if fountains were in her eyes? As I told her what the Lord was revealing, it was no word of consolation, for the more uttered, the deeper the sobs, as if each tear was part of a broken heart.

God was telling her that her future work would be among animals. Petula would have a ministry among sick and wounded animals. The deepest consolation her heart would ever know was sick animals being made well. They would bring animals to her from near and far. I was wondering if she was to be a zoo keeper, or even go on safari. The animals would find her to be a friend. It was this young person who would release the animals from pain and suffering into the realm of health, not in a farmyard, something more important and imposing than that. Her life would be as tied up with animals as feathers were tied into the wings of birds, and wool was part of sheep. No wonder the beasts that had been revealed looked healthy and well cared for. They were in their 'heyday', the prime of youth coursing through their veins. They looked more like household pets than marauding beasts.

When everything subsided — tears, laughter, sobs and strong prayers — Petula began to explain why she was so moved when God revealed this to the visiting speaker. From birth she had had an adoration of animals. From a child, as Timothy had known the Scriptures, she had known animals. She slept with them, ate with them, thought of them and dreamt about them. Her parents thought she was going to be a lady jockey, such was her interest in horses. It was more than an interest it was an obsession to a degree that could not be measured.

Petula was in the local college, studying to obtain qualifications in order to deal with sick animals. After seeking the Lord, asking what her future ministry should be, she had felt that the Almighty had spoken to her about this in the past and was leading her in a particular way. It was a matter of choice and calling that had brought conviction to her condition of faith. As the term in the college proceeded, a few doubts had appeared on the horizon. Was she doing what the Lord required of her? Was it all a mistake? The New Testament word used for 'doubt' means 'to be pulled two ways'. Had God really spoken? Was it her overworked mind that had played tricks on her? The devil had been twisting good English words and the English alphabet to alter what God had said. Good advice was becoming gibberish.

What had been commonsense suddenly did not make any sense at all. The girl required confirmation of the will of God, and this confirmation would be as a backbone of steel, helping her in the way she wanted to serve the Lord. If only the Lord would speak to her again, and confirm her heart's desire to work, speak and think for Him. When trial and temptation came, then His confirmation would hold her steady, keep her facing the wind. Like Jesus, Petula would set her face as flint, unflinching in the most challenging circumstances. (John 4:4.) If the Lord spoke to her this morning, there was a determination to live in the echo of that voice.

Unknown to the speaker, Petula was studying to be a veterinary surgeon. This was her heart's desire, the only thing she lived for, but even the strongest desire and conviction requires encouragement. What was uttered that morning brought great encouragement to her. No mistake had been made. God had sent someone to tell her that her future ministry would be among animals that were as dear to her as her own heart, as — and more lasting than — diamonds. She was dear to God, and these animals were dear to her heart. If the speaker had known her, he could not have explained the deep feelings of her heart any better. The things uttered were the things in her heart, and like Mary, the mother of Jesus, she had 'pondered'— turned them over and over because they were so preciou. (Luke 2:19.) Petula felt about her calling as David must have felt when he longed for water from the well at Bethlehem, or when he enquired about a weapon of war, and was told that the sword of Goliath of Gath was in the tabernacle. He said, 'Give it to me; for there is none like that!' Anyone who has a deep conviction of things they feel they must accomplish will know how she felt that morning when it was announced that here was Mrs Noah.

The Lord told her that she would open the door to a place of refuge for animals, as Noah did. They would come in during a time of threatened storm, only to go out when she decided the time was right. She would be in charge of a rescue centre, a place to dispense healing to sick animals. The weary sheep would come and find rest, and there would be no limit to the type of animal that would be ministered to. Many a story would be told of how she treated one dog, and a few days later it came scratching at the door of the centre, bringing another sick dog for treatment. There were many animals to be treated but she knew that the best cure, the healing power would be love. As the vet, hers would be the ability that would manage the Centre, for at the centre of it all would be the call of God that had been received. Each animal would be seen as part of God's creation.

20

THE LIVING AMONG THE DEAD

It was a small gathering of people, as if there had been a poor harvest, and all had not been gathered in. The local council had given the lease of a building to the local pastor, who was trying to build the church of Jesus Christ. It was so tough, like trying to build a mountain out of sand. The minister consoled himself with the thought that good things come in small packages —such as diamonds and jewels — and those gathered were precious to him. He had put his heart, body and soul into this work that had commenced at the cross for the glory of Christ. After much work there seemed to be a restricted growth, but they were thankful for the small mercies that were part of the mercies of God. The pastor and his wife had the assurance that mercies of the Lord would follow in the shape of people who had been forgiven, and whose sins had been forgotten. Tough it may be, but it was these conditions that brought out the best in him and his wife. Their character was more important than their charter; what you are is more important than what you say or do. These were kingdom people.

Joe had been an engineer in a local bakery, and knew all about machinery. He had learned from the textbook, and also in the 'school of hard knocks'. He was well adapted to strip a piece of machinery to its ball bearings, but when it came to dealing with human beings he realised that they were more than spanners, nuts and bolts, or computers. They had feelings, and these had to be considered. They were human not robots, but they sometimes moved to obey the command of God slowly. Most of the work in the church, he and his wife, Beryl, had to accomplish. He needed the tools for the ministry of Jesus Christ, so that he could work on the hearts of the people, who sometimes seemed to be made of steel, wood or rubber. He had found that the best way to help any one with a steel heart was to pray that it would melt. He had seen flour and yeast turn into dough and then bread, and so these people under him would pass through one stage of glory to another until they became like the Bread of Life.

As I prayed, I could see a cemetery, and this frightened me because never before had I been into a garden tomb like this one. There was a great gulf of darkness between me and this place of dead bodies and flowers. There were headstones all over the place, standing like soldiers in sentry boxes. There were rows of flowers, but you could not distinguish one arrangement from the other except by their sweet scent. The colours or types could not be distinguished, because it was midnight in the churchyard. The blackness of the hour, moment by moment, merged everything into blackness. Where was the janitor with his torch? All were aware of the midnight hour, because the sound of the village clock rang true across the dimly lit area, its sound as a challenge to all night seekers to return to their beds, for strange things were happening on this night. The clock struck, like a man with a hammer striking an anvil from one to twelve, as if telling of all the mishaps of the previous day. Each time the clock struck it sent an eerie echo across the graveyard, causing my spirit to shudder.

What made this even scarier was that, around these graves, shadows were flitting from one place to another, as if they were being chased yet not caught. They were like children playing hide and seek. There was no light, only the deepness of darkness that reminded me of Genesis 1:2, 'Darkness was upon the face of the deep'. It was as if, in the operation of a *word of knowledge*, I had stumbled into the kingdom of darkness, where torchlight and daylight are forbidden. In my spirit I peered through the gloom of the midnight hour to see what was taking place.

Each of the headstones was being pushed by a strong power of destruction. As they were pushed, it was as if they were being forced to bend in worship, doing homage to a foreign king. They broke into two pieces and fell, one piece following the other. I had heard of the pestilence that wastes at noonday, but this was night time, and things were being wasted into want. There were no names or history of the dead written on these marble slabs. If there had been any fond memories expressed in the etched words, they were smothered and covered as the slabs were thrown down, just as those who were demon possessed in the New Testament were thrown down to the ground. (Mark 9:20–24.) If these in the graves had a history it had been rubbed out, and there was an air of despair and finality about the scene. As they fell they crushed the flowers that had been put onto the graves. Every memory of the person in the grave was rubbed out as the marble slabs fell; the beautiful flowers of colour and variety were being covered by black marble, thick and heavy. Where there had been shadows, now there was broken marble covering any beauty. If you have looked at any object from afar, in the dark they may take on grotesque shapes. Here was a picture of desolation that had been visited by locust and cankerworm. This was the day of evil, the triumph of the powers of darkness.

There was a woman sitting before me who I was praying for, who obviously had been part of the occult. You could smell evil on her as prayer was made. Blackness filled the surrounding area. Wherever you looked, all you could see was that cloaked in deep darkness. There was such sadness about this woman that would only be complete when Satan destroyed her. I thought to myself, 'How amazing: the works of Christ result in life, abundant life, and eternal life, while the works of Satan result in death, endless death.' The initial evidence of death is the grave.

The scene reminded me of the story in the New Testament where a man called Legion had been in the tombs, cutting himself and crying out. (Mark 5:1–9.) This man was demon possessed, and no one could bind him until Jesus bound him with the cords of love by showing an interest in his deep need. The love of God is stronger than the grave and deeper than hell. The need in that man was as deep as hell — many demons were in him. This woman's face looked marked, as if a pencil had drawn lines on it, so that all could see the suffering etched in her face. There seemed to be the hand of the plastic surgeon at work, marking the areas that he was going to trim off and tuck in. God gives medals, but Satan lines the skin of your face and soul with furrows that tell where he has ploughed and sown his evil seeds, like the seeds Adam and Eve found in the forbidden fruit, seeds of doubt, fear, mistrust, anger, wrath, malice and pride.

Sheila had obviously been part of the occult. There was demon activity in her life. It had spread from one area to another, and now there was no stopping it. What had been meant to be as a flower, in its purity, colour and diversity, had been crushed by another power that was in opposition to the Lord. Sheila was trying to break out of this darkness, but the slabs of marble were so heavy, and as she tried to move them they had a grip of steel on her life. The mould of black, of darkness, must be broken forever! The marble slabs fell over and crushed her heart that was as a bunch of flowers. Even in the darkness she wanted to be a rose or a lily, not deadly nightshade that poisons all who reach out and taste it.

As I gazed at that broken ruin another power entered that cemetery. It was the power of the resurrected Lord. As He rose from the dead, so each broken slab was lifted back to its position, with the words written on each one: 'I love you'. The resurrection made an awful mess of that cemetery. Flowers began to grow that were not in water or placed on graves; the cemetery became a meadow of flowers, springing up and carpeting it with a multi-coloured carpet. Those lives of the dead were springing up like immortal flowers, perennial in shape and nature. The shale and the gravel pathway no longer hurt the un-slippered foot. Those flowers covered every grave and every pathway. This was like the paradise of God, black night became white day. The morning had broken, and instead of shadows and black clouds there entered the singing of the birds and the shining of the sun, as if it intended to set no more. Summer had come. It appeared as part of the creation of the Lord, to cover hill, vale, stone and straw. This was better than a stab in the dark or the switching on of a torch for light that would eventually dim as its batteries weakened. What power, diversity and freedom the resurrection brings when it takes place Instead of the village clock chiming there was the singing of birds to another. Sadness and sorrow were replaced by joy and gladness. Even the surrounding trees seemed to be clapping their hands.

For the broken and bent woman, the funeral and committal had taken place before she had died! From dust to dust and ashes to ashes seemed a fair epitaph of such a life. There was nothing left for her to live for. The way of escape was barred;

all was night around her as an invisible wall. Who would set her free from this torment and body of death? Sheila felt crushed and hurt. She was being pushed into an open grave before the end of life had come. The commencement of death had already taken place. She had become a creature of the night; the bat and the owl were her companions.

'Sheila had been part of the local church, and had resigned and joined another church,' so Joe, the local minister, told the visiting preacher after he had prayed for her, and revealed what the Lord was saying to Sheila. This woman had been part of a thriving church that had experienced a 'split'. Along with her husband, Sheila had joined another church, but that did not suit her. Anything that is 'split' from a boat will drift with the tide, will be misshapen and contain many splinters that can be used as spells to bind others with. As the years went by nothing seemed to satisfy, and the close walk she had with the Lord became an empty gap, a gap that could not be measured.

Sheila was looking for reality, and reality must be the name of that found by her. If it was magic or miracle, spirit or spirits, in her state of mind it did not matter. Both were appealing, and seemed to her to be holding out open hands in her moment of need. Sheila decided to get involved with a local group of those who were dealing in 'black magic'. She thought it would be alright just to try it. She thought that there was no harm in it really, and that it was only make-believe. The stories she had heard must have been made up after a night spent drinking alcoholic beverages. Others had tried it, and it seemed to bring relief to their aching hearts. Little by little she was influenced, until the influence became a rule and a necessity. Once tried, it would not let go. A price had to be paid, and this woman had paid the inflated price with interest. Here was a woman drawn into a spider's web, never to escape again. She was a convert of the devil! She would serve the cause all the days of her life. Sheila had wanted something and someone to live for, not to die for.

Suicidal thoughts, as black shadows, had flitted across her mind, leaving imprints on her spirit. Footprints were there that were saying to her, 'Follow me!' As she gazed to where they were leading, the edge of a sheer drop appeared. There was that beckoning her to follow the footsteps right over the edge, into an unknown abyss. These steps deepened until they became as deep as hell, before hell was arrived at. Sheila noticed that no footprints were coming from the precipice towards her. The only way out was in. Only one thing could be deduced: no one ever walked out of that place beckoning to her to come right in. These were things that frightened her, and having no power over them, she was invited— no, commanded — to follow as a lamb to the slaughter. There was no control in her life over this power, it was controlling her, squeezing the life out of her, as if she was between the devil and the deep blue sea. The sea was getting larger. The devil, with his forces of evil, was coming to claim her soul. There was the feeling that, without knowing it, she had sold her soul to the devil! It didn't take long: only one second, one decision, just to draw the curtains and shut the light out would be enough. Under the cover of darkness, the evil deeds of Satan could be carried out.

There was a certain stratagem about the way he worked until she was in his grasp. It could not be described as being 'at his mercy' for the devil shows no mercy, only cruelty, harm and despair, all threads in the web of deceit that had been flung around her, laughing at the woman as she fought a losing battle.

These things were all true, because after the *word of knowledge* had been in operation in that church, the pastor informed me what was wrong with Sheila, and how things had radically changed in her heart. That heart had spilled its contents into those around her. Here was a soul winner for Satan! Here was a disciple of a demon, a devotee to evil and the wiles of the devil. In the meeting she sometimes wandered around like a restless spirit, as if demons had been cast out of her, and she was wandering around looking for something to take their place. (Luke 11:24–26.) That morning when I met her, she had a face as if the sun had set and thunder had taken its place. If there was a fresh commitment to Christ, and a desire to be set free, then the Resurrection and the Life would do His work, scattering, smashing, and uprooting the works of evil in this life half-formed. Sheila could be set free to choose her Master and Friend.

21

VISION AND APPLICATION

Ruth's character was in her face: sure, strong and serene, with a smile, that extended across it. This lady was built to last, well proportioned, a woman with a mission. What God had said to her must be fulfilled. Souls must be influenced, people won to Jesus Christ whatever the cost or care. Here was activity in a woman, a mother in Israel, one who had good works in abundance and kindness that could not be counted. The whole of Montreal, Canada, where she lived and was now attending another church, was before her, spread out, waiting for those with zeal to set it on fire. There did not seem to be one place in a corner of her life which had space for a rocking chair in order to put your feet up. There was no time of rest, for in her discipleship there was only time to do and dare. Ruth was a woman of action, an action woman.

The *word of knowledge* began to reveal the need of Ruth's heart. There were areas where, although there was no lack of commitment, there was a lack of direction. It wasn't that she was not trying hard enough; in fact, here was a person who was trying everything and anything, yet accomplishing nothing. If there had been prizes on offer for attempting great things for

God, then Ruth would have won that prize. There was faith in operation, but that faith was not producing anything; it was faith weighed in the balances and found wanting.

There was not a lazy bone in her body; she would have outrun the sun and the moon in her desire to serve. Times of play and rest were as rare as a blue moon. Ruth as lady pastor worked day and night, mixing the two together for good to produce in others the Bread of Life. In her work and ability, help was needed. The face of the Lord must be sought, and what was revealed from that Source must be added to all the activity of an active life. Ruth was 'saved to serve', and 'served to save'. Others were her main thought and desire. If, after the feeding of the five thousand, the fragments that remained had been given to Ruth, she would have broken the pieces smaller so that more people would have been fed!

I saw this lady as worker and a saint. In her hands was a large bow with very large arrows. I was amazed that the arrows ever left the bow and flew through the air. This lady was large, and every ounce of her strength went into bending the bow of steel, and sending the arrows scattering. This created a problem, because they just flew and fell, they did not accomplish their mission. What was the use of firing so many arrows if they did not fulfil their ministry? So many people have zeal without knowledge, which leads to fanaticism, but zeal working with knowledge builds bridges and leaps across chasms. The ardent spirit required to be harnessed to something useful to produce a crop at harvest time.

Ruth knew the story of how Elisha asked King Joash to beat the arrows on the floor after he had struck the floor a few times and thought that was enough. Elisha had challenged King Joash as to why he did not beat the floor many times, because that would have been the number of times he would have defeated the enemy. (2 Kings 13:14–19.) Ruth was not even beating the floor, she was firing the arrows into the air and letting providence take them on the winds of change wherever it decided. These were less useful than a seed on the wind, because where seed lands at least it can be planted and grow. Wooden and metal arrows do not grow where they land. As an arrow falls, there shall it lie.

Here stood a person full of zeal, trying to serve the Lord with all her heart, soul and strength, but failing in the attempt. It was not the devotion that was questioned, it was not the ability or the commitment, it was the direction. Ruth had things to do, but did not realise what those things were. The circle was not complete. The whip, spur and trigger would have been fitting emblems to describe her attitude — the sweat of her brow the initial evidence of hard work. You could not fault her zeal. The Scripture was fulfilled: fervent in spirit, serving the Lord (Romans 12:11), 'fervent' meaning 'white hot with passion'. There was such intensity in what was being 'accomplished', but 'accomplished' is not the correct word, because she felt that after such endeavour very little seemed to have been done. It was as if she had run a mile and not taken a step in the right direction! This was leading to frustration and stagnation.

The activity was real without accomplishment or distinction, first moving to the right and then the left, moving in neither direction. This was not dereliction of duty, it was duty without destination. Ruth had done all the right things following the pattern that was written in her heart. The right buttons had been pushed, the expected results did not materialise, and in fact they were invisible.

Ruth stood facing an open field, and she reminded me of Abigail, the wife of David, who had been married to Nabal, that churlish man. This was another Shunammite woman who uttered the words, 'Slack not your riding for me unless I bid you' (2 Kings 4:24). In her actions was the suggestion that here was the servant of Jonathan who, when the arrows were fired, would either fall short of the target or go beyond it. When I saw what was happening, Romans 3:23 came into my spirit: 'All have sinned and come short of the glory of God.' The figure is that of an arrow being fired at the glory of God, but, missing the mark by a mile, falls as flat as the ground it came from, never to return to the quiver that held it. I mused within my heart: was the lack of success because Ruth was like Ephraim, who turned back in the day of battle? (Psalm 78:9.) The figure in the words 'turned back' is that of a 'warped bow'. You may be an excellent marksman, but if the bow is warped you will miss the mark by a larger margin than can be measured in the word 'warped'. This will throw you off the target. The activity in the life of Ruth was leading nowhere. If a woman wants to get to the moon, the empty sky is a poor consolation, be it ever so large and high. She was not taking second prize for archery; she was not wining any prize or receiving any plaudits. Surely she had not turned back in the day of battle? This woman was not for turning, but for going straight on, as straight and true as the arrows she was firing from the bow. Her ministry lacked salt, lacked achievement, lacked that vital to archery.

Ruth had fired many arrows, day and night. By her strength and dedication she had fired the arrow by night that could kill. There were many arrows flying through the air, as if a machine had been used. As the Psalmist says, if the quiver is full we are blessed. (Psalm 127:5.) Ruth was involved in this demonstration of skill and power, but it was skill without the kill.

The air was filled with arrows as if an army was firing, but to no avail. What a waste of a steel tip, of wood and feathers to balance the weapons of war! These wooden sticks of death were not accomplishing the desired intention of hitting the target. That target was everywhere beyond where she stood. If you fire a gun and a flock of geese is passing overhead, even without a specific target you might hit one, and send it crashing to the ground. Zeal was seen, without knowledge. Ruth was going to conquer the world, but there was no world within her sights to conquer. This was the day of visitation and battle, but with no objective in view, nothing could be accomplished. The arrows were sent out of the quiver as something on a day's outing, with no pattern, no thought of where they were going. They had been fired, and that was accomplishment in itself. What a waste of effort! Strength and purpose could have been put to better use.

I have never witnessed such activity for a long time. The last time I saw such activity was when a flock of geese were flying overhead on their migration journey to another climate. At least they knew where they were flying to, but not these arrows. They were as servants without a master. I saw Ruth replace the string of the bow, as if it might be the string that was too slack, and that was why she was missing the intended target. Here was opportunity without an object or accomplishment. No wonder the arms of the archer were as bent as the bow! Arrows and bows were not created as toys, or to refresh the spirit of the archer. A target was needed.

This was as bad as whistling in the dark or believing for something and not knowing what is believed for, just as if someone had prayed 'Lord, do something, and do anything.' Here was a display of zeal, good works, activity and service, which meant nothing, because there was no target to strike. Goal posts are essential if you are to score. It is good to have a target. Without goal posts no footballer, no matter what his value, will ever score.

Suddenly, two large hands descended from the sky, like aeroplanes landing on a runway. They did not taxi along, but came and took hold of Ruth's frustrated, quivering hands, and a target appeared at the end of the field. A stronger grip took hold of those feeble hands. At last the vital target had appeared. It was not shaped like the usual target with outer ring and inner ring of different colours, this target was cross shaped. The cross was coloured red and could be seen plainly wherever you were standing. There was no bull's eye; the centre contained the red blood of a lamb. The arrows now being fired were not the normal shape of arrows but smaller crosses than the target. As they flew, each one struck the shape of the cross, as if they were attracted by light to the larger cross. They did not stick into the wood, but disappeared into the main cross. Every arrow, every smaller cross, flew into the target cross, to disappear. It was as if they were arriving home after a long journey, and the larger cross was welcoming them with open arms.

The main cross was so large that the smaller crosses could not miss the target. Not one was wasted: none went beyond the target, and none fell short. Here in the cross was something that Ruth could not fail to strike. Here in the cross was the possibility of success. It was a picture of the target cross moving to where the smaller crosses were flying, and receiving them unto itself as if they were related. They were of the same nature and wood.

The message was clear to this lady minister. Her ministry was not to do or die, but to die. As she took up her cross daily and followed Christ, all that had been a waste would produce results. As the cross of Christ was expounded, it would become as flying arrows to the hearts of the people. They would be taken up with the larger cross. There had not been the cross to aim at in her ministry, but from this day on, all she did would be a success, because the principles of the cross were being added to her life. Her ministry must be spiced with the teaching and principles of the Cross of Jesus Christ, that would influence everything else. That Cross stood as the King of crosses. This was not simply a calling that had been received; it was the call of the Cross. In her future ministry, if she preached the Cross then others would reach the Cross. There was no gulf large enough to make any cross-shaped arrow fall to the ground. Every time she opened her mouth and presented the cross, a target would be given to her. It would not be Ruth who would fire the arrows; it would be those strong hands that had come to her aid. The target in the shape of a cross would make sure that she succeeded in her ministry.

A smile spread over the face of Ruth, a smile of assurance, a smile with a target in her eyes, as bright and as light as when the Lord had said 'Let there be light!' Something that had troubled her had been troubled. It was morning in her heart, and the shadows of the night had passed away. She now understood. It was not enough to serve, it was only enough to serve the Cross of Jesus Christ. It was not enough to fly through the air as a piece of wood in the form of an arrow. The Cross was God's seal of approval and her guarantee of success. Her future direction and involvement must be centred in the Cross of Christ. If it was, then every target would be struck, every army of opposition overcome. The target would not be struck nine times out of ten but always.

22

SHOES THAT DO NOT FIT

Often, as children, we would pretend that we were adults. We were totally convinced when, at Christmas parties, we were allowed to dress up in adult clothes, that we had suddenly become adults. The fairy that we mistakenly thought could change so much with her wand was on top of the Christmas tree! Put a cowboy hat on me, and I could conquer the West; with a toy gun in my hand I was a potential world ruler. I have often seen my children and grandchildren wear dresses that were far too big for them, and hats that seemed to be as large as the sun. They did not object to wearing spectacles, but the largest and loudest laugh was reserved for the moment when they wore shoes that were not the right size. They were not too big for their shoes; their shoes were too big for them! If the shoes had high heels, they would wobble as a drugged drunk from side to side, and finish up on the floor laughing at themselves. At the moment of wearing shoes too large, they walked into a mess.

When children play these games it is laughable, but when we play the same sort of games spiritually it is deplorable. When a mature person acts like a child it is not child-like but childish. It is centred in the word 'insincere', meaning stuck on or put on for the occasion. The Greeks would fix broken objects with wax that melted in the warmth of the sun or the home, and those pieces stuck on would fall off into the hands of the purchaser. Because of this, they were compelled to provide the buyer with a certificate that had the word for 'sincere' 'without wax' written on it. Sincere means the lack of play acting or being a hypocrite. Hypocrisy is an act, but not an act from the Acts of the Apostles. All that is worn in hypocrisy comes from the devil's wardrobe. Whatever it is you put on, if it is not you, then it is play acting. There is far too much passed as Christianity that is like a Christmas tree, or should I say a Norwegian pine tree where everything has to be tied to the branches to keep it from falling off. Many have tried to fight the giant Goliath by means of another's armour. (1 Samuel 17:38.) Some are more practised at being the hypocrite than they are at being a Christian. One is a profession yet the other can become an obsession. One is a performance the other is a practice of being like Christ in personal trust and purity.

I was surrounded by many nations, the meeting was packed with worshippers, and being in Canada I was asked to pray for those who were standing at the front of the church. Suddenly, as a *word of knowledge* began its skilful operation, manifestation and insight, I was in another world, the world of the Spirit of God, Who is full of eyes within and without, who sees all things, knows all things, and is able to perform all things. (Revelation 4:6.) Hagar said, 'You, Lord see me' (Genesis 16:13). I could see Maureen as a child. The mature woman had become diminutive in the picture that I was seeing. Suddenly the years were rolled back, as if an orange had been peeled or an apple pared with a knife, to reveal its core. Suddenly Maureen was back at infants' school. Physically she had shrunk into a child. Was this a picture of her spirituality?

The tricks that I mentioned earlier, of children dressed in adult clothing, was the way this woman was now seen. It was not clothing that my eyes were directed to, not even the fact that she seemed so small, it was the shoes that had been fitted to her feet. Maureen had sat and considered whether to wear these shoes or not. Time was spent deciding, as if her eternity would depend on it. Later I was to find out that her eternity did depend on the decision she had taken. They were adult, high heeled, that she placed on her feet. The colour, design or make did not matter. These were made for wearing and she would fulfil the designer's wish. They were not forced onto her feet as if they did not fit. Her feet slotted into them as if they were the cardboard boxes they had arrived in. They were large enough for her to twiddle her toes. Here was room for self expression.

The whole figure that was being revealed to me was one of delusion on a grand scale. Here was a woman appearing as a child, and here were adult shoes into which her feet were placed. Her feet had shrunk, while the shoes remained the same size. Her feet slotted in so easily, and it seemed to bring a smile of achievement to her face as if she had just competed in the Olympic Games, and had won a gold medal. This was not gold, but leather or plastic, and this was not the Olympic Games. They were the unreal thing, fitting someone who was not really a child but an adult. Maureen was stepping into something cosmetic and unreal. Small feet and large shoes could not work together; there could be no unity here, walking together as two that agree. These feet and shoes would never be as two peas in a pod. It was the act of stepping into the shoes that had caused her to diminish as if they had shrinking powder sprinkled into them. At first, Maureen tried to walk backwards in shoes that were too large. The shoes were facing one way, and she was walking another. There was a twist of irony in this story. Then I thought, 'How silly, to be wearing shoes that don't fit, and then to walk backwards in them', this was adding insult to injury. It would have been difficult enough to walk forwards, and here were backward steps into the past. Difficulty was added to difficulty; the sense of a donkey had entered into this childish mind.

To the childish mind, the fashion of these walking leathers did not matter. It was not the design that had attracted her, it was the adventure of being an adult yet feeling like a child. This was to result in childish behaviour. To my mind her choice was like trying to climb up the side of a mountain in slippers or wooden shoes. Now and again Maureen looked down, and when no one praised her attempts at being grown up, she would clap her hands with glee. This was self praise, the presentation of plaudits from her personality. By her actions she was saying, 'I am so clever', and maybe this is where the English colloquial saying 'clever clogs' came from! Caution was thrown to the wind as the box the shoes came in was discarded.

Obviously a miserable failure at walking backwards, Maureen then tried to walk forwards, and as she did so she fell backwards. By doing one thing there was the accomplishment and inclusion of the other. As there was an attempt to walk forward, she swayed from side to side, as that in a wind ready to fall. As in the case of the unwise man who built his house on the sand, 'Great was the fall of it' (Matthew 7:27). Then her feet, or should I say shoes, seemed to twist together, and she fell headlong onto the floor, hurting and bruising herself. Then she commenced treading on her feet, because the shoes were too large and her feet too small. Bruised feet would be part of her if she continued. This did not matter to this young girl with spring in her soul and a summer of delight to follow. First one trip then another, until a steely look of determination entered into her heart, and shone onto her face, 'If this kills me, I am going to do it!' Many attempts to walk were made, and all finished up as a complete mess on the floor, legs in the air, hands waving frantically, and clothes over her head! Now she was not only lame but also blind.

It did not matter how many times she fell. Each time she would rise, straightening her dress, brush herself down with her hands, and continue on her walk of exploration. By now she was getting more and more cross with herself. She was more cross than ten scorned angry women! More cross than she had ever been before when boys pulled her pigtails and spat at her. There seemed to be no blame laid on the shoes. This little one was blaming herself. Why could she walk straight in her own shoes but not in these? Surely size didn't make that much difference. If only a few steps could be taken, that would be the initial evidence of victory. It was a battle of shoes over mind, and being self-willed there was only going to be one winner.

What did all this mean? Maureen was not walking properly, yet she was determined to continue walking as she was. If she fell, then by her own strength she would rise up again to walk. What this lady was doing was causing a child to stumble, as one who was blind but without a white walking stick. There should have been an orange ring added to the white stick because she was blind and deaf. Here was a woman stumbling blindly in daylight. There was no shield over her eyes.

There was sin in her life, and that was associated with her sexual behaviour. A man using a scriptural definition was trying to pass himself off as something that he was not. When hypocrisy meets hypocrisy there is always play acting. Two bad seeds will not produce a good harvest. Maureen had not realised this, but she had the common sense to discuss it with her pastor. She had gone to bed with a man on a number of occasions, and felt uneasy about it, but what could she do?

What he was telling her was plausible. In her heart there was the ready acceptance of the lies because it would suit her desires. 'Birds of a feather flock together', and even when they gather together, feathers fall as they begin to moult. There is 'honour even among thieves'. Hypocrites are of the same profession.

The advice given to Maureen was that she must examine motives and actions in the light of the Scriptures. If an angel from heaven preaches contrary to the Word of God, that angel must be rejected. The man was so persuasive; she needed to remember that the word 'con' as used in 'conman' comes from a word that means 'heart'.

This man was a charlatan, pretending to be what he was not, so that he could get Maureen to sink to his level. Two bad apples falling to the ground will soon take root together. William Shakespeare, the English playwright, said, 'Misery acquaints us with strange bed fellows', and so does hypocrisy. The man was a 'quack', repeating empty words, and the listening ear was obeying. Have you heard the 'quack' of a duck? There is nothing in it. It is an empty sound. It is not music on any scale. It seemed as if Maureen had been deceived into living a hypocritical life, causing her to wobble from side to side, and to walk such a path that the broad way would have been ashamed of her. This is why there was constant falling. This was the cause of her immaturity. Wearing adult shoes caused her to hurt and bruise herself. She was play-acting, where pretence had found a home for its litter. It was where truth became stranger than fiction.

Suddenly a battle of the worlds began. A cross was thrown in front of Maureen, but her concentration was on her walking and keeping her balance. As the cross fell, it pointed to another path, a narrow way. She fell to the floor, giving a loud cry as if her ankle was twisted. She was not going to give in without a fight. This was not the fight of her life, but a fight for her life. There the body lay, as a rose in the dust. I reminded her that when the petals of the rose are crushed, sweet perfume worn by kings and queens oozes out.

As she wobbled and fell, I saw another pair of shoes being fitted to her feet. At least, someone was trying to fit them but Maureen was kicking and crying. These sandals were less fashionable than the shoes she was wearing. They were the sandals of Jesus Christ, lined with love and buckled with boldness, made out of strong assurance. With her resistance broken, she surrendered to these other shoes being added to her feet. As soon as the sandals of Christ, as gospel foundations, were put on, her feet began to grow to the size of the sandals. (See Ephesians 6:15.) These sandals brought comfort like well worn footwear worn by the pilgrims of the ages as they passed through this world. Now Maureen was taking surer, firmer steps as if she knew where she was going, and where the sandals were taking her. She began to dance towards the way that the Cross was pointing. The Cross had fallen onto the floor, and now it was giving its message. When she reached the narrow way, the dancing ceased. Maureen began to notice lots of other people were on this narrow way, all wearing the same sandals that had been offered to her, as part of their service for Jesus Christ. She saw John the Baptist with the sandals of Jesus. (John 1:27.) When the sandals were loose through travelling along this way, John stooped to tighten them.

While this girl had been wearing fashion shoes, tumbling and struggling, and hurting herself to the point of pain, it had been a lonely place with no one to help in time of need. These sandals were bound to the feet with slender cords of love, knotted with a promise knot that said, He would never leave her or forsake her. On each sandal there was a pattern of Scripture. It was as if these sandals had come from the Bible, and had kept the pattern of the Bible on the leather of love they were made from. The promises of God were on the leather uppers as part of the pattern. One of the promises read, 'This is the way; walk in it!' Maureen had to choose what she would trust in. Although sandals are flat, yet she would walk tall in them. There would be no reason for her to be on the floor looking up at the stars. There must be the walk of the Lord and not the talk of religion. Maureen was so thankful that only one shoe or sandal had not been offered. If it had only been one, then her walk would have been lopsided. These two sandals would bring balance, holiness and direction to her life that was being wasted on wobbles. Wearing the sandals she felt she could walk forward into eternity, never feeling tired. Sandals were so well fitting there was the feeling that when she was born they had been born with her. Maureen was at peace, walking in peace and talking peace that came from these outfits for her feet. They were part of her, where they went she would go. Their God would be her God. They would have the same goals and walk the same pilgrim pathway.

The sandals gave her a new quality of life and identity. If she wanted to run away from temptation, then she could run. If she wanted to fly, then she could fly. Whatever was decided in God, the sandals of sainthood helped her achieve the unachievable. They could be walking boots, climbing shoes, running shoes, skating shoes, shoes with a firmer grip, the shoes of a soldier and warrior, or of a princess. They were not cold as leather can be; they were warm, as if someone had just stepped out of them. From those leathers on her feet, a sense of the warmth of the love of God began to rise into her heart, until the love of God, and love for God, was shed abroad in her heart by the Holy Ghost. (Romans 5:5.) The words in her heart put there by the love of God were: 'They shall walk and not faint' (Isaiah 40:31). 'Faint' means 'to be weary', as if each step you take is as long as a thousand miles. The steps that Maureen was now taking seemed easy, for walking in light is easy. These were steps ordered by the Lord. The steps of a good woman are ordered by the Lord.

23

THE ISOLATIONIST

I saw Peter near a children's playground. I wondered if the playground belonged to the church and was an outreach for children. The facilities were modern, with swings, play area, roundabout, and a slide with the floor cushioned in case a child fell from the top step of the slide, and was hurt. The children were as happy as an anthem of larks singing as they soar in the sky. The sun shone in all its splendour, shafts of sunlight surrounding the area like golden spears thrown, not in anger but as if engaged in a javelin match. The scene was one of peace and quiet, despite children being involved! It reminded me of night time when children have said their prayers and are tucked up in bed. All I heard and discovered was part of a *word of knowledge* that had been revealed in the stillness of the heart.

Peter looked cold, forlorn and isolated, although it was a bright summer's day. He kept looking sideways towards the children's play area, as if he was afraid of facing it front on. If he turned his face fully towards it, there would be something that could not be resisted. Who can resist the pleading eyes of a child or the noise of laughter? When the children broke the summer silence with laughter or teasing, he turned and looked again and again, as if trying to make up his mind about an important event.

Immediately, questions went through my mind. Did he have a bad upbringing? Was he abused as a child? Was he afraid of children? The answer to all these questions was 'no'. Peter thought that if he responded, people might think that he was a child. His actions, which were speaking louder than words, portrayed the fact that he was immature and he felt that in certain situations he could not be a winner. 'Once a child, always a child' is what he thought. Now he had come to know Christ as his Saviour he was more than a child; there were certain things he was determined to stay away from. Children to him meant crises and calamity. He had lived next door to a large family, and knew the trouble that large families could bring if you got too close. The twins of Temper and Tantrum, with Trauma their sister, lived next door to him. He would keep himself to himself, and be like a closed book.

Peter had known the Lord for about four years. His conversion was as dynamic as it was dramatic. He began to read, but he only believed what he wanted to receive. He was like someone eating fish with bones in. He carefully took the flesh of the fish, and carefully put on one side what he thought were bones which might be damaging to his system. As a new convert he was aware how one had to be careful not to be drawn into something one could never extricate onesself from. He was very careful where he went, what he did, and with whom he mixed. He knew others could be an influence for good or bad, and even sometimes for good and bad! There had to be a separation from other influences, and the only way he knew how to limit influence was by leaving as large a gap as possible between them and himself.

His conversion changed him completely. He was a new

creature in Christ, and as such thought he was something a little bit special, totally different to anyone else. The mould was broken when he appeared as a Christian. No one walked with God, prayed, or read their Bible like Peter. This began to develop in him a spirit of being aloof, even pharisaic. He felt that he was an island. It is good to be an island if you learn to build bridges that reach others. On an island you have to dig very deep to reach those on the underside, for they are in Australia! You can only be in isolation for so long, not for ever and a day. If isolation teaches you to craft boats out of trees, make cups out of coconuts, hammers and tools out of rocks, then for that time in your life it can be good. Return to civilisation and you will know it is much easier to be where people are. The Book of Ecclesiastes states, 'Two are better than one, because if one falls then the other can hold him up' (Ecclesiastes 4:9).

This was foreign theology to the heart of Peter. He felt if he mixed with others they might be an adverse influence. Some of their 'worldly ways' could mix with his pure spirit. Consolation was his because he knew that light cannot mix with darkness, both must remain separate. He did not realise that the Lord was strong enough to keep him, no matter how strong the pull of the current might be. Proverbs 18:1 says, that the isolationist only thinks of himself. The Message records it as follows: 'Loners who only care for themselves spit on the common good.' They can discourage others, and become as spit to a small flame. Those they meet whose fire and devotion is small, the isolationist does not help, they simply spit on the smoking flax and crush the broken reed. Loneliness is an awful thing. Elohim gave Eve to Adam so that man should not be alone. Loneliness becomes an echo of yourself; you become as flat as the shadow that follows but never speaks or listens to you.

Those who do not agree with or like the church of Jesus Christ always forget, when it suits them, that Jesus Christ loved the church and gave Himself for it. If Peter was to influence children, then he must become as a child. The apostle Paul spoke of becoming 'all things' to all men that he might win some. (1 Corinthians 9:22.) You can come down to another's level without becoming like them. When I stoop to pat a dog, I do not become like the dog to snarl, bite and bark, unless I become a cynic, which means to 'snarl like a dog'.

In the *word of knowledge* I had seen Peter dressed smartly, as if going to a wedding, although by the look on his face he looked as if he was about to attend a funeral —his own! What had produced this was his persuasion that he must not mix with other people. He wanted to live as if he was the only man in the world. If the Lord had saved anybody, it was him and him alone. It was this sort of spirit that entered into Jonah, a Jewish prophet who could not believe that the God of Israel loved Gentiles enough to be sending him to the city of Nineveh. Jonah had to get used to fish before he could get used to the idea that God loves all men. In Jonah chapter 4 he had deeper fellowship and felt closer to a worm than to the Gentiles.

Peter knew his Bible from cover to cover, for he had read it through many times in the short time he had been a Christian. The folly was that he had not let that word enter into his heart and expand so that he could share fellowship with others. Often, to console himself when confronted, he thought of what the Lord had said about Abraham, 'I called you alone (Isaiah 51:2). It is quite amazing how we try to force part of a puzzle into a shape it was not meant to fit. When it suits, we squeeze things out of Bible texts that were never there in the first place. We always forget the context when we want to justify ourselves.

The children in the playground were now laughing, skipping

and making a noise, as if a band was playing. Peter stood on the outside of the playground, just looking, and deciding in his heart that it would not be good for him to join in. As he gazed, so he diminished into a child, whilst the children began to grow. Was it something the parents were feeding them on at home? Was it the mirth, the laughter and joy that was causing them to grow so rapidly? The picture suggested it was a combination of things, plus the fellowship that they were enjoying. As long as Peter stayed aloof, he would diminish. He would decrease while others increased. He would always be as the sand from his desert island, and others would be as stars to adorn the heavens. What he was thinking, so he was becoming, restricted and shrivelled up like a prune. The laughter and joy was making the children grow into adults.

Peter was for staying, standing and staring. To be a fisherman he did not have to dive into the pond or river. He would stand on the bank with a rod and do his fishing. If he joined in, as he was invited, part of it might influence him into the wrong channel. Those the tower of Siloam fell on were killed because they were too close to the tower. (Luke 13:4.) If they had moved away from it, as Peter was doing, then they would not have died. He had to keep himself reserved for the Master. He wanted to be as the loaves and fishes, multiplied, but what he did not realise is that for the miracle to take place the loaves and fishes, though few in number, had to mix with the crowd. The lad's lunch had to be within the reach of hands and lips, become part of the fellowship that took place around Jesus Christ. He would never know their joy or depth of experience until he joined with them and became accessible to one and all. Life, to him. would never be as a child on a swing going high, or coming backwards down a slide. It could never be as the challenge that comes to a child when it climbs a climbing frame and gets to the top, rejoicing as if it has conquered

Mount Everest. Slowly, as slowly as the snail entered Noah's ark, Peter plodded towards those children who were enjoying themselves. As the gap between them decreased, he seemed to be growing larger, the gap between them even smaller. In a moment, in the twinkling of an eye, he was mingling with the mirth of the minors. Only when he went from roundabout to swing, then slide, then climbing frame, did he begin to realise what he had been missing. These he thought were children had something to contribute to his life. The zest and zeal were with the child nature, the spirit of adventure locked in their hearts. He could only grasp for it, like grasping a handful of wind. Where he had been standing there was no such enjoyment. He could only guess what others were experiencing. It was in this play area that he began to get to know the needs of others. It was here that he was being developed from one level to another. For the first time in a long time, he saw the tears of a child, heard a sob and scream as a child tripped and fell. He was close enough to dash in and help, and realised that a child needs a hug more than it needs sticking plaster or bandage. He soon realised that a kiss covers and cures every sickness.

The glory of friendship and fellowship was beginning to appear in his heart. He was no longer a lonely figure, but had become part of a team. Peter began to realise that this is what marriage is all about, becoming part of a team, allowing the life in you to be stretched and used to meet the needs of another. Marriage is partnership in relationship. These children had something he had never had since becoming a Christian. Peter began to play with the children, and they played with him, and the last time I saw them they were like a happy family that time or ocean would never separate.

Three years later I went back to this church. Peter met me, and what a difference in his face and manner. He had the spirit of youth inside him, like a jack-in-a-box. The spirit of the child in him was crying to be set free, for life to him was an adventure. He took me by the hand drew me to himself and gave me a Pentecostal bear hug! 'Thank you so much for what you said to me the last time you came. It made me realise that when I was invited to join a team and work in the local church, my refusal was born out of my insecurity. I thought others would take away from me what the Lord had given. Since God spoke to me through you, I have become part of the ministry of the church. I feel that I have grown so much. In the past I thought the church needed to grow, but I realised it was not the church that needed to grow, but me. There is no thought of being isolated or relegated in my heart. I wish I had a thousand hearts; they would all be given to the Lord. I want to serve Him morning, noon and night. I did not realise that in mixing with others I was serving God. My body may grow old, but my spirit wants to remain as a child.' He looked even more radiant; it was as if fire was being rekindled as he spoke.

I assured him, 'if you had to take fat and eat it, it would not taste nice. If you had to take flour and spoon it into your mouth it might choke you. If raw eggs had to be eaten by you, that could make you sick. Salt alone is not a good thing. Mix together, add the heat to the ingredients, and through mixing and stirring you have a cake that, when tasted, cannot be left until it disappears. It can be a wedding or christening cake, a birthday cake or even simply a cake for a special occasion. Fellowship with others is special, and must be highly regarded. This is what fellowship and friendship means. The icing on the cake is when you realise your need of all the other ingredients.'

Peter is involved in the church. He visits first one and then another. He stands at the church door to give out papers with information on; he collects the old people and brings them to church. Like the colours of the rainbow, he is part of the whole spectrum. Without one colour, the rainbow would not be a rainbow, would not a sign of the covenant between God and man. He does not see himself as an 'odd job man' or as an 'odd man', but as someone who is building.

When a visitor was shown around Liverpool cathedral in England, he asked the people who were engaged in building this architectural masterpiece what they were doing. One man said he was wheeling the barrow full of concrete. Another said he was a bricklayer, another a carpenter. 'I am a labourer,' said one with modesty. Then the visitor turned to an older gentleman and asked him. 'Sir, what are you doing?' The older man, drawing himself to his full height as if to emphasise what he was going to say, said, 'Sir, I am building a cathedral!'

Peter had realised that he was one among many. There are those who as individuals see themselves as stone cutters, while another may see himself building a hospital! Peter was not called to be a lonely shining light; even stars appear in clusters, and birds sing in groups during the morning chorus. Geese, by their 'V' formation, give uplift to each other, calling to one another as they fly a great distance.

Peter would only be as great as the people he associated with. Each person in the church is a tool belonging to the Carpenter of Nazareth. Each tool, each person, is used to shape you into your destiny. Sometimes it could be sandpaper to smooth you down, other times a rasping file, or a chisel to cut out and shape. Only when joint meets with joint, dovetailed together, can they take on a new shape. What is a piece of wood can become part of the finest design. It is like that in the church: simply to stand and stare will neither help you· nor others. We need to be in the mine where diamonds are dug if we are to produce something rich and rare. Quantity becomes quality when we show we care. 'Peter, there are talents buried in you that can only be unearthed when you meet those things shaped like drill, pick and shovel.' We need each other as much as the body needs eyes, legs, lungs and heart. Peter was smiling because he fully understood what I meant. In his new role there was so much ministry and enjoyment. He had learned not to endure but to enjoy other people with their strange ways, he realising they must all converge into the Way, the Truth and the Life. Peter, in the church, had found a place of self expression through the love of Jesus Christ. True soul-mates were his.

24

THE DIRECTOR OF COMMUNICATIONS

I first met Robert when he was a young man in Quebec, Canada. His associates wondered what potential there was in his life. He was the youth leader, assisting the assistant pastor in a large church. In England, we would have described him as 'the dogsbody', meaning he could be used for anything and if a person itched, he had to scratch, even if they had itching ears. (2 Timothy 4:3.) He was a 'gofer' —he would go for anything if told to do so. Robert began to doubt his calling, and wondered about his potential for the ministry. Sometimes he seemed to be a round peg in a square hole, at other times a square peg in a round hole. Would anything good come out of his life? Robert knew that a butterfly evolves from an ordinary chrysalis, and yet is so beautiful when it appears. He contented himself with this though even for that to happen it involves a struggle on the part of the butterfly!

It was difficult to be the 'gofer' between the senior pastor and his assistant, who was older than Robert, and had far more experience. Robert was like a rag doll in the hands of two angry men, pulled this way and that. He felt as if one day he would be torn apart, one party would have his head, the other his legs, then he would be of no use to either. Would he ever become the real thing? The best policy was to keep quiet and let the Lord work it out. In the meanwhile he would apply grace to his aching spirit as an ointment for all the jars and knocks.

'All things work together for good to them that love God, and are called according to His purpose' (Romans 8:28). You can quote it, and believe it, but you have to receive it. Sometimes you have to see it happen before you believe and receive the out-workings of this promise. Robert in experience had entered into a phase where things were just 'working together' and he was not assured at all about the 'for good' part of the promise. Everything he prayed for seemed elusive, to the point of reaching without touching, never being able to take hold of that for which Christ had taken hold of him. It was as difficult as it was for the French authorities who were trying to catch the 'Scarlet Pimpernel'. 'They sought him here, they sought him there, they sought him everywhere...' He was elusive to the point of being invisible.

Robert prayed and pleaded before the Lord God Almighty, asking the Lord to give him something that would confirm his usefulness. Surely the carpenter of Nazareth could make something out of a boat that was already a wreck although it had never left the harbour! There was conviction in his spirit that made him feel easy as he approached the coming weekend. This could be the time of reconciliation. After prayer, instead of approaching the coming eclipse, instead of entering it as a man going into a storm, he would approach as a pearl diver going deeper into troublesome waters to find pearls embedded in the mud at the bottom. As the weekend of special meetings approached, he took a deep breath, expecting to find and know in his own spirit that which God was speaking into his situation. He wanted to move forward. He did not want to be as Eli who, on hearing that the Ark of the Covenant had been taken by the Philistines, 'fell backwards' (1 Samuel 4:18), and that was the end of his ministry. Robert had prayed, 'Lord, do not let my end be like his. I want to keep going forward, not as on a slide, but step by step with Jesus all along life's way; now the cross and conflict, then the perfect day. I do not want to be announced as a participator, I want to arrive.'

Robert came forward for prayer with a heavy heart. He was a tall, slim young man, but not as tall as I saw him in a *word of knowledge*. He had an abundance of life in that form presented; there was something caged up that required to be set free. The cage must not be rattled; the door must be opened to enable that which was locked within to fly free to any destination or determination. As he approached me, I saw Robert suddenly grow as long as a telegraph pole. It reminded me of the children's story 'Jack and the Beanstalk'. That beanstalk grew from a few beans given for the sale of Jack's mother's cow. Here was the beanstalk growing out of a man as a telegraph pole. The wind was blowing the pole, trying to bend it, but it was not for bending. The wind tried to uproot it, although the pole had no roots like a tree, but stood in a firm foundation. At first Robert was trying to hold his position as for dear life, then suddenly he realized that his security was not in holding his ground as a pole, so he let go; as he did so, the wind uprooted it from where it was and put it into another place, thrown like a spear from a hand, to land where it would be most useful. The next time I saw Robert, he was standing as a pole, but instead of wooden struts across the top, it was his arms that were outstretched, making the sign of a cross. He had realized that the only possibility of remaining and being of use was through the Cross of Jesus Christ. I began to wonder 'is this young man up the pole', off the beaten track, doing things that are mad and fermenting into that defined as crazy? The pole did not seem to be of much use where it was, but God was to reveal something further and deeper — deeper than the pole cemented into the ground, and higher than it reached to the sky.

Robert was not crazy. God was preparing him for a new role in life. These figures being applied to him by the natural mind were unfair, because he was to fulfil an important ministry. Remember, I knew nothing about the situation he was in. The Lord was telling him that he was to be as important as a telegraph pole that is not blown away by the wind. There would be as many opportunities coming to him as went into the wires that come to and go from any telegraph pole. The pole would be situated where the Lord determined. He would not have to go from pole to pole and sea to sea to find the will of God. Robert's greatest achievements would be where the Lord put him. It would be revealed here and now. He was to be God's mediator between man and man just as Jesus Christ was the Mediator between God and men. (1 Timothy 2:5.) As electricity went through those wires, so the power of God would flow through his life, and he would communicate with others. He would pass on what was passed to him. A pole does not have much personality, merely forwards what passes through it to another destination. Robert would re-route lives. People in distress would contact him for help.

At this moment in time, he was one pole with one wire stretching outwards from it, but with many coming towards it; and in what the pole was designed to do, it was not fulfilling its role. Messages were being received that were not passed on or translated into another language. There was a much wider ministry awaiting him than he was involved in at the moment. There would be as many wires leading from the pole as were coming into it. He would be a conduit for the message of the Lord and the power of God. The secret of any telegraph pole is that the nature of the pole does not enter into the message. What he received he would pass on. He would not change what the Lord was saying, he would be there, just as a telegraph pole, to receive and pass on the message.

From that pole many messages would be sent across the world. He would find himself in a position of administration, would become a Director of Communications in the denomination he was operating in. Robert would be a messenger with a message. That which was spoken to him would be passed on to others. Missionaries, ministers, messengers, evangelists, teachers, anyone engaged in the work of God would come to him for help and advice. He would be the one chosen to pass on what others wanted to communicate. Without him and his work, the work of God would not go on to its hour of glory. The position he would occupy would be an important one. Each telegraph pole has messages to receive and messages to communicate. Robert would never have to add to or take from what was said, he would simply be the telegraph pole, used to pass on grace and love, with kindness and longsuffering. The tongues of men and of angels would pass through him. Robert would be the one; if he received bad news, he would pass it on as good news after prayer. People would hang on to what he had to say. His heart would be the 999 or the 911 centre that in despair others could contact for help. This man would never be as natives who, on hearing voices coming from telephone wires tried to chop them into small pieces, thinking if you chopped the wires you would kill the voices.

When I met Robert, and his wife Susie and their small children, a few years later, I casually asked him what his position was within his denomination. He calmly told me that he was the Director of Communications. Anyone coming into the country, or travelling abroad, contacted him, and he did all the arranging. They saw him as their telephone directory and telephone wires. He by taking up his cross daily, and following Jesus Christ had become a blessing. The word of his mouth, and his skill at passing on messages, would help, bless and guide. With a twinkle like a diamond in his eye, he said to me, 'I remember what you said a few years ago about the telegraph pole and the wires coming and going from it. Only the other day my wife and myself were discussing it, and the relevance of it, and how the Lord has slowly but surely brought it to pass.'

The relevance of what was said to Robert had entered into his heart. He knew that it was from the Cross of Jesus Christ that God communicated His love to the world. While his life was lived in the shape of the cross, there would not only be Greek, Latin and Hebrew coming from that Cross, but many languages to many people. (John 19:20.) All he had to do was to convey in his preaching and through his position the love of God for a dying world. Robert saw Bible texts as telegraph poles that sent a message into the hearts of the people. John 3:16 is such a telegraph pole: 'For God so loved the world that he gave His only begotten Son, that whosoever believes on Him should not perish but have everlasting life.' Someone was required to pass that on to others, and here was the man. To Robert, each Bible text was filled with words that had to be passed on to others. As Director of Communications, he would communicate in his preaching all that the Lord had to say. He would send out the whole counsel of the Lord to anyone who would listen.

One day, a man who was not conversant with mobile telephones or sending text messages, decided to re-arrange an appointment with a client. On the front of his mobile telephone, he had inserted a few words of comfort. Every time the mobile telephone was switched on, the first words that appeared were: 'Jesus will always love you.' They are still on his mobile telephone ten years later. He thought he would send details to re-arrange the meeting. When he met the man he had sent the text message to the man asked, 'Will Jesus always love me? I received that before I received the message to re-arrange my appointment with you.' Through that the man was told about the love of God. This was the area that Robert had to move into. In communicating with others he would communicate Jesus Christ by word and deed and by word and wire whenever he used the telephone.

A minister felt led to telephone a certain person, but did not know the number he was to ring. In his spirit, put there as a treasure by the Spirit of God he felt the person who would answer the telephone was in desperate need. The telephone began to ring but all Charley could hear was the beating of his own heart. He half wished that there would be no reply. A woman, Doreen answered the telephone and spoke in a posh voice. 'Hello, can I help you? Charley felt like running a thousand miles, longer than the telephone cable stretched. 'I am telephoning you because I feel that you have a great need. I want to tell you about the Lord Jesus Christ, and how He can help you.' Charley heard the woman gasp, and he thought for the moment she had stopped breathing. There did not seem to be anyone on the other end of the telephone. Was Charley speaking to himself?

The woman and her husband Reggie had been in business, and that business had failed. They had cried out for help from God. They had no experience with the Lord but their business had collapsed, and their marriage was swaying in the breeze ready to fall and break into a thousand pieces. They were both on the verge of committing suicide. During the conversation Charley was able to make arrangement to go to the home, and lead Doreen and Reggie to know Christ as their Saviour.

Paul has a picture of an open Bible that appears every time

he presses the button to switch his mobile telephone on. He knows that whatever he says to anyone during his telephone conversation is based on the open Bible. His motto is: 'open up any conversation with your Bible at the ready.' What forms of evangelism these have discovered because another man saw a telegraph pole with all the wires passing through it, and used it as if every message spoken depended not on the telephone or the wires but the pole that held them all in place. Every life needs the cross that will keep lines of communication open between themselves and the Lord. The cross will save you from getting your wires crossed, or from speaking at 'crossed purposes'. What the telegraph pole does for communication, the Cross of Jesus Christ does for character.

Robert, apart from his position within the church, was able to help people. While his life was lived in the shape of the cross, becoming like a telegraph pole, he would be able to settle accounts or disputes and be a help to all who came into contact with him. The term Director of Communications meant a lot more than Robert thought it meant when he first heard the term mentioned. The larger picture was that he must win people to Jesus Christ. He must bring parties together that were thousands of miles apart. His was a blessed ministry, as he was able to bring messages from far and near, bringing people together.

25

AFRAID OF LEADERSHIP

We can stand in the shadows for so long that we eventually become a shadow. The substance of our fears can take on many shapes and sizes. What begins as a shadow can become a tormenting memory. In fact, three shadows can appear at once, and the question has to be asked, 'Will the real you step forward?' We require that which is not dependent on the position of the light or the sun. There are seven men (or women) in all of us: the man your wife knows, the man your friends know, the man your enemies know, the man your work colleagues know, the man the world knows, the man your children know, and the man God knows. The real man is the man that God knows, and that man knows God. The shadow we become requires to be turned into substance that is strong and durable. Not as putty or plasticine, not as 'playdoh' that children use to mould into the shape of hand or finger. The slightest pressure must not pressurize us. There is moulding that makes and marks out that person who is God's servant.

Betty was not one for taking on the role of leadership, or for being in the limelight. Here in Montreal, Canada, in this overflowing church, there were people with the ability to do most things. She was content to take a back seat and to work in the shadow of her husband. As long as Tony was in front she would push him on, as she had so often pushed a boat out in a seaside town. She would cover his back from those who were firing at him from behind. Betty would 'snip' the snipers and watch out for the snakes trying to perform as saints. Her discipleship and role in life was to follow Tony wherever he went, and to do whatever he suggested. Where he was she would be as one to protect him as the eagle protects its young with its wings. Even that was only acceptable as long as it did not include leading meetings of any description or standing at the front of the church to guide and help people in a public fashion. Betty would always be content to play second fiddle, as long as no part was found for the second fiddle to be alone. To be lost in a crowd was part of her disposition. This woman would have made a good wife for Nicodemus, the disciple who came to Jesus by night. (John 3:2.)

Whenever a crowd gathered, Betty was content to melt into it and be hidden among the stuff of life. The ability had been born in her to melt into the background. The impression must not be given that she did not help others. If they had a need, then she saw that need as being related to the wounds of Jesus Christ, and Betty must wash, bathe, bandage and see them through to healing. There was a conviction in her heart that signs would follow them that believe. She worked as a skilled surgeon from the back room. Betty was part of the back room staff. She pulled no strings, because that might have brought her into the foreground, and she believed that background material described her ministry. In her disposition you were reminded of the 'Punch and Judy' shows at British seaside's, where the person activating the puppets is never seen, only the voice is heard.

The church was growing. Betty was a busy mother with

children to feed, clothe and wash, which seemed to be the pinnacle of her life. Yet deep within her was something that was longing to 'be' and 'do' what the Lord was demanding of her. As a 'secret disciple' she would be a regular visitor to the 'secret place' of Psalm 91. In the past, it had been acceptable for her to take a back seat, to be at the back of the queue or to pass the reins into another's hands. They knew where they were going, and Betty was following as tail follows body. Betty's theology was in the words of Jesus that if we diminish then we shall grow. Humility, to her, meant being last of all, the least of the least, and not to seek a position that you were not made for or called into. John the Baptist had said, 'I must decrease and He must increase.' Even when eating she would never take the first cake, or be first in line when numbers were counted. Dressing her family for school or play, Betty would wait until they had been provided for before she would step into her Sunday best. She felt this was the way of life until her work on earth ceased. 'After the sun, the rain, after the rain, the sun, this is the way of life until the work is done.'

The mould was about to be shattered! Betty would be awakened out of this lifestyle, and find herself doing things that she had never thought possible. The words used by Jesus of the prodigal son describe what happened, He 'came to himself'. There were lessons that the Lord was to take her into that she would come through, and find herself doing what others only dream of. A hand would bring her from the dark areas and her position at the back of the choir, to make her into a lead singer. Betty was about to take the role of soloist and main singer on the stage of life. When she first heard the words, she shuddered, as if a ship had made contact with rocks. To do what was being said of her would take far more courage than Joshua or Gideon put together! Add to those others from the Acts of the Apostles who spoke the word of

God with boldness, and this would only be enough to get her to the front of the church! That shawl of retirement would be thrown off. The garments of those who serve would become part of her living and thinking. The leading role would mean that she would not know where she was leading them to! It would take a 'baptism of boldness' for her to enter into the role of leadership — standing, thinking and working on her own.

A *word of knowledge* to Betty was that the days of standing in the background were over. The background disappeared, as if it was broken off as a piece of bread from a loaf. The days of being at the end of the queue were over, for she would stand at the front of the activity and organize it. Sheep would enter the pen under her direction and leadership. Betty had been as a root in dry ground, and as the root responds to the call of spring to blossom, so she would spring forth from the shadows into His most glorious light. Betty would have an expanding ministry from this day on. Shy would become shine, backward would become forward. There was to be a re-birth and a revolution in her heart. Betty thought within herself, 'Is the speaker talking of somebody else, because what he is saying doesn't fit into my thinking. It is as different from me as chalk is from cheese. Maybe mistakes have been made, and it is the woman next to me that the Lord is speaking to.' Betty did not want hell pouring into her soul to torment her day and night for the rest of her life, for in her natural state this is what it would have meant. To be in leadership would be the worst thing she could think of, rather like drinking poison while in the prison instead of water. Jesus said, 'If they drink any deadly thing it shall not harm them' (Mark 16:18). The Spanish inquisition would be easier to accept than leading and preaching! All those people staring at her was too much for this self effacing woman.

The word of the Lord to her heart was straight and true, as true as the sky is blue. Betty did not know how it was going to be fulfilled. The man of God had said he could see her leading worship and speaking to crowds of people. Betty thought to herself, 'I can barely manage the children, how can I be expected to take on this new, larger and dynamic role?' God would not lie to her, for He had been faithful through many years of drought, despair, storm and suffering. It must have been a shock for Gideon when he had been told to chop down the idol that people were worshipping. God had called him 'You mighty man of valour', when he had been hiding corn from the Midianites. (Judges 6:12, 25.) Gideon had gone from chopping down an idol to blowing a trumpet, then emptying pitchers, and putting a light into them. He broke the vessels, and the light within them shone out as the light of the Lord. (Judges 7:16, 19, 20.)

It would be difficult but it was achievable. A *word of knowledge* had declared that she would occupy the pulpit as her husband did, would see many souls blessed and restored through a public ministry. Leadership was to become her third love, after God and her husband. To do this would have been like a mole coming out of its hole with blind eyes and leading a charge into battle. It seemed so far removed from her nature and character that Betty could not quite believe it. She could believe after it happened, but the challenge from God was to believe Him before it happened. It is strange how, in unbelief, we always put the cart before the horse, or night before the day.

Even the clothes to be worn by her were described. They would be rich, rare, colourful and beautiful. Betty would not appear before the people of God as a timorous mouse, but as a bold lion. There would be no sense of stress or nerves as she stood to proclaim boldly the word of the Lord. Betty had done none of these things before; they were as foreign as that overseas. Where, when, why and how? All marshalled into her mind, as a crowd pushed into a small room. God would have to make a new woman of her. Even now, in this condition and this day, she trembled as she thought about it. Suddenly her trembling was replaced by the Holy Ghost, as the Spirit of God came upon her like the force of a mighty rushing wind. Betty felt like ten women, with all their best qualities rolled into one. This woman was being redrawn by the Spirit of the Lord. That which had been reticent was made into that which was resistant. 'I can do all things through Christ Who strengthens me,' thought this dear lady. Betty suddenly felt like the woman with the issue of blood who, fearing and trembling, touched the Lord, and came before Jesus to tell Him all the truth. (Mark 5:33.) The woman in the story is not given a name, but she came behind Him to touch Him, then *before* Him to tell Him all the truth of her trust.

Like Mary, the mother of Jesus, Betty began to 'ponder' all these things. (Luke 2:19.) To 'ponder' means to turn them over and over as a sweet in the mouth, rolling it backwards and forwards on the tongue. Betty began to ponder as one with a plan, to see carried out what had been said to her. Noah had been called by the Lord to build the ark. God had provided the wood and the pattern, but Noah the carpenter must get his tools and begin to work out what he had been told. Betty would do the same, but she felt that the tools were missing. Where would she commence? It seemed as if the Lord, when He spoke, had put truth as a tool into her hand. As she took it, then from that small implement first one thing and then another would grow and grow until the whole plan was executed.

Some time later, the man who had uttered a *word of knowledge* was again at the church for ministry. Betty was looking forward to meeting him after so many years. Last time he had come she had been a shy housewife, now she was a mother in Israel, a woman of substance, as strong as steel and flaming as a torch for the Lord. She felt like the cherubim in the Garden of Eden with a sword that turned this way and that. (Genesis 3:24.) When she met this friend of the family she would tell him the truth of what the Almighty had done, how great things had happened since he was last here. He would hardly believe what she had to tell him.

As he was ministering, Betty was busy taking notes. He was speaking from the Book of Ruth, and the thoughts he was presenting were challenging and heart changing. 'These thoughts could be used for my Bible study,' thought Betty. The woman now had her own Bible class, teaching the women wonderful truths from the word of God. The following weekend they were conducting a women's rally, and she was one of the speakers. Suddenly everything became so dramatic. The visiting speaker did not know, but such a change had taken place in the heart and disposition of Betty. They were asking the similar question to that which was asked of the blind man in the Gospel of John: is it really her, or is this another? It seemed as if the disposition of angels had been given to her, flying here, there and everywhere, doing things that she had never thought possible, for the Lord. There was no end to her boldness. It had come from the Lord, it was in the Lord, and it would be maintained by the same God who had granted it.

Whatever had been lacking, the confidence was now there in abundance. To Betty's heart it was as if one of the trees in the paradise of God, the garden of Eden, had been named confidence, and had been uprooted and planted in her heart, never to wither, only to prosper. Not one good thing promised by the Lord had failed. It had been more than a success. Here was an absolute miracle! The visitor, using the *word of knowledge* had uttered the words, and now this lady was the book containing those words. She told the visitor, 'Those who know me will tell you what you said during your last visit by a *word of knowledge* has been fulfilled. It has been pressed down, shaken together, and it is running over. Wherever I go, my confidence touches lives. My life before was a nightmare, it is now a dream in reality.

'I do not have to spend time fearing and quaking in my shoes. My knees are no longer like rubber, they are as steel as I stand to proclaim for the Lord. I have been let loose, set free to do what the Lord has called me to do. Before you gave a *word of knowledge* I was not like this. I was a fly; every opportunity was a spider's web which I got hopelessly entangled in. I felt that I would surely die, because the confidence was not there to take me through an experience.' Here was a woman who had been a little girl. A minor had become a master, a mature person, and an example for all to copy. Through her was a revelation of the power of a *word of knowledge*, revealing the purposes of the Lord before they were even thought of. That conceived in her was of the Holy Ghost. Betty moved with ease, as she stood before crowds to tell of the wonders of her God and King. The only thing for her to fear was fear. There was no place in her heart for doubt about leadership. What the Eternal had said, she would do, carrying it out to the last order. Every day was filled with opportunities as a sunny day is filled with sunbeams. Betty had increased as she decreased; there was no need to hide or be ashamed, to run away as a shy animal going underground. Resurrection life had been poured into her soul, and she was standing on holy ground. God who had put the stars into space had enabled her to find her place in the church of Jesus Christ. No longer as a voice crying in the wilderness, she began to water that wilderness with her tears, and to shine upon it with her sunny disposition until growth appeared in others, the same growth that was making her great. As Betty stood in the shadow of Jesus Christ, she shared His shoes, and let them take her into ministry that brought consolation and fruit. From His shadow came her substance of sainthood and womanhood. There was a relish about her service spiced with the realism that through God 'all' things are possible. The word 'all' meant the ability to lead God's sheep to greener pastures and soft flowing waters.

26

FINDING THE MISSING PIECE AND COMPLETING THE PUZZLE

He looked the part. If he had taken part in a play, the role could not have been better acted by William Shakespeare. His face looked long and drawn, with shadows on, as if the sunshine had passed him by, the radiance of his life had set, and he had been left with the marks of a hard life indelibly etched onto his skin, markings which made him look much older than his birth certificate indicated. Here was a man with many burdens. John would not mention them, because in his generation you always had a 'stiff upper lip', and suffered in silence with pain as your only friend. The burden of the work of God had been added to as the years had passed. When morning light broke, it seemed to carry some of the darkness of the night into this man's life, as if night time left its calling card in the heart of this servant of the Lord.

I had been praying for a number of people who were part of the flock of God of which the Lord had made him overseer. I noticed that he himself held back, as a parent wanting the children's needs to be met. He thought that a *word of knowledge* was for the people and not for him. He did not realize he was part of what the Almighty wanted to say. He would be spoken to this day through the tongues of men, angels and a *word of knowledge*, bringing help to him, pouring strength into his body, soul and spirit. The manifestation of a *word of knowledge* made him realize that God was the Lord of every realm right, left or centre; the Lord speaks to you in the mother tongue about Father's kingdom.

As he was approached to be prayed for, he seemed to take a step backwards, as if a light had suddenly put the spotlight onto his soul, and he could not stand the light that had entered into him. He blinked as one entering a room full of light after being in the dark. What would the Eternal have to say to this man reluctantly reaching out, yet rich in grace? More grace was about to be poured into his heart. A fountain would be opened in his heart that would refresh and rekindle all that the Lord wanted to accomplish. His hands were taken hold of, and he was drawn nearer to the speaker, as if no one else should hear what was being said to him. John had prayed on another occasion that the Eternal would give him a listening ear to hear words of wisdom and knowledge that would help him with his building plans.

The land next to the church looked like a mud bath. It was a wet Sunday morning, and it was as if the heavens had been reserving the rain for this day. This day was the birthday of rain, and how it was celebrating with rain pouring from every quarter! Some new buildings that had not yet been completed were in the background. Evidence of hard work was everywhere. A builder had bought the land and he wanted to knock the church building down. John had been given a limited time to find a new piece of land. The church were searching everywhere as wise men seeking Jesus Christ. (Matthew 2:2.) It was so difficult, he had tried many avenues; he found that every avenue had become a cul-de-sac. All roads led to a brick wall. It was not a brick wall that John required, it was bricks on a piece of land that could be erected as a church building. There was no way through, and time was passing. He felt like a boat waiting for the tide to come in.

As the Spirit of God began to reveal what was in the man's heart, a picture of John kneeling over a puzzle was revealed. The picture had no frame; it was a reflection of what was happening at the moment. The puzzle was not complete. John was studying it as an accountant would his figures or a solicitor his letters. His face was whiter than chalk. John was swaying backwards and forwards as if rowing a boat. He knelt there for a long time, until his back began to ache. If he stayed there much longer his bones would set, and they would have to carry him home in that position!

John was trying to fit missing pieces into the puzzle. As he did so, the real puzzle was in his heart. What should he do next? A number of pieces had been left to one side, and the puzzle was incomplete. Here was the man that Jesus mentioned who went to build a tower and could not finish it. (Luke 14:28.) This minister was stretching forwards and backwards, and then scratching his head, as if the answer to the problem was in his head. If he scratched it enough, he might unlock the answer. At times he held his head between his hands, as if he had a headache. Would he be the 'Jack of all trades and the master of none'?

John reached towards the missing pieces of the puzzle and tried to make them fit. He had no idea which piece would make it complete, and because of his ignorance he required a *word of knowledge*. There was concern written all over his face. He picked up one piece and tried to make it fit. He was very forceful, but did not seem to grasp that the piece he was putting in place was not shaped to that contour. John would then ruefully try another segment of the puzzle, trying to squeeze it into the rest of the shape. When he forced it in, it made no sense, and the picture on the puzzle was distorted. It was as a child mixing paints together. Hands and mind were not working in unison as ship and sails. He believed in try, try again, and if at first you do not succeed then try again. Wasn't it Robert the Bruce who had watched the spider in the quiet corner of a cave trying to get from one side of the web to the other? When it failed it tried again. The spider tried as many times as Robert The Bruce had tried to defeat the English, and eventually it was successful. Bruce went out to defeat the English. If prizes were to be given for trying this man, the pieces of puzzle would have won first prize.

Eventually, John seemed to bend lower, as if the burdens were becoming too much for his frail back. I never realized that an incomplete puzzle could torment a man both day and night as if hell was in his soul. He adopted the posture of surrender. He had tried his best but had not succeeded. History would record that he failed. Maybe another would follow on to make a success out of his failure. He could leave the pieces of this puzzle for someone else to slot into place. As these thoughts passed through his mind, as water through an open hand, he began to cry out to the Lord God of Israel to help him with this matter. Where would the pieces fit to complete the vision that he had been given? The burden was covering his mind and eyes, and the result was he was as blind as Bartimaeus. (Mark 10:46.)

John had been on his knees, as Elijah was when seeking the Lord to send rain. (1 Kings 18:42.) The young man had been dispatched to look for a cloud the size of a man's hand, and here was this man, John, looking for a piece of puzzle that was smaller than a man's hand, to slot neatly into place. When the cloud was seen by Elijah's servant, this signalled an answer to prayer, and when this man of God found the right pieces, and places for each piece in the puzzle, all would be well.

Suddenly there shone a blazing light, the light of glory, so dazzling that you had to close your eyes, because its force was so strong it would have burned them. It was the same as the light that threw the apostle Paul from his donkey onto the ground, proclaiming 'Who are you, Lord?'(Acts 9:5). It was more brilliant than the midday sun or white electricity, the kind of light that comes from lava as it trickles down the side of an erupting volcano. As this light entered the room where John was kneeling over the puzzle, it threw him backwards, as if a wrestler had taken hold of him, and thrown him to the ground to jump on top of him. John gasped and groaned with fear, amazement and delight, the three emotions taking hold of his spirit. He fell backwards, but not as one who is flung and can land anywhere — it seemed as if in eternity it had been decided where he would land. As he fell backwards with his arms outstretched as one in worship, he fell in the shape of a human cross, making the sign of the cross with his body and arms.

Then a hand came from the light that had appeared, like the hand that had written words of judgment and warning on the plastered wall of Nebuchadnezzar's palace before he was judged. (Daniel 5:5.) This hand did not grasp or grab to take hold of John who was flat on his back. It did not write, it began to put things right. It lifted a piece of puzzle from those on the floor. Here was sovereignty at work in choice and pleasure. It was done with deliberate intent, as if someone was counting the pieces. Each piece of the puzzle, one after the other, was lifted, and each was put into its correct place in the puzzle, adding colour and contour to that which had been incomplete. Now it was complete; the Master had been at work, without any force being used.

As the final piece was fitted, it was as if an empire had been built by a hand. John had gone quiet, as quiet as a baby feeding from the breast. That hand was feeding his spirit with lovely answers to his prayers. The hand that had taken hold of pieces of the puzzle was also feeding living bread to the heart of this disciple. Here was the echo of his heart, responding to what he required. His longings were being filled, and he was satisfied. That as deep as a well found in his heart, and as difficult to reach as the bottom of the deepest ocean, was being filled and ministered to. God was saying to him, 'Leave things to me that are too difficult for you. What seems like a puzzle and pain to you is a plan to me. I work "all things" after the power of my own counsel.'

By this time John had regained his posture, and was leaning forward to see what the complete picture of the puzzle represented. I do not know what he expected to see, but a look came on his face as if the light that had entered the room had suddenly been painted on it. The puzzle was a puzzle no more. It was complete, with a beautiful picture. It did not just contain one picture but three, which changed one after the other. It was as if the picture had gone right through the material and would appear on both sides. These pictures could not be rubbed out; they appeared in Technicolor and paramount vision.

The first picture to appear was that of a large congregation at worship. As they worshipped, they sang songs that were not yet created by writers. They sang like those choirs from the valleys of Wales. Here was a massed choir, singing in tune, and all playing their part. It was in unison, but each person had their part to play, each one was an instrument of worship. The singing was deep, each word soaked in a tear. The emotions of those singing had entered their music, and each person worshipped as if in the presence of God, with arms outstretched. This was revival singing.

The next picture was not as moving as the first because it did not include the emotion or the voice of the people. It was the figure of a new building, standing in pristine sunshine as if it had just been built. Each brick, door and window looked as if they had been erected by love. There was such a cleanliness about that building. It was large in size, and yet it was not too big. It was as long as it was large, and as wide as it was tall. It reminded me of the Apostle John's vision of the new Jerusalem descending from the heavens. (Revelation 21:16.) The complete thing had come from that hand of light that entered the room through walls, ceiling and doors, the hand that did not knock and asked to be admitted. It was the hand that suggested the sovereignty of God. Jesus said, 'I will build my church' (Matthew 16:18). John had to let Him do it not with bricks and mortar, wood and glass but with light and glory. This was what John was being exercised about. Here was the building completed by the hand that had taken hold of pieces of the puzzle, and put them where required. There were no joining lines in that puzzle, all fitted together as if it had been born as part of the whole.

The final picture appeared as if I had been watching a slide show. This one was more glorious than the other two. It was a picture of the full head of a man. It had a suffering face and had seen many traumas. I immediately recognized the man on the face of the puzzle. It was Jesus Christ. He had been busy working as a hand of light to complete what was in the life of this under-shepherd. There was long hair coming down to the shoulders, and the picture reminded me of the description of the Beloved in Solomon's Song 7:5. Without this final picture the puzzle would not have been complete.

The Lord, in grace, was revealing to John that all he would do was based on the person of Jesus Christ. Worship, congregation and building were all in the plan of God. John had to take a back seat, to let the Lord reveal His Lordship in every area of the church. The puzzle would not be complete until the hand of God did its work. John had to sit on his hands, and set free the hand of the Lord. 'Many hands make light work', but here it had to be just the one hand that made the light work. The Almighty leaves nothing in pieces, He says it, and it is done, He commands, and it stands fast. The last time I saw John he was on his knees sobbing, as if his eyes contained too many tears.

27

FILLING THE CUP
TO THE BRIM

Mavis was holding a small cup made out of silver. On the side of the cup was an assay mark which formed the shape of a cross, a lion, a throne and a crown, denoting where it had been manufactured and the date of production. I could see many lips drinking from that cup. And everyone who drank of its contents was refreshed. Coming to the cup as weary wanderers, they moved from it as pilgrims with staffs in their hands. After drinking from it, some seemed to sway from side to side like drunken sailors. Merriment and joy had been squeezed into that vessel, a vessel unto honour and not dishonour. It had not always been like this. Weary folk had come to drink, but instead of refreshment, as seen earlier, they were adding to their weariness. It seemed to me rather like a prisoner who was hoping to find freedom, only to find it was another door into another prison cell! When they had tasted the contents of the cup they spat it on the ground, as if it was lukewarm water. They had come to the chalice with such high hopes, only to discover that it did not contain what they thought. Their hopes, as their spit, were dashed to the floor.

The silver chalice seemed to me as if it could have been

borrowed from Joseph when he ruled Egypt. It was like the cup that was hidden in the sacks of corn that his brothers took home with them. There was a spiritual lesson here! That cup contained corn, chaff, and straw. It did not contain the real thing. That which is contrary to the nature of the cup was found in the top of every man's sack. (Genesis 44:2, 12.) When you take things from Egypt (as a symbol of this world), the cup remains with a few straws in, and it will never taste like sweet wine, no matter what you do. You can wash it thoroughly, stand it in a place of prominence, but there will be no flowing wine of the highlands of Canaan. Instead of 'winner' written on the outside, 'loser' will be etched on the inside. The cup is for filling and drinking from. It was through such a cup as this that Joseph had interpreted dreams, and through a *word of knowledge* God was revealing the secrets of a woman's heart.

Mavis had come to the silver cup to taste of its contents for herself. What passed through her lips was bitter, as bitter as Marah (Exodus 15:23) and as brackish as the River Jordan with the taste of leprosy in it that Naaman had washed off himself. (2 Kings 5 and Luke 4:27.) This was not what had been expected. It was like opening a package to find that it does not contain a present, but a 'trick present' like those used to fill a stocking with at Christmas. A carrot wrapped in shiny paper to make it look like a bulky present is no present at all.

Mavis was disappointed. She thought that cup in her hands had good tastes within; grapes of Eshcol had been squeezed into it. At least there was the expectancy that the first communion wine that Jesus and His disciples drank from in the Upper Room would have been in it. Now the wine content was disappearing faster than waters of the flood that Noah experienced as they abated. (Genesis 8:3.) Like her life, the cup had the wrong content. It was giving to others who were parched the wrong taste of things to come. Here was supposed to be the wine of the kingdom, new wine in a new wine cup. The content did not match the asking or desiring. The thirst would not be quenched but stretched. Those who had been to the cup would not return until a better testimony of the contents was heard and received. They had come to a wedding and found it to be a funeral!

It left me wondering if Mavis worked in a pharmacy, because before her were many bottles on shelves. She was dressed in a white garment, fit for the righteous to wear. After tasting what should have been wine from this silver cup, Mavis had gone away so disappointed. She felt that something needed to be added to that cup. Others were drinking from the cup and spitting out the contents. When the contents landed on the ground, weeds and flowers faded as they were christened by this liquid. It looked as if autumn had come early and was blighting leaf and flower. There was death in the pot! A remedy must be found!

I had the feeling that, if prayer was made, liquid would be poured down into the cup-shaped object which would be sweet to the taste, and people would drink it and 'taste and see that the Lord is good.' This was not to be so. The order of things would be changed. It was like reading a story with a twist in the tail. The obvious was not so clear. What should be done was being shunned, and truth was becoming heresy of the first and second admonition. Because of her background and training, Mavis would do the sensible thing, which at this moment was far above the spiritual. There must be something that could be poured into the cup to complement what was already there.

Mavis was swiftly moving among the row of bottles —bottles for this and bottles for that. To some, life must be pill and bottle shaped, but we were dealing with a silver cup, not a glass bottle. As she read words in Latin, I could hear her muttering the English equivalent (here was a woman with a gift of interpretation) and saying, 'That will not do, that might do; let us try this and see if it works.' I strained to see what was written on the bottles, and saw clearly words that amazed me. Words like 'self effort' 'good works', 'service in the church' 'help and kindness', 'listening to another's problems', 'self righteousness', 'religion' and 'tradition'. There was no end in sight of the bottles standing on the shelves as soldiers on parade. They looked as if they had been reserved for such a day as this. Some were only half full; others were a quarter of the way down the glass. In the past there must have been great demand for what the bottles contained. The name on each glass shape sounded good to me, until realisation gripped me, and I became aware that Mavis thought she could sweeten the contents of the cup by her own efforts.

Taking different coloured bottles, a small part of each was poured into the cup that she held. As the liquid entered, the cup did not seem any more full than it was before. With a look of triumph on her face, taken from the heart of Richard 'the Lionheart', Mavis took the cup and put it to her lips, expecting what had been added to change it in sweetness and depth. Her lips pressed the side of the cup as it was tilted, until the cup was almost upside down. Was she trying to drink all there was in the cup? She had only intended to have a sip. As the cup was turned upside down and removed from her lips, there was not a drop of moisture in it. The proverbial church mouse would have been disappointed with the contents. Not even the sweat of the brow was in that vessel. It had now become simply a show-piece. It served no purpose only to be given as an empty cup as a team triumphed at sport. The contents of many bottles were tried, but to no avail. As the liquid was poured in, it was as if there was a hole in this silver chalice. As fast as it went in, it disappeared. This liquid from the bottles was a wasted ministry. The cup was a bottomless pit. Whatever was poured in was never poured out; the metal seemed to have a mouth and was stealing the contents. How could Mavis get the wine to flow again?

Mavis thought that if there was a low ebb or tide, then it could be supplemented by what she could do. The message from the Lord was that good works and manners, along with kindness, religion or ceremony, can never meet the thirst of the soul for salvation. God has to be included in what we do. Mavis must pray for a fresh vision of the cross and Jesus Christ. The contents of the cup of salvation must not be added to or taken from.

Mavis began to pray and to weep. As she prayed, her tears began to fall into the cup, as if being collected. The Jews collected their tears into a bottle (Psalm 56:8), but this was into a silver cup. These were tears large enough to sail a boat on — not crocodile tears, but tears to measure the repentance of her heart. What a fool she had been not to realise that the salvation of the Lord and its sweetness cannot be supplied by people. It is a gift from the Lord. As Mavis repented, so the cup took on a new sheen, and began to shine with a glory that resembled the glory of God. This was not added glory to the outside of the vessel, as the fire that burned on the burning bush when Moses heard the voice of God calling him to set God's people free, before taking a stick from that bush that would part the Red Sea and bring plagues upon Egypt. (Exodus 3:2–10.) This was an inner glory moving to the outside of the container as a burning fire illuminating the silver cup. Each of the assay marks began to glow: the cross first, then the lion, followed by the throne and crown. All glowed far more than if they had been polished. This was not glitter, it was glory!

As the glow intensified, Mavis slowly moved towards the cup with a new reverence, in order to have a look inside. Was it empty, an empty dream that had been experienced on a bad night? If not, would its contents be bitter or sweet? Her mind was awash with thoughts. Mavis gazed deeply into the cup, as young lovers gaze into each other's eyes. It was the twin gaze she had used when looking upon Jesus Christ and coming to Him as her Saviour. It was the gaze of wonderment of a child seeing something for the first time, a look of wonder, love and praise. Could this silver metal be used again, and would sweet wine come from it when those who were thirsty came to drink?

Mavis looked, and it was obvious by her amazed look that she had witnessed a miracle. Was there healing or a Divine hand inside the vessel? Were angels dancing around in a circle, small enough to fit into the cup? What she saw would take some believing and even more receiving. Would her friends believe her? The sweet wine was there, the cup was filled to the brim. It was wine as red as blood and sweet as honey. The miracle was that it was not being poured into, but from the sides it was as if there was a secret fountain, a source of supply in the cup itself. The whole vessel was oozing wine into the cup, and it would never be empty again. Mavis began to drink of this new wine. The more she drank, the more wine poured from the sides. Here was a wine cup filled with wine that would never run out. Here was a reminder of the wedding at Cana in Galilee. When that wine ran out, Jesus turned the water into wine. (John 2:1–11.) I was reminded again of the widow woman with a jar of oil that wasted not away, oil that continuously filled the vessel. (2 Kings 4:3–6.) The day of miracles had not ended. There was no end to this story, no end to the wine, only that beginning again and again.

Mavis would be able to offer something to others that would not dry up or die down. It was a constant supply. As many lips as would come and taste of this sweet wine would have their fill. There need not be any additions; all had been supplied by the Lord. His salvation of which the silver was speaking, was enough. 'I will take hold of the cup of salvation' (Psalm 116:13) is the Scripture that could be applied to this miracle. At last, here was something there was enough of. Everyone could drink from a flowing stream and a full salvation. It did not depend on human resources or human supply for it to taste like wine. In this silver chalice was the real, deep and flowing new wine. Mavis realised that all her efforts to add to the work and supply of the Eternal were in vain. We cannot add to what the Lord has already done. If we do it would be to gild the lily. That work of Jesus on the cross was sufficient in every degree. Adding to it actually takes away from its nature and fullness. Mavis had learned a lesson, thus becoming a disciple of Christ, doing whatever the God of Israel suggested, because she was full of new wine from a full cup.

28

THE MULTI-COLOURED RAINBOW

The storm had been ferocious, tearing up trees and tossing them about as if they were straws. The tornado had struck with an iron fist. Much damage had been done, but now a calmer climate had entered the landscape. The woman who stood before me was young, vivacious and attractive. With her raven hair, she showed no sign that she had been in a struggle with trouble. Sheila would have made a good advert for the beautician, but now she was going to advertise the Lord, with His glory being the centre of her expression of life.

Before God had spoken to her and put a rainbow arch under her to give her support during the overwhelming flood, the marks of Jacob who wrestled with God had been part of her features. Instead of jewels she wore furrows on her face, neck and hands. This lady had been engaged in a battle, not a natural one, that was spiritual and eternal. It had left her cold and grey, with disappointment in her heart that no colour can express. In the past, to hide her fears, Sheila simply reached into her make up bag. A few dabs here and there, with a little lipstick added to her lips, and who could tell how she felt? In this modern world it is easy to create colour, and it is a matter of choice and mood how you appear to others. Whatever colours you carry in a case, they can never reach the heart that can be so bland.

The wonderful thing was she was a winner. The Lord had decorated her with the sun that was shining and the rainbow that had appeared, as if He was saying in splendid colour, 'Well done, you good and faithful servant, enter into the joy of your Lord.' The rainbow was expressing the feelings of Almighty God to this simple soul. God had become the Master of decoration in creation. A rainbow appeared as a mystery in the picture that was revealed by the Spirit of God. It was not in black and white, with grey thrown in for good measure, but was so colourful there was no space for doubt or fear. The rainbow in all its glory had broken the monotony of the colour of the clouds; it appeared framed in the blue of the sky, filling the eye of the beholder and the landscape.

Now all seemed as serene as sunshine, but this was only a quarter of the whole story. What had appeared had not been there earlier. That which was ordinary was replaced by something extraordinary. As Sheila stood there, the sun began to shine in all its strength sending out rays as spears of light to enter into every realm. In the foreground was a beautiful rainbow, drawn by the Divine for her benefit. It had one message written in many colours stretched across the skyline. 'I love you. If you can find the end of the rainbow, then you can find the end of My love. If you can measure it then you have measured My covenant with your heart.' It was so brilliant I thought it was like the first rainbow that appeared in the Book of Genesis. I looked to see if Noah could be seen, filling the space under the rainbow arch because of his fine physique. (Genesis 9:13, 14, 16.)

In Genesis the 'rainbow' is described as a 'bow'. It is the

tool by which arrows are fired. In Sheila's life it was where encouragement, hope and faith were fired from, the target being her heart. They were let loose to set her free from depression and fear. That heart was filled, with hope without measure becoming her treasure. Shafts of colour were fired from the rainbow that sent positive thoughts into a heart that had wandered.

The storm had passed, the singing of the birds had come, and the dark night of despair was over. This rainbow looked like a tunnel of love painted in many colours. Sheila was beckoned to enter into that tunnel, and to find a new, colourful life at the end of it. For her changing moods, there came a rainbow, the colour of delight taking her from despair. The rainbow had come to her rescue. The sign of the covenant of the Lord was filling the sky. What the Lord was saying to Sheila through the rainbow could not be uttered in words, so He had provided a rainbow. It could be shown in a picture rather than be explained. One picture is worth a thousand words. When men begin to stutter and cannot express the love of God, then the Eternal will draw that love in the most outstanding colours. As each colour in the rainbow blended into the other, so the life of this Christian lady needed the life God gives. Those of every tongue, colour, tribe and nation could find their place in the covenant of the Lord. Rainbows are throughout the earth, whatever nation you are in. What holds those colours in place? What keeps the rainbow hanging in the sky, as if held by invisible threads? That is God, and that which is held by God does not fade or fall like a leaf from a tree.

This was no small rainbow; it stretched from where she stood right into the future. The future looked bright and colourful, stretched out before her in a particular shape. The rainbow in all its splendour was touching the present and the future, suggesting to her that her future would be as bright and as colourful as the rainbow was. It was as a great archway, inviting all who would to come and walk through the rainbow after the rain. This rainbow was a carpet of welcome, woven with dexterity in the most vivid colours.

That picture alone would have satisfied the heart, but this woman had a deeper longing than that. Now the storm had passed she wanted more of the covenant of the Lord in her life. Sheila wanted a life as colourful and as plentiful as any bridge of colour in the sky. From where she was to where she wanted to be, there was a need in her life for the many colours of the grace of God as defined in the word 'manifold'. (1 Peter 4:10.) Instead of looking like an inverted rainbow for people to walk over, this sister wanted those things in her life that would make people stop and look up to heaven to thank God from Whom all blessings flow.

The salvation that once entered Sheila's heart had lost its appeal. There were many difficulties that she had faced, and they had been like 'blood suckers', drawing the colour out of her life. Christianity for her had become bland grey of colour and of nature. It should have been yellow, pink, orange and red, but the difficulties in her life had washed away the colours of her salvation, like one of the seasons before its time. There was a need to replenish what she had lost. Who could add the colour or paint the colour of salvation? Who can paint hope? Who can put heaven into a colour? That which had delighted her had merged into one colour. Salvation had lost its appeal, and Sheila had been asking God to restore the colours of joy, peace, righteousness, and longsuffering back into her life.

A *word of knowledge* was in operation which would add to her life all that had been prayed for. The Lord was about to re-paint the picture of the life of Sheila. The weather outside the church gave no indication of what was going to happen. It was pouring with rain, as if the plug had been pulled out of the sky. Water like that, and conditions like these, did not stop the Almighty working. He was about to do what He does best, and that was to perform a miracle that would bring all the colours of the rainbow into this drab, dreary lacklustre life.

The rainbow arch was there in the colours of its glory, unaltered by time or testing. I saw colour, taken from the rainbow and placed into the heart of Sheila. I did not realise that so many colours could be put into one life. At the moment the colour entered in, pulsating radiance came from her heart. Then another colour was added. It was as if a painter was choosing colours for a masterpiece. First one colour and then another was taken from the rainbow, and slipped into this lady's heart as if it was a box for coloured crayons. God was restoring the colour of her salvation. The faded paper would not be 'touched up', but a new colour would be added to replace the old. It would never again be grey; it would be a riot of colour as any garden in July. The colours were taken one by one and put where they belonged. I knew that God was restoring His covenant with this one. He was putting back into her life what the stress and sheer grit had taken out of it. Nothing of the colours appeared in the dress that she was wearing. This had nothing to do with outward adorning; it was the hidden man of the heart. (1 Peter 3:4.) God's best was being put into this soul. That representing a sabbath of rest was being dispensed.

The delightful thing about all that happened was that as you gazed on the rainbow it was not diminished, did not lose any of its shape or colour. In fact, the more colour that was taken from it, the more colour seemed to be added to it. This rainbow was self propagating. God was saying it does not matter how much He does for us, we will never make Him smaller. His reach will not be diminished. Whatever the colour taken, the rainbow would still act as an arch, as a covering for those who trust in God. It reminded me of the outstretched wing of a hen waiting for her chicks to run to safety. All that the Lord achieves will add to His glory. That put into you does not make God smaller but larger. More is added when more is taken away. When a prayer is answered, that answer does not impoverish God, does not shorten His arm to reach out and bring you in. If He gave away a million stars, another million would line up to take their place. When angels travel to earth to deliver us, heaven is not made smaller or less able by their absence. Your need gives God an opportunity to display His glory. The wound becomes a depository for His healing power.

The future for Sheila would be filled with that supplied by God. All her troubles, storms and fears would have rainbows as attendants. Her life had been an overcast sky with thick cloud blotting out the refreshing blue. God had put the colour back into living. This convert could go into the most appalling conditions and situations, but whatever the colour, black, blue or red, she would take with her that which she had received from the covenant of God. God would minister colour through her life in the most blank and bland areas. Every experience would be a blank canvas waiting to receive colour. What Sheila had in the Lord would become a ready transfusion to change anything that was boring, day after day, week after week, and year after year.

Within her heart was the coat of many colours that Joseph had worn. (Genesis 37:3.) The King's daughter was all glorious within, and her clothing was of wrought gold. (Psalm 45:13.) The future would reveal a 'colourful character'. Having her around would be like having a garden filled with flowers, a sort of flower box. Sheila would become attractive to children, because children love colour and diversity. They love chasing and being under a rainbow. How different this was to what Henry Ford, the creator of the 'Ford Motor Company' in America, said: when he was asked what colour should they paint a certain model of his car, he replied, 'I do not care what colour you paint it as long as it is black!'

All that was part of God's salvation was entering into her soul. She would be stretched to the size of a rainbow. Her ministry in the future would not be of one colour, but in grace she would minister many colours that would add other dimensions to any life presented to her for help. Some pregnancy crisis departments refer to themselves as 'The Rainbow Club'. There is nothing like the colour of an answer to prayer to give you cheer and comfort.

God was reminding Sheila that the colours of His covenant found in a rainbow would not fade with time, would not grow old as we grow old, but would shine with the stars. Nothing fades that the Lord brushes into our lives. Even when the clouds appear, somewhere in the background there will be the rainbow. Sheila's life was the telling that the storm had passed. Jesus had said, 'Peace; be still!' There is a certain colour for faith that is part of the covenant of the Lord within each soul.

It began to rain. Not as it rained during the flood that Noah experienced. The fountains of the deep were not broken open. This was like fine spring rain. Not a lot of it, but rain that could saturate and make you more uncomfortable than heavy rain. The reason for the rain was that, as I spoke, Sheila began to weep, as if to provide rain for the rainbow to appear. That in her life would be the shape of a rainbow, not just one colour, but a diversity of colours. Her ministry was to be as varied as the colours of the rainbow.

Some of those colours had been put into Sheila's heart. The rainbow was also a reminder of the rainbow encircling the throne in Revelation 4:3. Around that throne, with all judgement and storms passed forever, will be found that which will complete a faithful life.

The Lord is Sovereign, giving life to any who cry out to Him in repentance, and faith in Jesus Christ crucified. By grace were you saved, and grace will be given so that you can reach your goal in God, which is to be in His presence forever.

29

THE ATHLETE

As I laid my hands on George, I distinctly heard the loud crack of the starter's gun. It broke the stillness of the morning air as if an aeroplane had broken the sound barrier. It was fired right on time, and this young man was in a race. I whispered to myself, 'I wonder if he will win this race?' George set off at a pace as if he relished what was before him, mile after mile of running track. There were other competitors running by his side who were familiar to this athlete. George was dressed in a red velvet top and white shorts, and he looked determined to win.

As the race progressed, he began to wheeze as if he had a punctured lung, or was having an asthma attack. He was gasping for air and short of breath, and began to slow down. What had begun as a race between humans had become a race between tortoises, the pace had become so slow. Other runners were passing George on the right and on the left. Using the air around him as a rope, he was pulling on it, but making no progress. The only person to catch up with George was the ambulance man with his first aid bag slung over his shoulder. As this athlete began to fade, so he began to fall on the track, and was left with legs motionless, and hands and arms wildly grasping the thin air. He had not run out of track but out of fresh air. His capacity had not increased, it had decreased as his lungs demanded more and more air.

George looked as if he was tired of being tired. He wanted to go on, but the track was so long and his legs were so short. It was not the first time this had happened. You could set your clock or watch by this happening in his life. Whenever he attempted great things for God, he seemed to die in the word 'attempt'. He never received what he attempted or expected from God. The look on his face said 'I have been here before.' The starting line in his endeavours had become the finishing line. He had fallen short of his objectives. It all seemed too much and too far for him to make it to the end of the race. His life in the Spirit seemed to be as the cycle of the butterfly or dragon fly.

This athletic man had spent weeks, month and years in training. He had tried different running tracks and a new diet. Even his clothing had been re-arranged because he thought that what you wore made you into a winner. The only ground he seemed to cover was that under his feet — no further. Discouragement had tripped him up yet again, for he folded up as a box lid being closed. All he had succeeded in doing was running into the open arms of the first aid man stationed at the track to meet such catastrophes and medical emergencies. The ambulance man would be able to practise his skills on the fallen hero, even though the fallen hero wanted to practise his running skills on the track.

Every time George had made a move forward, he commenced running the race like an ostrich, but finished like an elephant with five legs! He had so much to give, and wanted to take so little, but it never seemed to work out. He was in deep despair. Remorse was not in that he had fallen and, short of breath, had crumpled into a heap, it was in that he had failed again. He would never wear the coloured jersey the leading cyclist wears in the Tour-de-France. The rosette of the winning horse would never be in his show cabinet. Silver would never be on display. His achievements would be moulded in tarmac! Instead of reaching out and touching the finishing line, he reached out to touch the outstretched hand of the medical man who had come to assist him. The only gold medal he received would be tablet-shaped, offered to him by this man who had come to help. He had a desire that could not be measured, to be a winner, but he was always the loser. Instead of first over the winning line, George was usually carried over on a stretcher, or guided, step by step, by one trying to console him. First love was missing, and the lack of zeal did not carry him over the line to break the tape of truth at the end of the track.

What happened reminded me of the man in the Bible who fell among thieves, described by Jesus Christ in the parable of the Good Samaritan. (Luke 10.) George did not fall among thieves; his own faculties let him down. His legs, feet, lungs and arms sat down on him! In the moment of need, the needy one was left bleeding and dying where he fell. 'As a tree falls there shall it be.' (Ecclesiastes 11:3.) The Red Cross meant nothing to him at this moment. It was not a helping hand he required but running feet, the feet of a Cushite or Ahimaaz. (2 Samuel 18:21, 27.)

Was it his training that was wrong? Was it that he should not run a race? Was he to be consigned to the scrap heap? Must he become a paradise for those who were rejected, and never made it in life? Even the apostle Paul feared being rejected. (1 Corinthians 9:27.) If prizes were handed out for losing a race, George would have received enough to decorate his cabinet! The consolation letters he had received had been too many to count; he almost felt he had the beginning of a library! Stretching them side by side they would have stretched from his house to this race track, which was quite a distance. Thoughts might have been enlarged by his brain, but in discouragement everything gets out of kilter, and you become your own killer. George spoke within himself words of deep discouragement. Suicide was being committed in the open as George tormented his heart with thoughts as sharp and penetrating as any dagger, sword or sharp blade. Here was slow poison.

Who would deliver him from this body of death? He felt like those in the Galatian church who had been 'hindered'. (Galatians 5:7.) The way had been broken up before them. If this did not work, then hurdles far too high to jump had been placed before them. He had to run the race of life, looking unto Jesus. George had tried to lay aside the 'weight' that had beset him. (Hebrews 12:1.) The word 'weight' describes 'superfluous fat' — fat that is not required. George was short of energy and wind. He felt in his heart that what he required was in the wind of God that came into the upper room in the Acts of the Apostles, wind that sent them everywhere, preaching the word. He required 'wind and 'flame'. He had become like a boat in the doldrums, lacking wind and will to be driven before the fresh breeze. There had to be 'times of refreshing' from the presence of the Lord or he could not go on. (See Acts 3:19.) The figure used of Caleb who 'wholly' followed the Lord filled his heart. That picture in the word 'wholly' is that of a ship with the wind in its sails, going out to sea.

Here was a fallen saint who needed someone to come to his aid. The first aid he required was that found in Jesus Christ. Jesus would help him in the race of life that was moving faster than George ever moved. Every time he had attempted to do something, he had achieved nothing. Because of negative thoughts, whatever he attempted would achieve nothing, and

George was not winning the race because of the thoughts of his heart. He was a loser even before he was a starter. He hit the floor before the floor hit him. There needed to be some stability and continuity in his life. Life was running out of his life. He was losing impetus; it seemed as if judgement had been passed on him and he was doomed to failure. What he required was help.

Could not Luke, the beloved physician who wrote the Gospel of Luke and the Acts of the Apostles, reach into his medicine bag and give him something that would comfort him, something that would deaden the pain of failure. He required someone to be a 'paregoric' as they had been to Paul in Colossians 4:11. ('Comfort', 'paregoric' — the drug that soothes pain and eases suffering.)

From his position on the floor looking up, he could never carry the baton to the next stage. The fire that was lit in the torch kept going out. Instead of George showing others the way, he felt he was becoming an obstacle to them, tripping them up because of his inconsistency. Of all men he felt most miserable, like the child reaching out for the reddest apple in the dish, then someone slapping his hand, causing him hurt, grief and pain. He felt he was melted tarmac, and as others running the race came to him, they found that he held them back. It was if when they met with this man, they were trying to run through tar or treacle.

As I began to pray for George, I knew that his expectation would not be cut off. I had the deep conviction that, whatever was wrong, the Lord would put it right. Jesus would become his Great Physician, and He would offer more than the whole of the medical profession ever could. The realisation had gripped my heart that what was wrong with George was not physical but spiritual. He kept letting God down; in doing so he took a whole lot of other people down with him. The earth, the next step, the few yards had become his goal; the members of his body, lust, lasciviousness, indulgence, desire, pride and malice were what was wrong in his life. He was achieving what his heart wanted to achieve. He was not for going the whole way and thereby travelling the whole ten yards. The falling places had become the finishing places. His goals were so small that a child could reach them. There was nothing wrong with his body, it was his head and his heart ruled him, bringing him close to destruction. He had been built for the kill, but the kill was killing him. The hare was chasing the hound. The things he was allowing in his life were becoming a hindrance. He could not travel far without some mishap becoming part of his life. He had to be released from this strife.

The Jericho Road, the Roman Road, and the Emmaus Road had to be opened up to him. He had to go to another track, and run the race of his life. George was on the wrong track. He was running everywhere, going nowhere. He had spent time running after first one preacher or teacher and then another. The latest fad had become his one desire. He had never realised that these things and his attitude were holding him back from the altitude that the Lord wanted him to reach out and take.

This had all been seen through a *word of knowledge*. As I turned from George, to look to the future, I saw another man step from what had been the crumpled body on the track. It was George, but now with a look of realism and determination on his face. He was as a man who had received his second wind. I felt in my spirit that this man was now on the right track and could become a winner. He was dressed in the livery of love. This looked more like the George who would slay the dragon!

In the past George had tried to have goals that were far beyond him. One thing I knew about the Lord was that if we will let Him, He will cut the cloth according to the measure.

He will not allow us to be tempted above that which we are able to bear. George had reached out for far more than the Lord had intended. We always fail and get hurt when we bite off more than we can chew. What was the use of George trying to run a four minute mile if he could not run a few yards in an hour! When we take on more worries than the Lord wants us to, we begin to draw our own plans in the dust of the road. We are bent on failure; and travelling what we think is 'light', we travel without light.

As this new figure emerged, sleek and handsome. I knew that a winner was born out of a loser. The 'old man' had died this morning, as George had surrendered. The new man had been set free to accomplish so much in God. He was not interested in running his own race with his own grace and finishing in the same old place. Here was a man, in George, who was a born winner. He had the marks of accomplishment on him. He would, from this day, run the race with patience, but he would travel at God's pace and not his own. The way he would go, and the path he would travel, would be of the Master's choosing. He could not lose. There was no more shortness of breath, with the Holy Spirit breathing new life into him; He was receiving the 'breath of lives' (Genesis 2:7), 'life' plural: 'lives'. The shoes he was wearing were gospel shoes. (Ephesians 6.) All his flowing garments were tucked neatly into place, as well formed and shaped as a baby's napkin. He ran as Elijah before the chariot of Ahab.

The secret of George's success was not in what he wore or how he ran, but in whom he obeyed. There were certain tracks, certain places, that George should not go. The result would be loss of face and disaster if he travelled a way different to that chosen by the Almighty. His heart was gently pushing him on, coaxing him into success. That put in his heart by the Holy Spirit was like a good mentor, a spiritual advisor and special coach running alongside him. Bread and water along with fresh, deep air was given to him so that he would not falter, trip or fall.

As he ran, he was leading the rest of the field. They could never catch a man like this! You had the feeling that George was so enamoured and armoured that he could have carried every other runner on his back and would still have won the race!

He was no longer alone. Crowds were gathering around him, as large as a football crowd. They wanted to know the secret of the success of a winner. They came to him as birds to bread. They wanted a slice of his success. If the story of his achievements were to be written, they wanted to be the writers, editors and publishers, because he had something to tell. He was a man who knew how to endure to the end. He had an end in sight. He did not have tunnel vision, but vision that allowed him to see further than his competitors. George was worth following because he knew where he was going. The sweet smell of success travelled with him, as scent in a flower. He breathed, smiled, ran and thought success. He had moved from the track of failure into another lane called success. He was running the race with patience that had been set before him (see Hebrews 12:1), pressing towards the mark (keeping to the lanes on the running track as part of his discipline) for the prize of the high calling of God in Jesus Christ. (Philippians 3:14.)

It was the same order as the wedding in Cana of Galilee (John 2). Whoever had arranged this was keeping the best wine until last. As George ran forward, instead of the goal and winning line being way ahead, it seemed they were within the next few steps. The track grew smaller and smaller as he moved as swiftly as the wind. The finishing line appeared and he began to run towards the tape stretched over the end of the track, as a cord of love. When you touched it, you knew you were a winner. God's love would enable him to cross the line in triumph, not tragedy.

As George ran, he became fitter and more capable. His legs became stronger, and he powered his way through the air and along this track. Every straight now seemed to be the home straight; the race, a hop, skip and a jump — and he was there! Every step he took resulted in the running track becoming smaller and smaller. The Lord was telling him that no distance was too long. He could and would make it. God would make the track to his measure; God would decrease the distance, so that George would reach every goal that God gave to him. His God-given ability would make every task asked of him as short as a stroll along his own garden path. George realised what a fool he had been. To leave it with the Lord meant everything would be measured as the wind is to the shorn sheep. The past that had seemed so great would now be reduced to the size that this athletic man could achieve. When we cannot make it, let God make it, as He controls it, and if He makes it we shall make it — not to the floor, but to the end of the race. God had granted George something that he could be successful at.

30

THE OINTMENT OF LOVE

The trials of life take something from our frame which affects not only the physical formation but the spiritual dimensions as well. Jack was a physically strong man — from the outside of the door, built like a door, and from the outside it was impossible to tell his inner suffering, until it was revealed by a *word of knowledge*. The weather outside was stormy and bossy. If you were not careful you would either slide into the church building on the mud or come in forced by water as it swirled around. God is not regulated by weather conditions, or the conditions of the human heart. He operates far above what we can see, feel or know. There was no gauge in the church to show you whether it was the right temperature for the Lord to move, or if it was cold enough to have reached 'dew point'. God acts independently, even as the architect and engineer do not work according to feelings, but with facts that are presented to them and which are demonstrated in the dynamics of building.

It was a fact that God had decided to crown this coming together. More than two or three had gathered, and it was noised abroad that Jesus was in the house. Here, healing, happiness, helpfulness and usefulness could be found. Those who came seeking would find what was required according to the promise of Jesus in Matthew 7:7.

The atmosphere was impregnated by the Holy Spirit. The presence of the Lord was so real it was as if you could reach out and touch it. Those wanting what the Spirit brings felt they could reach out and receive. It was so real it was tangible, a reminder of the time in the New Testament when 'the power of the Lord was present to heal' (Luke 5:17).

The man presenting himself for prayer was unshaven. He was last in the line of despondent disciples, his hands outstretched as if he were reaching to heaven to pull something down from the skies, or climbing a ladder one step at a time. I could not decide which he was doing. He was appealing to everyone to help him in his need. With upraised hands he was making an appeal for help from above.

It seemed as if his whole body was opened up before my eyes. Was this the gift of discernment being operated? I do not think so, but by the Spirit of the Lord taking and using what little I had to offer, He was revealing the true heart of this person. With my natural eyes, I saw the outer form of Jack, but with the eye of my understanding the inner self of this man could be clearly seen as a grey light on a misty morning. This had never happened to me before. Previously I had seen all sorts of shapes and sizes, there had been more pictures hung in my mind than in any art gallery or exhibition. I, too, had been a pavement artist, the pictures put out for all to see.

This was a new experience, and was a warning to any who think that God has revealed all that He has, that He has used up all the anointing oil as found in the Person of the Holy Spirit. God is creative; He creates new things all the time. Every time a person is healed, God has revealed the abundance of His care and power. Abundance is another word for variety. Here was the variety of life revealed through the God of life and all living things. God never comes to the end of Himself. He never comes to that place where He can go no further. He does not run out of land, sea, stars or sky. His creative nature just keeps on creating and living. He reveals what we understand and do not understand, and this particular morning was the day of a revival and fresh revelation of what the Lord can do. He can do all things, but He chooses to do some things for a particular time to lead us into triumph when we feel that we have tainted the truth.

The need of the hour demands something different from the Lord of variety. For Noah it was an ark. To Gideon it was a mantle soaked with dew, to Joshua He revealed Himself in the sun that was delayed as it began to set at the end of the day. (Joshua 10:12.) To Moses it was a rod. The list of God's diversity reads like the faith chapter, Hebrews 11. We limit what we receive from Him when we are lacking in faith. When we trust Him we discover that He is so trustworthy. He has been like that all the time, but we have not appreciated it. When Jehovah does something new, we think it is brand new, but it is only new to us. God has known about it all the time. He has produced it from His repository what is as deep as the ocean, or as high as the sky.

When we cannot receive any more impressions of the Lord, He simply arranges the canvas, or takes us to another height, of the heights of Abraham, or Nebo, to where Moses stood to look again into the land of Canaan. Sometimes, during sacrifice and surrender in our spirit, we are taken to Mount Moriah, and from there we view Jehovah Jireh. Then He teaches us: You have dwelt on this mountain long enough. Turn and go to a warmer climate. Go where you will see manifestations of love and power. Go to the area where God is unfolded before you as He was when Moses spoke to Him as a man speaks with a man, or a friend speaks with a friend. (See Exodus 33:11.)

This is why we have thirteen epistles in the New Testament. The same reason is applied to having four gospels, because no man sees God from every angle. Not even the angels know Him in His fulness. Paul said, after serving the Eternal for many years, 'That I might know Him, and the power of His resurrection' (Philippians 3:10). A man opens his Bible and new truth seems to leap from the pages and slap his face. He feels that a new ointment comes from the open page. Each page is seen as for the first time. The length of time you are married does not tell you all things; we see something new in each other almost every day. A gardener walks through his garden to admire the flowers that he or she has seen a thousand times, but this time it is different. He notices a rose he has never seen before. At the garden tomb, Mary saw Jesus standing in the shadows. She had looked, and thought she had seen everything in that garden, but she had not noticed the resurrected Christ. (John 20.)

We might mistakenly think that the Eternal has changed, yet He has said, 'I am the Lord, I change not' (Malachi 3:6). It is not God who has changed; we have been changed, and are being changed from one stage of glory to another. If the Lord works in one way only, why is there is no end to the words that we speak? We repeat some, and new words enter our vocabulary every day. God gave us speech, rich, rare and colourful, to describe the things we see.

This morning praying with 'Jack the lad', the lid had been lifted off his life, just like the top of the Ark of the Covenant could be lifted off. I was looking inside from the outside, waiting for the Lord to decide what new thing He would reveal. Here was the 'house that Jack built' standing before me. Viewing him from the outside, there was just the physical frame. 'Beauty is in the eye of the beholder', but that only deals with outward observation. In New Testament days they could discern the weather by what they could see, yet they got it wrong time and time again. (See Matthew 16:3.) None of us knows what is around the next corner; we do not even know what the next corner is.

What I was attesting to was not physical but spiritual. The Lord, in grace, was showing me hurt, pain, emptiness, lack of love, an aching void that could not be filled. This man's spirit, not his body, was in tatters, it was bleeding and dying for the want of love. There was the appearance of having been mauled as a mouse in the claws of a cat. It was not the body that the man wanted to be taken hold of, he had no need in that area. It was his spirit that required the healing power of the Lord.

Jack was of a large physique, well proportioned, and outwardly you could not tell what was wrong with him. Seeing him in the street, you would have greeted him as one of God's men doing the work of an evangelist. How wrong can you be? With God's revelation, how can you be wrong? You can be wrong if you judge from the outside, as wrong as when men told us that the earth was flat instead of round, believing that if you sailed far enough you would sail off the end of the world!

It was that which was revealed by the Lord that was the correct assessment of Jack. When Jesus said, 'I know my sheep', He meant not only outwardly but also inwardly. The hand of God is not only seen in the outward colours and design of a flower, but inside that flower where no one sees. If it is cut open, you will find that it is as beautiful inside as it is outside.

The spirit of Jack had become the habitation of every strange creature. It was like a cave for bats, as grudges, anger, wrath, jealousy, malice and pride found a hole in which to reside. I could tell that these things tormenting his spirit had not come on holiday; they had taken up permanent residence, bringing lock, stock and barrel.

Jack's troubles were not as a chip on his shoulder. He did not wear his heart on his sleeve. There was nothing disfigured about the body standing before me. It went much deeper than that. This was not facial or physical, it was spiritual. The man had a broken heart. Something had penetrated the armour plating, the veneer had been torn, and whatever it was had entered into his spirit. That spirit had been torn from top to bottom, just as the temple veil had when Christ died. (Mark 15:38.) Here was a man suffering in spirit those things that many suffer in their body. Was there a plaster large enough, long enough, and strong enough, to encircle the spirit of a man?

Jack required ministry to his aching, hurting, bruised and torn spirit. It was in tatters, as if it had been passed through a shredder. Who could knit it together or stitch something so torn? It was as if what Goliath had threatened to do with David (tear him apart and feed him to the dogs) had happened to this man's spirit. (1 Samuel 17:44.) How would the Lord deal with this unusual situation? It was unusual for me, but not for the Lord who deals with all things. He neither slumbers not sleeps; nothing catches Him off guard or takes Him by surprise. He is the surprise that catches us out when He supplies our needs. He has said, 'All things are yours' —which applies to body soul and spirit.

I felt when dealing with 'Jack the lad' that my hand should be turned upwards into the shape of a cup, as if that hand was to receive something from the Lord. A voice was heard speaking in the most tender tones, that even as the voice was speaking sounded like the music of the 'Hallelujah Chorus' and Mendelssohn's 'Elijah' added together. What would Elohim do with the old creation? A creation was taking place in the spirit of this man standing before me. 'There is love as ointment in your hand.' As the words ceased there was such a calm as when Jesus said to the storm, 'Peace; be still' (Mark 4:39.) 'Be muzzled', as if a mad dog had been muzzled to bite and snarl no more.

Taking my left hand (I am left handed), and putting it into my upturned right hand, I began to put this ointment of love onto my fingers, and then applied it to Jack's body, making strokes upon and down his back. My hand was acting as a relief for every pain and torment in this man's spirit. The number of times I dipped my hand into the ointment and applied it was the number of times that he had suffered. As my hand swept over his body, the pains were smeared away into oblivion. Many times my hand moved up and down, and my hands and arms were aching, but this was nothing compared to the distress in this man's spirit. Each time the ointment of love was applied, healing took place. What was in his spirit seemed to fly away, as crows disturbed by the firing of a gun in the rectory woods.

It was the love of God shed abroad in his heart by the Holy Ghost. (Romans 5:5.) It is a picture that refers to the Roman contest between gladiators. When the victor stood over the body of the defeated, and looked to the crowd for them to decide the fate of the defeated, to raise the thumbs meant 'let him live'; thumbs down meant 'kill him'. As this happened, the stench of blood, guts and death filled the air, despite the fact that the amphitheatre attendants had vessels filled with flowers and scented water, and threw flower petals, and sprinkled water everywhere to cover the scent of death. This is what the writer to the Romans is describing when he writes about the love of God shed abroad in our hearts.

Jack began to groan and to grow. These were the 'growing pains' of Jack. Whatever had been troubling him was troubled.

All that anxiety of spirit, the pain and frustration, the deep seated hurt, was dealt with. This ointment of love had a deep penetration, better than deep heat treatment. This was acting as a laser of love to the spirit of the man. Every disjointed part of his spirit was pieced together by the Spirit of the Lord. Who knows the mind of the Lord like the Spirit of God? Here in this ointment of love the Holy Spirit had become a Comforter not only to the body but to the spirit. The chaffing, the sores were gone; the man was healed through and through. My hand could resume its normal position. Enough ointment had been used, its ministry was complete. Here was a man clothed and in his right spirit ready to follow the Lord. He had a new spirit of dash and dare within him. What had been painful was substituted by the plentiful. What had been hurtful was now beautiful in harmony with God and man.

31

ONE DROP OF BLOOD

I do not know if Anne was educated, whether she was a university graduate or had a degree in English. What was being revealed to me by a *word of knowledge* did not reflect on her writing or education. If she had a talent for writing then she had buried it very deep, not in a grave but in a pit! Maybe, when she wrote, what was there was nervous tension doing its unsteady work? Word after word appeared on the page, as if the hand could not rest, or its work never be complete. Her writing was so untidy it was as if a spider had crawled over the page. I have seen better writing scrawled on the walls of a mental asylum. This was no neatly typed essay handed to a tutor after an English examination. The computer had not been switched on to punch out its dictates. No one could write so badly and still claim to have been through the education system. The page was turned over, and I was expecting to see a better display of English grammar, but all that was seen was more of the same. Then pages were turned vigorously, page after page, yet not one had any neat writing on it. They were replicas of each other. Had Anne been treating pages of this book as a shopping list, and in her rush to complete it had not bothered? It was not that the 'ts' were not crossed or the 'i's dotted, it was all as untidy as a child's bedroom, jumbled together as if the alphabet had rebelled against the writer and was pleasing itself concerning what appeared on the page.

This person required tuition in calligraphy! Of this there was no doubt. If Anne had attended the school I went to they would have put the dunce's cap on her head, sat her in a corner, and given her a thousand lines to write. She would not have been allowed to go home until the writing improved into recognition. Anne would have been expected to master that which was mastering her. Had Anne sat as we did in past years at school, before a large blackboard where every letter of the alphabet had been written in chalk, which we had to copy, her writing would have been much improved. At the same time the teacher would give the pronunciation and meaning of each word. 1 Peter 2:21 says that Jesus Christ has left us an example to follow. The word 'example' is taken from the Greek education system. In the tablet of clay, one word or line was written by the tutor, and then the scholar had to copy it underneath. This was as simple as 'A' 'B' and 'C'. There was no excuse for bad writing. Your whole life can be interpreted by how and what you write.

This one seemed to have remained in her childhood as far as her writing was concerned. Would she remain childish forever? Was her writing going to be in the nappy stage no matter how old she was? There was the requirement of maturity that needed to be expressed in her thinking and writing. She was not an old woman, nor a child, but a young lady, and what was expected, was writing that would grace any page. That well written could be well spoken. The greatest discoveries began with a thought and then were translated into the mastery of the pen. 'The pen is mightier than the sword.' Anne's writing would have deserved only condemnation. Words can be 'lords'. What was in Anne's book did not make sense. It was as the markings of David, who scrabbled on the door, pretending he was mad in order to escape from the clutches of the evil king in whose country he had come to reside (See 1 Samuel 21:13.)

Anne's book of white paper was filled with dark ink, as if her pen had a will of its own, and had moved across the page ignoring the lines. This seemed as if a Pharisee who opposed Jesus had decided to become a scribe. The man who penned Paul's epistles had not been at work here. There was no improvement of Anne's writing from commencement to conclusion.

This woman could have done with another hand taking hold of hers as she wrote. If this had happened then maybe the writing would have been better. Intelligence and academia had been shut out of this book, had been refused entrance. It looked as if the person did not want to receive help. The spelling was not the issue; it was the formation of the words, appearing as if ink in some places had been splashed onto the page from a bottle. Scholar and lecturer, pupil and teacher, would reject this writing as unintelligible. It looked as if it had been deliberately written in code; no one could read or understand it. It looked to me like a hieroglyphic, written in Egyptian with a mummy writing it and trying to read it!

What was being revealed through a *word of knowledge* as the Holy Spirit began His work of interpreting the heart, with its moods, fears and thoughts, was the life of Anne. It was there as a note on a public notice board for all to read, being presented to me. The diary of the heart was being seen without being understood. I know that young girls like to keep diaries private, because of the silly things they write into them. At least you can usually read and interpret what is meant.

I felt I needed the gift of interpretation for this writing. If my work involved translating, then maybe something could have been made out of this jumble of words. At that moment there was not one word that could be called handsomely written. Then I tried to form the words written, but there was nothing in my brain corresponding to the words that I was trying to read out. What was written was so bad it brought shame to a tongue.

Jeremiah 11:20 (The Message Bible) says, 'Life is as an open book.' If that is so, then it depends on who is the author. What we allow to be written in it is of importance. When I tried to read what was written, it was an impossibility As I attempted to read the writing and pronounce the words, a hidden hand appeared, and the book was closed to prying eyes and long lasting memories. The Holy Spirit was saying that what was contained in these pages was not for human consumption. It should have been sealed with seven seals. This should not be made public. It was private, and private it must remain, until something better was written. The sacred page was waiting for the handwriting of a king. This writing would be turned into the written laws of the Medes and the Persian which could not be changed. It would be a masterpiece in writing. The speech writer would become the story teller through the medium of writing.

The book opened by itself. There are 'talking books' for the blind, but this was a 'self opening' and closing volume. As it opened, I looked to see if there was just one page where the writing had improved, but to my chagrin, they were all the same. Page followed page, all was stained with ink, for that is all the writing could be described as. It was quite a large book, more in the style of an exercise book than one produced for publication.

This was the opposite of what God had said about the believer in Jesus Christ. We are 'epistles' read of all men. (2 Corinthians 3:2.) We are His 'workmanship' created in

Christ Jesus unto good works. (Ephesians 2:10.) That word 'workmanship' is where we obtain our English word 'poetry'. It is the same Greek word 'poiema' translated in Romans 1 —'handiwork'. It suggests poetry and the weaving of a lovely pattern of light. This book was more like the 'empty and void' of Genesis 1.

When Jesus Christ was on trial, and Pilate the Roman governor had put above His cross, 'Jesus of Nazareth the King of the Jews' (John 19:19), the Jews wanted it removed. Pilate seemed to be mocking them because of the writing on this headstone in wood. Pilate replied, 'What I have written, I have written.' When the pen has written it moves on. These pages in Anne's book had been written, the pen had moved on, but it was in the same direction and was doing the same thing. It had a life of its own to write or scribble that which no man could read. I felt like calling in Daniel or Joseph, because they were interpreters of handwriting and dreams. 1 Corinthians 13:1 indicates that tongues of men and of angels can be used. I wondered if it was possible to write with the pen of angels and of men! I thought: does the devil have his own school of handwriting?

The interpretation of what I was looking at was that this book presented the life of Anne. This scribble was a token of the undisciplined life she was living. The small book spoke volumes, but no one could understand the language! To write neatly you have to be disciplined, and takes a lot of practice, for in every word there is a picture. One picture is better than a thousand words.

As the book opened again, I saw one drop of red blood drop onto the page. Immediately, the colour and contour of the writing was changed forever. This blood did not stay on one page. It was so powerful, and it went from page to page until it had gone right through the book. The poverty of the writing did not mean a thing to this red drop of blood. It did not stop to try and read what had been written, did not seem to have to stop to catch its breath — as a rider on horseback, it went with the wind.

This one drop of blood among so much writing did not turn back, nor think the task assigned was too great. It moved from page to page with relish, as if zeal was its family crest. It sped along, and as it did so each letter, each word, as they appeared on each page, was wiped out, as if they had never existed. I looked blankly at the lank page, as you looked at the page untouched by pen or hand. The writer knew that all the things she had done wrong were not just crossed out, but expunged. There was no tale left to tell. There would be no beginning or ending.

The Bible says the 'handwriting of ordinances' that was against us has been taken and nailed to the Cross. (Colossians 2:14.) It refers to those who owed debt. When in debt, that debt was written on parchment, and nailed outside the house on a post. When the debt was paid, the parchment was folded, nailed on the post so that all could see the debt had been repaid. The debt could not be seen by the prying eye. Where I was born, if someone owed money to the local shop, and refused to make a payment, their name was put on a list, displayed in the shop window. Many times I read that list, and cried all the way home, vowing that I would never owe anyone a bean.

What I was seeing was better than this. The pages were not doubled over, they were wiped clean. John, writing in the book of Revelation (he wrote in the poorest Greek of his day, the Greek of the man on the street), says, 'He has loved us and washed us in His own blood' (Revelation 1:5). The obvious reference is to the fact that in the days parchment was used instead of paper; there was no acid in the ink, so what was written did not bite into the parchment, and consequently it could be wiped away. The slate would be clean. This is what the Lord was doing for Anne. I often wondered, as I watched my teacher at school wipe words from the blackboard, where those words had gone. In my young mind I thought they must be somewhere. 'The blood of God's Son, Jesus Christ, cleanses us from all sin — *keeps cleansing*; the Greek tense is in the continuous tense, and it refers to an act in the past which is constantly being repeated in the future. (1 John 1:9.)

Anne began to write again after the cleansing, but not with the same ink, and not in the same way. The pen seemed to be shaped like a cross. The words were neat, and the writing was an indication of the beautiful life she intended to live for the Lord Jesus Christ. You now had sainthood in writing, purity in a pen. Because of her love for the Lord, each word was a picture of love. Here was a sonnet of love. Poetic words instead of pathetic words from a pure person were being formed, as if an architect was perfecting a building or a sea captain sailing a ship. Each word was shipshape and 'Bristol fashion'— all neat; everything in its place. What had been disorder was now order. God had blotted out the past. The God of pardons had pardoned this one (see Isaiah 55:7), and it did not matter how deep or long the sin was, it was all wiped away. Anne could begin another day as if it was her first. This was the first day of the rest of her life. This was not the 'turning over of a new leaf', not even the turning of a page, but a completely new start with an empty page on which she could write.

32

THE BEST BOOK OF ALL

Ruth was taller than most women. She must have been six feet. When she walked through the door, she filled that door with her humanity. Items on the top shelf which would be out of the reach of most women, Ruth could easily reach. Wherever she moved, there was a presence about her that had to be acknowledged. Even when she had left, you felt as if part of her was still in the room. Strength had been poured into this frame of a dame. In God's garden, Ruth would have grown head and shoulders above all the other flowers. Here was beauty and symmetry combined in clay. I had never seen her before, so had no history of her life before we met. Through the Spirit of God it was being suggested to me that this woman was associated with a farm, I could hear the noises that come from a farmyard. The quacking of ducks, the hissing of geese, the braying of a donkey and the neighing of a horse, along with the cluck of a hen and the noise of a tractor on the move. Cows mooed and sheep bleated. Each sound was as clear as a bell on this fine sunny morning, confirming that it was good to be alive.

The *word of knowledge* had taken me in my spirit into a

farmyard, though physically I was in a church meeting praying for many different people, with needs as varied as a market stall on a Saturday. The queue was endless, as was the power and knowledge of God. Diverse people had gathered together, some tall, some small but all were part of the Fall through Adam who lost his way in Genesis. Some of these had never found that way back into the presence of the Lord. Now the gate was being opened, and sheep were coming into the pasture, sweet, green and plentiful, provided by the Shepherd. (See Psalm 23.) Abundant life provides abundantly for the people of God.

Suddenly there were just two of us; the others seemed to have melted away. The noise of the farmyard went into a silent hush, as the *word of knowledge* began to reveal the heart of the Sprit of God to my heart. The building we were in was like a barn, old, empty with a hollow sound every time you tried to speak, as if you were in competition with your own voice. The battle commenced, and we were in a fight for life! I had no idea what had prompted Ruth to come for prayer, but whatever it was had pushed her forward, to the place and point where she could hear what the Lord was saying to her. Her ears had become as large as her body, as she waited to receive something precious from the Eternal.

The building was so high that it was impossible to see out of the windows, I wondered who had put windows into a building that you would not be able to see through. The windows were as a brick wall when light should have been let in through them. They were so arranged that a ladder was necessary to be able look through to the outside world. The doors were the same, so high that you could not enter through them or leave. It seemed as if somebody in their lack of carpenter wisdom and knowledge had set the doors far too high for people to get in or out. The strange thing was that if you did walk through the door you would fall to your death. These were the windows and doors of death. Doors were closed and windows were shut. The windows and doors were not fulfilling the purpose for which they had been designed. These were false windows with no light coming through, and false doors, trap doors that you would go through if they had hanged you for murder. Even Ruth, with her giant-like tallness, was unable to reach either the window or the door. I wondered what a person would see if they had been stretched like elastic, and were able to see through the windows. These windows had blinds drawn over them, and although there were no blinds to be seen, yet no light was shining through as a revelation. Were the doors locked or open? If you managed to obtain a ladder, climb it, open a door, what would you see on the other side?

Ruth was crying because she was in desperate need. There was a desire in her heart to get to the windows and look through them. I saw her move to what appeared to be a pile of old books in the corner of the barn building. There were as many as sheaves of corn. These books were not laid one upon another, they were on the floor as if an angry person had read them and, not finding what they were seeking, had thrown them down onto the ground. Most were well worn, and it seemed as if many people had read them in the past. History and time, along with thumb marks and finger prints, had marked them. Was this the family history of the woman in the barn? There was a library here of ancient books. Maybe it was a monastery or a college that we had discovered?

The books were all shapes and sizes. Some had pages torn from them. Some were paperbacks, others hardbacks. Some had letters of gold at the beginning of the chapters. I thought that these must be important ones, worth lots of money. Some were thick, others thin, while others were small and wasted.

Ruth was taking far more notice of the books than she was of anything else, gazing at them. In them she saw her hope of reaching the windows and doors, her ability to go through the doors into a new experience. Ruth moved away from my side, bent over the books, and picked one up. To my amazement, she stood on it and tried to reach a window. I knew that the book would not be large enough to enable her to reach a window by standing on it. Books are to be read, not to be used as ladder rungs to stand on, although as a child when I could not reach the top shelf I would use a chair or a stool to give me the height required, but rarely would I stand on a book.

When Ruth found that there was no privilege in standing on a book, she turned her attention to the others. They were not going to be read by her, they would act as an improvisation to reach for things that were higher than the arm or hand could touch. She tried each book for size, using them as a foundation to reach the light that should have been coming through the windows. I could see that each door had a key in the lock waiting to be turned, but they were rusty, as if no one had ever reached the doors or turned the keys. I knew they never would if they used these books to stand on to reach their goal. These keys would be difficult to turn, even for a strong woman.

First one book then another was tried; they became as steps in a book ladder. Ruth felt these were the 'Thirty Nine Steps' (an English book telling the life of a spy). She had seen the old film 'Room at the Top', and wanted to get there. Usually ladders are made from steel or wood, but Ruth did not think of these things. She had zeal to get to where she wanted to go; she was going to use anything within her grasp. At first, if one book was not large enough then Ruth tried another. All the time, tears were coming from her eyes, using her face as a launching pad! One or two tears were christening these volumes. When one hardback was not large enough to give her the height required, another and then another volume was tried. No matter how glossy or full of information the book was, the end result was the same. This woman would never be a scholar when it came to mountaineering or climbing. The gap was too great and the books were too small. Even a leap of faith that was required would have to be a large one.

In her wisdom, the larger books were put at the bottom. It seemed as if this woman was building a ladder from the books so that she could get out of this place. All turned out to be Babel. (Genesis 11:9.) If she had opened a book, maybe there would have been a chapter on 'How to reach high windows and doors'? With zeal mixed with sweat and tears, I was looking for the blood added to the sweat and tears. The books could only be built so far, and each time they reached a certain height, Ruth would try to stand on the top. Even if she could have stood on the top book, I doubt she would have been able to turn the key or open the door or see through the window. Each time there was an ascent, she fell unceremoniously back onto the floor with the many books scattered. With her hands, feet and legs sprawled in books, there was no progress, only regress.

Ruth kept looking up, as if praying silent prayers. Then she would look down, as if pleading for the books to become as firemen with a ladder that could be rested against the wall of the building, and she could then escape. After trying so many times, she seemed to be resigned to what fate had decided. There was no way forward, backward or upwards —only downward. Here was a person incarcerated in a barn with blank windows and closed doors. Unlike the apostle Paul, she was handcuffed and handicapped. Paul, in prison when he began to write, was handcuffed but not handicapped, because many epistles came from prison, containing deep revelation. He had the light of revelation in a dark prison cell.

As a person making a last attempt, Ruth began to dig deeper among the books, and to her delight she found an old Bible. I wondered, 'How is the Bible going to help her when these other books could not?' The Bible was just as old as the other books, but not as marked, as if someone had stopped handling it years before. Had someone thrown the Bible to one side, thinking that the other books contained better information? The others had well worn pages, twisted and turned at the corners. Some had been heavily scored with pen or pencil. These thoughts were like straws on the floor, and needed gathering together before anything could be built from them.

Ruth took the Bible, and stood on it. As she did so, my eyes turned to the other books, and I began to read the titles. There was one on philosophy, another by Hackett on Evolution; there were the thoughts of David Attenborough on Creation and Evolution. I knew that this particular book was not so old, because this man was still telling people how the earth had been formed, and how we had ascended from animals. Then there was Russell Grant's book on Dreams, which I have heard him read on British radio, trying to convince people what their dreams meant. Another was Gibbon's 'Rise and fall of the Roman Empire'. There was a well read book on the history of the world, one on 'How to Find a Lost Relative', a book on steam trains and engineering. There was an almanac for 1740 among the books, along with a book on the merits of herbal healing. One book had the title' Ten Easy Ways of Living'. There were books in Latin, Greek and Hebrew that we could not read, books by scientists that had never been read. The 'Encyclopaedia Britannica' was laid to rest here. There were books on all matters of life but nothing about death or how to ascend to the windows. I did notice that there were one or two religious books that had not helped Ruth. In fact one of them had toppled the rest stacked up for the climber to stand on. That book was called 'Awake' and its companion was 'The Watch Tower'. There was a book on Spiritualism. The 'Book of Mormon' by Joseph Smith was in paperback.

On a crumbled piece of paper I saw a list of the hundred best selling books.

As Ruth stood on this Bible, suddenly she was lifted up to where she wanted to go. The book seemed to grow and grow with this lady standing on the top of it. As she was lifted, light broke through the windows like a revelation; the whole barn was flooded with light, like the light of the midday sun that surrounded the early persecutor of the church, Saul of Tarsus. (Acts 9:3.) As the light streamed through the windows, the sign of the cross in light appeared on one of the walls. It came through the light that shone through the window. I saw the keys dripping with fresh oil as they turned, and the doors opened onto a beautiful garden, so beautiful that it cannot be described. The perfume from the flowers scented the air, and the scent was glorious, overpowering the smell of cow and horse dung that had been on the floor of the barn.

Ruth stood in a blaze of light, the look of a pilgrim on her face. She had received a revelation in her darkness, that no other book could bring to her.

The only book that provided a revelation of God was the Bible. All the other books were written by men. From the Bible, light for life had streamed. As the book lifted up Ruth to where she wanted to go, and allowed her to see what could be seen, so it does for any one who will come, take it, and use it as a foundation for life and living. Every part of that building was filled with light as jewels in a casket.

Ruth had tried many ways to get to know if there was a God. If there was a revelelation to be had, where it would be found? In her humanity she thought that scientist and philosophers had all the answers, but all her searching, reading, comings and goings, had been in vain. These other books borrowed from the local library had only given her headaches! Ruth had entered the meeting that morning bound, feeling that she had been locked into a prison and the key had been thrown away, never to be found. God had revealed to her that through the Bible she could receive a revelation of another life and another world.

I left Ruth gazing through the windows, enjoying this new revelation of God, received through His word. I saw her then going through one of the open doors with the charisma of the converted on her face, singing as a soul set free. The light she had found was Jesus, the Way, the Truth and the Life.

33

THE LAST CHAPTER

The area of Manchester where Desmond and his wife were called to work was notorious for crime, prostitution, theft, rape and gun running. The locals said that to walk the streets at night in this area you required a Churchill tank and a suit of armour. Even the 'rent man' went door to door wearing 'body armour'! It was like the town of Nazareth where they asked so often that it became a proverb, 'Can any good thing come out of Nazareth?'

As many congregations do, Desmond was given a nickname. They called him 'Dizzy, Dozy Dezzy,' (though not to his face!) because he could be quite forgetful when making specific arrangements for meetings. He had been known to arrive an hour late, an hour early, or even not at all. On one occasion he actually turned up a week later! Desmond had a heart of gold and a will of steel, both very necessary in this particular area of Manchester. The spirit of the pioneer would never die while he was alive. He loved to see the Lord bring 'beauty out of ashes' —'roses from ashes', as one translation renders it.

Desmond had come to this particular Pentecostal church when there were few members. It was so small that if they had a split, then they would have to close the church down. The local authorities had contemplated closing the church down anyway because of the scarcity of its members, but what had been dross and waste, through the preaching of the gospel had been turned into diamond quality in the new people who had gathered. During a period of fifteen years the church had grown from that defined as small into something that can only be described as a multitude of people from all walks of life. So much so, that they had to build an extension. The work had been tough, but worth all the tears, sweat and prayers. What had been patiently born had taken its toll on Desmond's human frame, and now he was beginning to feel exhausted. Where once his stride was straight and his body erect with shoulders high, he walked with a stoop that told its own story of the suffering and the carrying of heavy burdens. Life had marked his face with lines of weariness. He had decisions to make, and before the morning meeting he had made those decisions. The time had come for him to retire.

Desmond was called to the front of the meeting, and the visiting speaker laid hands on his shoulders, and looked into his lined face. A *word of knowledge* began to be revealed to the visiting minister, the contents of the life of this man of God. Desmond was carrying a book, the size of an old pulpit Bible that was large and heavy. He was gazing at an open page, and seemed to be worshipping at it. He had opened it at the page of his choice. He was delving into his memories of the past, and while doing so forgot the present and the future. Surely if you keep reading one page of a thick volume you will get bored or weary. Even the Scriptures say, 'Weariness of the flesh comes through much study' (Ecclesiastes 12:12).

At first I did not appreciate what sort of book it was. Could it have been a ledger? Was it the church accounts that had been totalled incorrectly? Was Desmond contemplating writing a book about the miracles he had witnessed in the growth of this church? I gazed at its well worn cover. Because of my experience in churches, and seeing heavy Bibles in some pulpits, I was looking for the words 'Holy Bible' on its outer cover. Unable to see the word 'Bible', I looked for some other indication of the nature of its contents. Could it be that the author was holding it?

It was not a glossy magazine or a romantic novel, not even a book on science or bird watching, because it was much larger than these. The mystery must be solved. While I was meditating on what the Spirit of God was revealing, Desmond began to flick through the pages, as one who was familiar with its contents, and it was then that I discovered the nature of the book. Each page was a 'pigeon hole' of records. Each page had been scored, some words were underlined, and there were comments in blue and red in the margins. Desmond had drawn sketches in between some of the lines, and some of the pages had corners turned over as if there to remind him of past memories. It seemed strange that there was no bookmark in the book. I was puzzled, it seemed as if someone had taken a pen and added different colours to the book. Was it the work of a time wasting artist, who had nothing better to do than use the pen as a spider's foot? These markings did not enhance the chapters; rather it defaced them, leaving them as a battlefield stained with blood.

In my despair, I called to the Lord to help me to discern what this book was. There are times during the operation of a *word of knowledge* when God reveals a picture, and you describe what you are seeing. The danger is that you can put the wrong interpretation on the right picture. You have to pray that what you see and say is what was intended by the Spirit of the Lord.

Human personality is never extinct when associated with the gifts of the Spirit. The Spirit of God whispered into my heart that this was the book of Desmond's life. I was not ready for that revelation because I was thinking that the volume could be anything but the man's life. Someone had appeared with a book that was a mousy colour, and said, 'Desmond, this is your life!' The marks in the book were the 'red letter days', and the days of suffering, dark days of doubt, even the days of fear, had been scored on each page. Each experience had been gone through with a fine pen instead of a fine comb. Desmond had spent time there, reminding himself of the past with its many hurts, the time of the rose garden, and the purple mountain. Looking at this book, he was in the process of closing it, and putting it onto the shelf in his library. The book was being closed, not only to be put to one side but to be forgotten as many books are after we have read them. He moved his hand along other volumes, and made a space for it on the shelf.

Before Desmond shut the book, I took a closer look at what was in it. As he flicked through, it was like a game show at a funfair, where you place a coin in a slot, turn a handle, and still pictures, because of the movement, come alive. It was a miniature film show of his life. Some pictures were in black and white, while others, the happy moments and days of Desmond, were in red, yellow, pink and blue. I saw him being born, and then he moved into childhood, puberty, manhood, and now into senior years. Only the Spirit of God can reveal a life to you in seconds. Each page told a story that was part of this man's life. I was given the pleasure and insight by the Spirit of God to look into that life, to see things that no one else had been allowed to see, because they had been kept between the covers, and the book had been closed.

As Desmond closed the book, I understood by the Spirit of God that he felt he had come to *the last chapter*. Everything he ever attempted had now to cease. He was intending to retire, and hand the work of God on to somebody else. He was ready to pass the baton. In his heart Desmond had come to *the last chapter*. All that had been written about his life was finally written, and he felt as Pilate might have done when he said to those who were wanting to alter the inscription over the cross of Christ, 'I have written what I have written' (John 19:21,22). The full stop appeared where Desmond's tear fell on the open page. There was a finality about the action that Desmond had taken. The book of his life must be put away to gather dust and cobwebs, the home of a bookworm, never to be remembered any more.

As Desmond closed the book and was prepared to put it away forever, a hand appeared from nowhere, and took the book from him. I recognised that hand as being like the one I had read of in Daniel 5:5. The book that Desmond surrendered had been read thoroughly, and in his mind he had come to *the last chapter*. There was no longer any space left on which to write — the end had come. I was disturbed by what I had witnessed, because I felt there should have been more pages, more volumes. It was an unfinished work and, like the 'Acts of the Apostles' should continue from generation to generation.

Throughout the years it has amazed me, how many people have felt that the end has come, but He whose name is Alpha and Omega has taken hold of the end and turned it into a new beginning. The eyes of the beholder have been on *the last chapter*, while the eyes of the Lord have been fixed on the horizon. Some fix their eyes on the ditch, while the Lord is looking to the horizon, where new things appear. When Jehovah wanted Abraham to see new beginnings, He told him to look to the stars. (Genesis 15:5; 22:17.) Our endings are God's beginnings. Taking the last seed, He plants it into a harvest. He takes hold of the end of our tether, and spins it into a cord of love, winds it around us, until we are closely bound to Him for eternity. End was just another terminus in the life of a man, where that coming to the end of the line is redirected onto another line, and continues on its way. The word 'terminus' is from a Latin word meaning 'boundary', it does not suggest an end, just a line of demarcation before moving over the next furrow.

The hand that took the book began to create new pages that were blank. Then I saw Desmond beginning to write on these pages, after he had dipped his pen into something that looked like red ink or blood, each word, sentence and paragraph chosen with great care. Every time the name of God was entered, the pen was wiped clean, lest that name should be stained. As Desmond wrote, the Divine hand came over his hand, guiding that hand as if guiding the hand of a child who is having difficulty understanding the alphabet and forming each letter into a word. Here was a form of discipleship, as if the hand was on a plough as it passed across the field. The old book with its many pages had been in the handwriting of Desmond. That is why there were so many mistakes, seen in the blotches and pictures revealed. In the future, he would be directed by God what to write. With the help of Jehovah Jireh he would write a love story, the story of his soul and the love of God. There is no *last chapter* of the love of God!

Desmond thought life had come to a halt, as when an officer commands a soldier to halt. God was adding extra pages to this book. Now was not the time to give up but to get up and go on, and let his life become like the pen of a ready writer. (Psalm 45:1.) No more volumes to be written, but in this book there were certainly new pages to be added. Here was the wonderful thing: those old pages did not remain, but went from the book as the new pages arrived. The only pages in the book were those that the Hand had put there. The past was forgiven, the old had gone, and the new had come. (2 Corinthians 5:17, a modern translation.)

Desmond had decided to lay the work of the Master on one side, and release himself from any obligation. The tired hand must write on, not until it came to the end of the book of pages, but of life. This was not the end, it was not even nearly the end; was not even the beginning of the end. The Eternal had much more for him to do, and Desmond, as a willing son and servant, must operate as the Lord was guiding him. With a smile of acceptance he received what the Lord had said to him. In God he was as new as a book unopened, fresh from the printers. This man must not write his own Last Will and Testament; he must not think he had come to *the last chapter*. As life goes on, so he must go on.

At a future date I learned that Desmond had actually installed a co-pastor before that morning service, arranging to surrender the reins of leadership of the church. I am pleased to say that, to date, he is still allowing God to write those extra chapters! He will not arrive in heaven with a book that has the *last chapter* missing. Had the *last chapter* not been written, he would have missed so much. The best wine (John 2:9, 10) would never have passed through thirsty lips and into a parched soul.

Desmond is letting God do the writing, as he surrenders his life, day by day, as one page after another.